T0252260

Programming Language Fundamentals

A Metalanguage Approach in Elm

Martin Erwig

Oregon State University
Corvallis
USA

Copyright © 2024 Martin Erwig. All rights reserved.

Published by John Wiley & Sons, Inc., Hoboken, New Jersey.
Published simultaneously in Canada.

No part of this publication may be reproduced, stored in a retrieval system, or transmitted in any form or by any means, electronic, mechanical, photocopying, recording, scanning, or otherwise, except as permitted under Section 107 or 108 of the 1976 United States Copyright Act, without either the prior written permission of the Publisher, or authorization through payment of the appropriate per-copy fee to the Copyright Clearance Center, Inc., 222 Rosewood Drive, Danvers, MA 01923, (978) 750-8400, fax (978) 750-4470, or on the web at www.copyright.com. Requests to the Publisher for permission should be addressed to the Permissions Department, John Wiley & Sons, Inc., 111 River Street, Hoboken, NJ 07030, (201) 748-6011, fax (201) 748-6008, or online at http://www.wiley.com/go/permission.

Trademarks: Wiley and the Wiley logo are trademarks or registered trademarks of John Wiley & Sons, Inc. and/or its affiliates in the United States and other countries and may not be used without written permission. All other trademarks are the property of their respective owners. John Wiley & Sons, Inc. is not associated with any product or vendor mentioned in this book.

Limit of Liability/Disclaimer of Warranty: While the publisher and author have used their best efforts in preparing this book, they make no representations or warranties with respect to the accuracy or completeness of the contents of this book and specifically disclaim any implied warranties of merchantability or fitness for a particular purpose. No warranty may be created or extended by sales representatives or written sales materials. The advice and strategies contained herein may not be suitable for your situation. You should consult with a professional where appropriate. Further, readers should be aware that websites listed in this work may have changed or disappeared between when this work was written and when it is read. Neither the publisher nor authors shall be liable for any loss of profit or any other commercial damages, including but not limited to special, incidental, consequential, or other damages.

For general information on our other products and services or for technical support, please contact our Customer Care Department within the United States at (800) 762-2974, outside the United States at (317) 572-3993 or fax (317) 572-4002.

Wiley also publishes its books in a variety of electronic formats. Some content that appears in print may not be available in electronic formats. For more information about Wiley products, visit our web site at www.wiley.com.

Library of Congress Cataloging-in-Publication Data Applied for:

Hardback: 9781394251537

Cover Design: Wiley
Cover Image: © Martin Erwig

This book was set in Sabon by the author using the LaTeX document preparation system.

Contents

Preface   vii

About the Companion Website   xi

1 Introduction   1
1.1 The Role of Programming Languages in Computer Science . . .   2
1.2 Why Study Programming Language Fundamentals?   4
1.3 What Are the Fundamentals of Programming Languages? . . .   5
1.4 How to Study the Fundamentals of Programming Languages? .   8
1.5 About Programming Paradigms   9

2 Functional Programming with Elm   13
2.1 Getting Started   14
2.2 Expressions, Values, and Their Types   18
    2.2.1 Naming Values and Expressions   19
    2.2.2 Tracing Evaluations   20
    2.2.3 Tuples   25
2.3 Functions   26
    2.3.1 Function Application   26
    2.3.2 Currying and Partial Function Application   27
    2.3.3 Function Definitions   29
2.4 Iteration and Recursion   30
2.5 Lists and Pattern Matching   34
2.6 Data Types   40
2.7 Higher-Order Functions   44

3 Syntax   49
3.1 Context-Free Grammars   50
3.2 Parse Trees   54
3.3 Abstract Syntax   56
3.4 Abstract Syntax Idioms   62
    3.4.1 Factoring   63
    3.4.2 Replacing Grammar Recursion by Lists   65

| | 3.4.3 Grouping Associative Operations Using Lists | 68 |
| | 3.4.4 Representing Optional Syntax Elements | 70 |

4 Denotational Semantics — **73**

4.1	Defining Semantics in Three Steps	76
4.2	Systematic Construction of Semantic Domains	80
	4.2.1 Error Domains	82
	4.2.2 Product Domains	86
	4.2.3 Union Domains	87
	4.2.4 Domains for Modeling Stateful Computation	89

5 Types — **97**

5.1	Inference Rules	98
5.2	Type Systems	102
	5.2.1 The Language of Types	102
	5.2.2 Typing Rules	105
5.3	Type Checking	109
5.4	Type Safety	115
5.5	Static and Dynamic Typing	117

6 Scope — **123**

6.1	The Landscape of Programs: Blocks and Scope	124
6.2	The Runtime Stack	130
6.3	Static vs. Dynamic Scoping	134

7 Parameter Passing — **139**

7.1	Call-by-Value	141
7.2	Call-by-Reference	144
7.3	Call-by-Value-Result	146
7.4	Call-by-Name	148
7.5	Call-by-Need	150
7.6	Summary	152

8 Logic Programming with Prolog — **153**

8.1	Getting Started	154
8.2	Predicates and Goals	157
	8.2.1 Predicates	158
	8.2.2 Goals	159
	8.2.3 Repeated Variables (aka Non-linear Patterns)	161
	8.2.4 Conjunction	162
	8.2.5 Expressing Joins	163

8.2.6   A Simple Operational Evaluation Model for Prolog . . .   165
8.3   Rules   166
8.4   Recursion   171
    8.4.1   Trees as Computation Traces   172
    8.4.2   Left Recursion   173
8.5   Prolog's Search Mechanism   174
    8.5.1   Unification   175
    8.5.2   Scan, Expand, and Backtrack   177
8.6   Structures   179
8.7   Lists   186
8.8   Numbers and Arithmetic   193
8.9   The Cut   195
8.10 Negation   196

Index   203

Preface

Programming languages are indispensable tools for the development of software, and all good programmers know the languages they use very well—like all other professionals master the tools they need for their work. But computer scientists are more than programmers. They are a *scientists*, and as such they have learned to study the phenomenon of computation. Since programming languages are the predominent way of describing computation, it follows that computer scientists should know what programming languages *are*, what they consist of, how they work, what they can and cannot do, and what is needed to describe and analyze them. And that is the topic of this book: The general structure of programming languages, their individual components, and how they can be defined.

Audience

This book is primarily aimed at upper-level undergraduate students who have already some programming experience and who have basic knowledge of data structures and discrete math. The book can also be a useful resource for programming practitioners who want to learn the basics of functional or logic programming. Moreover, programmers who want to gain a better understanding of the tools they are using may find this book beneficial as well.

Content

The topics covered in this book are a selection of the most salient aspects of programming languages to be understood by undergraduate students and that can be covered within one quarter or semester.

One important feature of this book is the use of Elm (a typed functional programming language) as a *metalanguage* for expressing formal definitions in executable form. This approach facilitates the experimentation and exploration of different designs for a wide range of language aspects. In the past I had used

Haskell as a metalanguage for this, but I switched to using Elm because it is less demanding on the learner and provides a gentler slope to typed functional programming. In particular, in the context of a one-semester course in which the functional language is (a) only part of the curriculum and (b) must be mastered to the point of being employed as a metalanguage, Elm seems to offer a good compromise of clarity, expressiveness, and simplicity.

Another feature of this book is coverage of logic programming using Prolog. Learning about logic and functional programming expands students' understanding of computation significantly, since it introduces two new models of computation (often called *programming paradigms*) that differ considerably from the prevalent imperative programming style.

Some additional material, in particular, exercises and program examples, can be found on the accompanying web page.

Prerequisites

First, the book assumes some basic *programming knowledge* as obtained, for example, in an introductory programming course. This can be any (textual)[1] programming language. Even though for most students this will probably be an imperative language such as C, C++, Python, or Java, the actual language itself doesn't matter so much as having experience with representing a problem using data structures and expressing the solution by using the abstractions offered by the programming language.

Second, since representation plays a key role in the study of programming languages, it is important to have a solid understanding of basic *data structures*, in particular, lists and trees. Specifically, familiarity with basic notions of trees and operations on trees will be helpful, since we will represent (the abstract syntax of) programs as trees.

Finally, the book assumes knowledge of basic *discrete math* concepts, such as sets, relations, and functions, which constitute the framework through which programming language concepts are explained.

Acknowledgements

This book evolved out of my lecture notes for the class CS 381 that I have taught at Oregon State University for over 20 years.

---

[1]Having experience in only so-called "block-based" languages such as Scratch is insufficient; some experience with textual syntax is required to appreciate and understand Chapter 3.

First, I'd like to thank the many students in my classes for their engagement and interaction. Their feedback, and especially their questions, have helped me with identifying more effective ways of introducing concepts and explaining ideas as well as crafting exercises for testing the understanding of the material.

During this time, a number of committed teaching assistants have helped me with some of the exercises and solutions. Their suggestions have contributed to improving the presentation of the material as well.

I am also grateful to Cyrus Omar for his many helpful comments and suggestions on an early draft version of this book, which have been of great help.

Finally, I owe a great debt of gratitude to Iain Moncrief and Christine Lin for proofreading the book and providing valuable comments and suggestions.

About the Companion Website

This book is accompanied by the following companion website:

www.wiley.com/go/ProgrammingLanguageFun

This website includes:

- Exercises with solutions
- Programs with source codes

1

Introduction

Chapter Summary

The importance of representation and abstraction. The role of programming languages in computer science and the difference between computer science and software engineering. The need for metalanguages to study programming languages. Also, a short comparison of the three major programming paradigms.

Computer science studies the phenomenon of computation, where computation can be defined as the *systematic transformation* of *representations* for the purpose of *solving a problem*.

Let's consider as a motivating example the *problem* of determining a valid meeting time for a group of people on a particular day. The first step is to gather from each participant information about their availability, which raises the question of how to describe each participant's available times, that is, what *representation* do we chose for this information?

One possibility is to use a set of time intervals, which raises the further question of how to represent time points and at what granularity. Let's assume for simplicity that we are planning a one-hour meeting and that the available hours are numbered from 8 a.m. to 5 p.m. Using this representation, Alice may have the times $8-10$, $12-1$, and $2-3$ available; Bob can offer $9-10$ and $1-5$; Carol is available from $9-10$, $11-12$, $1-3$, and $4-5$; and Daniel can make it $9-12$ and $1-3$. Typically, in this representation an interval $a-b$ means the availability of the hours a through $b-1$.

The next step is to find a method for extracting from this set of interval sets a (maximal) set of intervals that are covered by, or contained in, them. While

Programming Language Fundamentals: A Metalanguage Approach in Elm, First edition. Martin Erwig.
© 2024 Martin Erwig. Published 2024 by John Wiley & Sons Inc.
Companion website: www.wiley.com/go/ProgrammingLanguageFun

this is not a very difficult task in principle, it can be quite tedious, in particular, if we have to do it without tool support.

An alternative representation that lends itself to a computation that can be easily performed by humans is to use a simple array of available hours in which unavailable hours are shown as "-". After aligning all availability arrays vertically, the potential meeting times are immediately visible as complete columns of hour numbers.

```
Alice   8 9 -  -  12 - 2 - -
Bob     - 9 10 -  -  1 2 3 4
Carol   - 9 -  11 -  1 2 - 4
Daniel  - 9 10 11 -  1 2 - -
```

The two possible meeting times $9-10$ and $2-3$ immediately stand out in this representation (as does the third-best option $1-2$, which works only for three of the participants).

This example illustrates that the choice of representation can have a significant impact on its effectiveness for solving a problem, and thus awareness of representational variety is an important skill for computer scientists – or problem solvers more generally.

As it happens, the question of representation has also played a significant role in writing this book, namely: *how to represent programming languages to facilitate the explanation of their fundamental concepts*. In the remainder of this introduction I will discuss this aspect and lay out the contents of the book.

1.1   The Role of Programming Languages in Computer Science

One driving force of computer science is the goal of automating computations by letting machines perform them. To that end, a *programming language* is an interface between humans and machines that enables the description of algorithms in a form that can be understood and executed by machines. Programming languages are thus one of the most important tools for computer scientists.

Computing technology evolves rapidly with new application domains challenging programming languages to provide new or different features. Consequently, the field of programming languages constantly evolves in many different directions. Estimates of the number of programming languages range between 700 and 9000, which is evidence of the fluidity of the field. This fact has direct implications on how to study programming and programming languages. In particular, it is impossible master all or even a large subset of these

Abstraction level	Example
5 Meta	Regular expressions, grammars, rule systems
4 Feature	Syntax, semantics (scope, types, parameter passing schemas)
3 Model/Paradigm	Lambda Calculus, Turing Machine, Predicate Calculus
2 Language	Elm, Haskell, Lisp, C, Java, Python, Prolog
1 Program	`fac n = if n==1 then 1 else n*fac (n-1)`
0 Computation	`fac 3` $\implies$ `3*fac 2` $\implies$ `3*2*fac 1` $\implies$ `3*2*1` $\implies$ `6`

Table 1.1 Programming language abstraction hierarchy. The level of abstraction of computer science concepts that are especially relevant to the study of programming languages.

languages. Therefore, to keep pace with the development, it seems more effective to study general principles of programming languages that apply to a wide range of languages instead of trying to learn individual languages one by one.

In addition to being indispensable as a tool for automated problem solving, programming languages play a central role in computer science as a substrate for *abstraction*. Computer science is suffused with abstractions. For example, an algorithm is an abstraction of computation: one algorithm describes many different computations by using parameters, and a specific computation is obtained by executing the algorithm with arguments substituted for the parameters. Turing machines, pushdown automata, and finite state machines are abstractions of physical computing machines: the exact physical details of machines are ignored, and their important characteristics are instead represented mathematically. Types are abstractions of values. And the so-called *big O notation* is an abstraction of run time.

The description of a programming language is an abstraction itself, an abstraction of all of the programs that can be written in the language. In studying the fundamentals of programming language we abstract from individual programming languages and focus on individual features that are abstractions of specific algorithmic idioms (loops, parameterization, scope, etc.). Moreover, in the description of programming language features we often use formalization tools, including grammars or rule systems, that live at an even higher level of abstraction. Table 1.1 shows the range of different abstraction levels. As you can see, programming languages involve many abstractions.

Since programming languages play such a pivotal role in computer science, it is obvious that they should be studied and understood well. But why should one study the *fundamentals* of programming languages and not just simply learn a few individual languages?

1.2 Why Study Programming Language Fundamentals?

Programming courses teach how to effectively *use* a particular programming language. By taking such a course combined with lots of practice and experience, one can become an excellent programmer in a specific programming language. Given how many languages exist and how quickly the landscape of languages evolves, this may not be an effective strategy to stay informed. In contrast, understanding the general principles that underly all languages empowers one to quickly grasp new features and whole new languages.

Nevertheless, to be a successful programmer, a viable strategy is to master the most popular language, or the one needed for a particular job, and then retrain whenever needed. This utilitarian view of programming languages is certainly adequate for programmers and software engineers, and it seems to be the strategy employed by coding boot camps.

However, being a computer scientist means more than to be just a programmer or a software engineer. No one would expect a physicist to be just a good car mechanic who understands the particular workings of a specific set of car models. Nor would we expect that a civil engineer is only able to build one specific kind of house or bridge. In the same way, we would be selling computer science short by expecting computer scientists to be just good programmers.

Computer science is still a young discipline and incorporates many different applied subjects that over time will likely spin off into separate disciplines. This is what happened in scientific disciplines with a longer tradition. For example, physics has led to mechanical, civil, and electrical engineering, and biology has led to medicine, agriculture, and ecology. Similarly, we will likely see software engineering in the future viewed as one specialization of computer science.

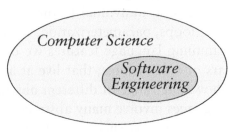

A computer scientist must understand the underlying principles of computing and how they are reflected in the languages used to describe computation.

	Objects at abstraction level	Who creates them?	Who uses them?
4–5	Meta & Feature	CS researchers	*Computer scientists*
3	Model/Paradigm	CS researchers	*Computer scientists*
2	Language	*Computer scientists*	*Programmers*
1	Program	*Programmers*	Everyone
0	Computation	Everyone	Everyone

Table 1.2 Abstraction users and creators. Most users of abstractions are also abstraction creators. In particular, any user of an abstraction at level $n > 0$ creates an abstraction on level $n - 1$.

The study of programming language *fundamentals* abstracts from one programming language and looks more generally at the concepts that can be found in many or most programming languages. Such a more general understanding of programming languages also makes you a better and more flexible programmer, since it allows you to learn new languages more quickly. It also supports you in assessing the scope of existing language features, puts you in a position to better judge the need to switch to a different language for a new task, and helps you select the best language for a particular task.

Table 1.2 shows the involvement of different groups of people with abstraction levels. In particular, we can observe that computer scientists generally work at one abstraction level above programmers.

The study of programming language principles provides an excellent exposure to identifying, understanding, and applying abstractions. These are crucial activities in the work of any computer scientist. If you are successful as a computer scientist, it is very likely that you are very good at dealing with abstractions.

1.3 What Are the Fundamentals of Programming Languages?

A language is typically characterized by its *syntax*, which defines all its valid sentences, and its *semantics*, which defines what each sentence means. This is also the case for programming languages. In addition, however, the necessity for programs to be executable by machines demands that the semantics of a programming language specify a lot of details that other language descriptions can often ignore. This includes, in particular, rules for the applicability of operations (that is, *types*), the reach of defined names (that is, *scope*), and the handling of values that are referenced by names (that is, *parameter passing*). In the following I will explain these aspects in a little more detail.

How do we tell a calculator to compute the result of $(4 + 1)^2$? Assuming a sophisticated natural language interface, we might try the command *Compute the square of 4 plus 1*. But how can the calculator decide whether to compute $(4 + 1)^2$ or $4^2 + 1$? Instead of using English, we have to adopt a notation that is unambiguous and that can distinguish between the two expressions. Not relying on a semi-visual notation with exponents, etc., we could write the first expression as square(4+1) and the second one as square(4)+1. The difference matters, since the two expressions yield different results.

In general, the definition of a programming language has to specify the *syntax* of programs because only well-formed programs can be executed in a way that results in predictable behavior. For example, an expression such as 3+square should be rejected, since it is not clear what the intended meaning is.

As another example, consider the task of determining which expression denotes the greater value, 2^3 or 3^2. While calculators provide a rich set of arithmetic operations, they often lack comparison operators such as > or < and the notion of Boolean values. Therefore, we can't directly express this task in terms of the operations offered by the calculator and instead have to simulate the computation. This is not difficult in this case: we can simply compute the difference $2^3 - 3^2$, and if the result is positive, the first expression is the larger one; if the result is negative, it's the second one.

While the encoding of Boolean values as integers might seem like a clever idea, it can lead to unexpected program behavior. For example, if we add a > comparison operator to the calculator language and have it return integers, what should be the result of expressions such as (3>2)>1 or (3>4)+5? A programming language definition has to decide whether these expressions are valid, and if so, what they evaluate to. It is a non-trivial task to define a large set of operations on a single type in a consistent way. One purpose of introducing *types* into programming languages is to rule out nonsensical programs and catch programming errors early on. A particular design decision for a programming language is *when* to check whether the operations in a program are used in a consistent way with respect to their types. This can be done before the program is run (*static typing*) or while it is being executed (*dynamic typing*).

To know what can be expressed in a particular programming language and to decide how to express a specific algorithm, one needs to know what values and computations the language provides and what the *semantics* of the language constructs are. Machines offer only a limited set of operations that can't directly support every imaginable computing application. Therefore, programming languages offer advanced programming constructs to facilitate higher-level descriptions to make the programming of machines easier and more reliable.

Every programming language offers some form of the naming for parts of a program. Even in the case of a simple calculator, one quickly encounters situations in which one wants to use names in expressing computations. Consider, for example, the task of computing $(371 \cdot 47)^2$ with a calculator that doesn't have a predefined square operation. Of course, one can simulate square by entering `(371*47)*(371*47)`, but that's inconvenient and prone to errors. It would be nicer if we could assign a *name* to `371*47` and then use the name for computing the square, as in `let x=371*47 in x*x`.

Factoring repeated program parts using names gets more and more important the bigger programs become. Names are used for simple values, for functions and parameters, for modules, etc., and with the definition and use of names, the question arises whether the same name can be used in different parts of a program, and if so, which of its definitions will be visible where. When a function uses a non-local name, that is, a name that is not defined as a parameter or locally inside the function, an important question is which non-local name to use: the one that is visible where the function is defined (*static scoping*) or the one that is visible where the function is used (*dynamic scoping*). These two strategies yield, in general, different results.

Directly related to the concept of names is the question of when and how expressions are bound to names. For example, in `let x=371*47 in 0*x*x`, the expression `371*47` could be evaluated and its resulting *value* 17437 bound to x *before* the expression `0*x*x` is evaluated. Alternatively, a language definition could bind the *expression* `371*47` unevaluated to x and evaluate it only when x is needed. In this example, the evaluator could determine that x is actually not needed to compute the value of `0*x*x`, and so the computation of `371*47` could be avoided altogether.

In summary, to understand and judge a programming language, you have to understand its syntax and semantics (which includes a potential type system, the scoping rules, and available parameter passing schemas). How can we accomplish this task?

1.4   How to Study the Fundamentals of Programming Languages?

To understand any technical subject, it is not enough to look at examples. Instead one needs to comprehend the fundamental principles that underlie the subject matter. It is no different for programming languages: to understand what a programming language is, it doesn't suffice to look at a handful of examples. In other words, programming in a few languages won't lead to a principled understanding of programming languages.

The definition of a programming language generally requires a definition of its *syntax* and its *semantics*. Technically, the syntax of a language is defined by the set of all of its valid sentences. In practice, the syntax of a language is given by rules that describe how sentences can be assembled from smaller parts, characterizing the different ways in which language constructs can be combined. The semantics of a language defines the meaning for each of its sentences. Specifically, the semantics of a programming language describes the computational effect of all of its constructs.

Thus, to understand a programming language, one has to understand the rules to construct valid programs and what computations such programs denote. Therefore, to be able to understand an arbitrary programming language, we have to understand how to define the syntax and semantics of a programming language in general.

The formalisms for syntax and semantics definitions happen to be themselves languages, and thus any language definition necessarily requires the use of one or more so-called *metalanguages*, that is, languages that can describe other languages. The language that is described by a metalanguage is then called the *object language*.

One important metalanguage that is used widely in computer science to describe the *syntax* of languages is the formalism of *(context-free) grammars*. For the definition of the semantics of languages we have a choice of several different approaches. We will employ *denotational semantics* for this purpose, which identifies a set of semantic values and then maps programs to these semantic values. Why denotational semantics? Because it reflects our intuition about (one aspect of) computation quite well: a computation transforms a representation of a problem into one of a solution. If we are not interested in the details of how this is done but only in the input/output relationship, we regard the computations described by a program as a function. Denotational semantics describes exactly this function.

As mentioned before, computer science is about the automation of tasks by writing programs that can be executed by machines. Now wouldn't it be great if we could automatically execute language definitions? This would allow us to experiment directly with different variants of syntax and semantics and thus explore the space of programming languages by observing the effects of language definitions.

This is indeed possible by choosing a programming language as a metalanguage for performing language definitions, and we will do this here as well. It turns out that functional programming languages are particularly well suited for this task, especially for expressing denotational semantics. We will employ the functional programming language Elm for this purpose. Since we need Elm as a metalanguage, this will have to be the first topic to be explored after this introduction.

The approach of understanding programming language concepts by being able to define them follows Richard Feynman's maxim:[1]

What I cannot create, I do not understand.

Or in the words of Albert Camus:

To create is to live twice.

1.5 About Programming Paradigms

Programming languages can differ notably by the *programming paradigm* they subscribe to. A programming paradigm defines an idiosyncratic view of what computation is and how to describe computation through programs. In other words, a programming paradigm describes a *model of computation*. Understanding different programming paradigms is an important part of understanding the landscape of programming languages and making sense of the variety of programming abstractions that exists because the view of *what* computation is determines *how* to describe it (by programs in a specific programming language).

In general, a computation is a transformation of a problem representation into a representation of a solution for that problem. A model of computation, and thus a programming paradigm, has to define the structure of these representations as well as the details of how transformations between representations can happen. The three major basic programming paradigms take the following points of view.

---

[1]https://web.archive.org/web/20211109060801/https://archives.caltech.edu/pictures/1.10-29.jpg

Imperative Programming. The main idea of imperative programming is to represent a problem as a state using a collection of named memory locations and to compute a solution by manipulating values in these locations individually through assignment operations, under the control of conditionals and loops whose behavior is determined by expressions that are based on the values in memory locations.

- *Representations* have the form of named values that are subject to repeated modification. The collection of named values is called a *state*, and parts of the state can be manipulated by individual *assignments* that access the state through the names, which are also called *program variables*.
- *Computation* is a step-by-step transformation of a state that results from a sequence of assignment statements.
- *Programs* consist of *statements* that are organized by *control structures* for selecting between different (groups of) statements and for repeating them.
- *Execution* of a program requires initial values for the program variables (often read through `input` operations).
- *Results* of program executions are the values of the final state.
- *Formalization* of this computation model is through the *Turing machine*.

Functional Programming. The main idea of functional programming is to represent a problem as an expression that is systematically simplified into a value that represents the solution.

- *Representations* of data have the form of atomic values and trees of values. The representation of a problem is given by an expression built from functions applied to data and other functions.
- *Computation* is a step-by-step transformation of an expression into a result value (tree). The transformation of representation essentially happens through the systematic decomposition of trees into components and the construction of new trees, directed by function definitions.
- *Programs* consist of *function definitions*. Control structures are realized by recursion and higher-order functions that take functions as arguments and return functions as results.
- *Execution* of a program requires the application of a function to arguments.
- *Results* of program executions are values (or trees).
- *Formalization* of this computation model is through the *lambda calculus*.

Logic Programming.   The main idea behind logic programming is to represent knowledge of a problem area by a collection of facts and rules. A problem is formulated as a query (also called a *goal*), which may contain variables and describe a pattern to which a solution is found by matching the pattern against the relations using the rules.[2]

- *Representations* have the form of terms built from atomic values as well as relations of terms and values. The representation of a problem is given by a term (the "goal") that may contain values and variables, and the representation of a solution is a *binding* for the variables in the goal (as well as an indication of whether or not the goal could be satisfied).
- *Computation* is the construction of a tree of rule instances (called a *derivation*) by repeated generation of bindings through the selection of rules. This process also creates bindings for variables. The systematic exploration of all rules and the process of *backtracking* allows alternative rules to be tried when the search for a solution gets stuck.
- *Programs* consist of *rule definitions* that define the relationships between inputs and outputs. Control structures are realized by the structure of rule definitions (multiple premises of a rule require the execution of all of them, whereas alternative rules provide choices).
- *Execution* of a program requires a goal, which consists of a term with values and variables.
- *Results* of program executions are bindings of values to variables contained in a goal.
- *Formalization* of this computation model is through *first-order logic* (also known as *predicate logic* or *predicate calculus*).

Computations can be captured in so-called *traces*, which are structures that arrange snapshots of the states a computation went through. It is instructive to compare the different kinds of traces that are produced by the different programming paradigms. The structure of a trace reflects the essence of the paradigm and can help get a better understanding of the differences between programming paradigms. Simplified example traces for the computation of a factorial are shown in Figure 1.1. Again, the trace for logic programming makes sense only after having studied Chapter 8.

Understanding different programming paradigms not only helps with evaluating and selecting a programming language that is best suited for a particular project, it also provides a broader, more diverse understanding of the notion

---

[2]This description may make sense only after having studied Chapter 8, so you may want to re-read this explanation later.

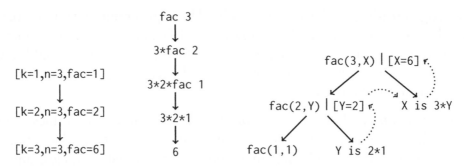

Figure 1.1 Computation traces in different programming paradigms. On the left: a sequence of states characterizes computation in imperative languages. In the middle: a sequence of expression simplifications characterizes computation in functional languages. On the right: a tree of goals and bindings captures (part of) the computation as it happens in logic programming languages.

of computation itself and is therefore an important part of computer science education.

While some languages try to support multiple paradigms, many programming languages fall into one of the three categories in the sense that most programs are written in a style that fits the underlying computational model of the paradigm. One can take a more fine-grained view of programming paradigms and identify further paradigms (such as object-oriented or constraint-based programming), but most of these classifications are built on the three mentioned paradigms.

Most students have extensive experience with imperative programming but haven't written a functional or logic program. We will therefore also explore the basics of functional programming in Chapter 2 and logic programming in Chapter 8. Those chapters also provide more details regarding the differences between paradigms (see, for example, Tables 2.1 on page 14 and 8.1 page 154).

And in case you are wondering about the ordering of chapters (functional programming in Chapter 2 and logic programming in Chapter 8): we start with Elm because we need it as a metalanguage in the discussion of syntax (Chapter 3) and semantics (Chapter 4). On the other hand, the discussion of Prolog requires an understanding of some technical ideas that are discussed in earlier chapters, such as rules and rule systems (Chapter 5) and bindings (Chapter 6).

Functional Programming with Elm

2

Chapter Summary

An introduction to the basics of functional programming using the language Elm. Working with expressions and names in the Elm interpreter. Definition and use of functions, in particular, the concept of currying and partial function application. Recursion and how it relates to iteration. Lists, pattern matching, and the basics of general data types. (More details and examples of data types to follow in later chapters where they are used for representing syntax, semantics, and type systems.) The concept of higher-order functions and their use as as control structures.

In imperative languages, such as C, Java, or Python, computation is expressed as transformations of state, that is, the underlying programming model views a program as a series of statements that perform successive changes to a state, which can be accessed through names called *variables*. For example, if a program declares an integer variable x, then the assignment x = 3 has the effect that referencing the variable x afterwards will yield the value 3, at least until x is changed by another assignment.

The functional core of Elm does not have an underlying global state that can be manipulated. Specifically, Elm does not have an assignment operation for changing the values of variables. It doesn't have *while* or *for* loops either. Elm is a *functional programming language*, in which every computation is expressed as a function. A function has one or more parameters and is defined by an expression (also called the function's *body*) that can refer to these parame-

Programming Language Fundamentals: A Metalanguage Approach in Elm, First edition. Martin Erwig.
© 2024 Martin Erwig. Published 2024 by John Wiley & Sons Inc.
Companion website: www.wiley.com/go/ProgrammingLanguageFun

Concept	Elm	C, Java, etc.
Algorithm	Function	Procedure/program
Instruction	Expression	Statement (+ expression)
Input	Function argument	read statement
Output	Function result	print statement
Iteration	Recursion	Loop
Computation step	Expression simplification	State update
Computation	Sequence of steps	Sequence of steps

Table 2.1　How algorithmic and computation concepts are realized in Elm compared to in imperative programming languages.

ters. A function is thus another example of an abstraction, an abstraction of an expression in which one or more parts have been replaced by parameters.

Thus writing a program in Elm amounts to defining a function, and running or executing a program is applying a function to one or more arguments. A function application is evaluated by evaluating the function's body where all references to the function's parameters are substituted by (the values of)[1] the corresponding arguments. The differences between Elm and imperative languages regarding the realization of algorithmic concepts are summarized in Table 2.1.

2.1　Getting Started

Since you can't learn how to program in a new language by just reading about it, it's best to work through the following examples by trying them out on a computer.

To this end, the first step is to install an Elm interpreter. There are several ways to do this. Probably the easiest approach is follow the instructions given at https://guide.elm-lang.org/install/elm.html to download and install the implementation for the operation system on your laptop or desktop computer.

To use the Elm interpreter as shown here, Elm must be initialized in the directory that contains the program files to be used. To this end, execute the following command in a terminal window.

```
elm init
```

---

[1]Under call-by-name and call-by-need parameter passing, argument expressions are bound unevaluated to parameters whereas under call-by-value, which is used by Elm, arguments are evaluated before being bound to parameters. See Chapter 7 for details.

```
module Grading exposing (..)

type alias Points = Int

type Grade = Pass | Fail

alice : Points
alice = 65

grade : Points -> Grade
grade p = if p>50 then Pass else Fail
```

Figure 2.1   The file Grading.elm contains Elm definitions for two types, a value, and a function.

After providing some information and asking for confirmation, this will create a file elm.json containing configuration information and a subdirectory src where Elm programs (that is, files with extension .elm) are to be stored.

It is important to understand that the code presented here occurs in two principally different places, namely (1) in *Elm program files* (stored in the subdirectory src) and (2) in the *interpreter interface*.

First, an Elm program contains definitions of types, values, and functions that can then be used in the Elm interpreter. A small example Elm program is shown in Figure 2.1, which defines the name alice to be a number, here representing the number of points Alice received on a test, say. In addition, the file contains the definition of the function grade for computing the grade for a particular point score. The value definition for alice should be obvious, and I will explain later in Section 2.3 how function definitions work; the details are not important at this point. The file also contains definitions of two types: the type synonym (or alias) Points for Int, and a data type Grade containing two grade values. Again, the details will be explained later.

Second, starting the Elm interpreter presents a command-line interface for loading Elm files and evaluating expressions.[2] The Elm interpreter is started by executing the following command in a terminal window.

```
elm repl
```

We are presented with a short message, followed by an input prompt.

---

[2]Interpreters of this sort are also commonly called "REPL," which stands for "read-eval-print loop."

```
---- Elm 0.19.1 -------------------------------------------------------
Say :help for help and :exit to exit! More at ...
-----------------------------------------------------------------------
>
```

At the prompt, we can enter expressions that the interpreter then evaluates, like so.

```
> 4+5*6
34 : number
```

The result is a value, 34, of type number. The colon can be read as "has type" or "is of type." In this case, number is a type variable that indicates that 34 can be either an integer (type Int) or a floating point number (type Float). I will have much more to say about types in Section 2.2 and type variables in Section 2.5.

We can load Elm files containing type, value, and function definitions into the interpreter. Definitions are always part of a module, and the first line of Figure 2.1 shows that a module definition consists of the module's name and a list of exported names (put in parentheses), that is, names defined in the module that are in principle visible to the outside world. The abbreviation (..) means to export *all* names. To make the definitions from the module Grading accessible in the interpreter we have to import the exported names. Again, we have the choice of importing only some or all of the definitions. We choose the latter.

```
> import Grading exposing (..)
```

After importing the definitions, they are available in the interpreter, and we can use, for example, the function grade to compute the grade for Alice's point score.

```
> grade alice
Pass : Grade
```

Again, the resulting value and its type are presented. You will notice that the syntax for applying functions is different from what you are used to in math. In Elm (and many other functional languages), applying a function f to an argument v is written by simple juxtaposition, that is, f v. In particular, parentheses around v are omitted unless f is applied to an expression.[3]

When we change the definitions in a file and want to use them in the interpreter, Elm reloads the definitions. If this doesn't work for some reason, we can always re-load the definitions by repeating the import command.[4]

---

[3]Thus we write grade alice to compute the grade for Alice but grade (alice-15) to compute the grade when we want to deduct 15 points for a late submission. Note that the expression grade alice-15 is type incorrect, since it is parsed as (grade alice)-15 and tries to subtract a number from a Grade value.

[4]Fortunately, the interpreter keeps a history of expressions and commands that we can scroll through with the up and down arrow keys.

> **INCREMENTAL PROGRAMMING**
>
> In many cases a functional program *f* can be effectively developed by following a divide-and-conquer strategy that tries to *simplify* and/or *decompose f*, whichever is applicable.
>
> *Simplify*: If *f* is too complex to be defined directly, try to identify special cases or make simplifying assumptions and implement (several versions of) *f* for the simplified case(s). This may include reducing the number of parameters for *f* and using constants instead of parameters in the definition as well as only dealing with a subset of the possible input cases. It may also include defining *f* for arguments that have a less general or structurally simpler type than required.
>
> Then test the function on several examples. (These test cases should be stored in the Elm file for easier reuse.) After that, try to gradually generalize the definition.
>
> *Decompose*: If the problem to be implemented consists of several subtasks, try to express *f* as a combination of functions $f_1, f_2, \ldots$ that solve these subtasks, and implement and test the functions $f_1, f_2, \ldots$ independently. Then test *f*.
>
> Note that both these strategies can often be employed in parallel.

The important thing to remember is this: when definitions of types, values, and functions are shown, such as for Points, Grade, alice, and grade, these appear in some file that can be loaded into the Elm interpreter. On the other hand, expressions to be evaluated must be entered into the Elm interpreter, which is indicated by the > prompt that precedes expressions and by the result printed on the next line. For how to effectively develop functional programs, see the box *Incremental Programming*.

Oh, and then there will be errors. Inevitably, you will enter an erroneous expression into the interpreter or place an incorrect definition in a file. Since machines are so picky in what input they accept, talking to a machine can be a frustrating experience. Errors can be simple misspellings, which are easy to spot and correct, as in the following example.

```
> grades
-- NAMING ERROR ---------------------------------------------------- REPL

I cannot find a `grades` variable:

4|    grades
      ^^^^^^
These names seem close though:

    grade
    abs
    ...
```

But some error messages can be more difficult to understand. In general, though, Elm's error messages are mostly quite helpful.

2.2   Expressions, Values, and Their Types

We have already seen integer values and expressions and how expressions are evaluated to values in the interpreter. Other basic types include floating point numbers (type Float), characters (type Char), and Booleans (type Bool). When we evaluate expressions, the type of the result is always shown as well.

```
> grade alice   |  > 7 == 9      |  > min 'a' 'b'  |  > not False
Pass : Grade     |  False : Bool   |  'a' : Char     |  True : Bool
```

Working with number types can be a bit tricky sometimes, since the number symbols and arithmetic operations are overloaded. For example, 4 can stand for an integer or a float, and + denotes both integer addition and float addition. As we have seen with the evaluation of the expression 4+5*6, Elm responds with the type number, which says that the result is of some type Int or Float. When the type of a name or symbol is known to be more specific, that type will then be reported. For example, we have defined alice to be a number of type Points, which is a synonym for Int, and if we use it in expressions, we see the specific type as a result.

```
> 65            |  > 65 + 2.0    |  > alice        |  > alice + 2
65 : number      |  67 : Float     |  65 : Points    |  67 : Int
```

Elm tries to infer the most general type of any expression, which provides some flexibility in programming. For example, we can use generic number symbols and operations in different contexts to denote integers or floats.

Finally, note that there is an important difference between conditional *expressions* (in Elm) and conditional *statements* as found in imperative languages: in Elm the arguments of the then and else branches are expressions to be evaluated depending on the condition.

```
> if 1+2==3 then 4 else 5
4 : number
```

Exercise 2.1

(a) Write an expression that computes the larger value of 5 and 2*3 (without using the function max).

(b) Write an expression that tests whether 2*3 is equal to 3+3.

(c) Is the expression (1==2)==(3==4) well defined? If so, what is the result?

(d) How about (1<2)==(3<4)? Is this expression well defined? If so, what is the result?

2.2.1 Naming Values and Expressions

An expression may contain names that are to be replaced by values during evaluation. A name, also called a *variable*, must start with a lowercase character and may contain characters, numbers, or the underscore _.

Of course, only if the names are defined (and in scope) can such an expression be successfully evaluated. As shown earlier, names can be defined in Elm files, but they can also be defined "on the fly" with so-called *let expressions* that have the form let x=e in b. Such an expression evaluates e to, say, a value v, and associates v with x during the evaluation of b, the so-called *body* of the let expression. The variable/value pair (x,v) is called a *binding*, and this binding is consulted when references to the variable x in b are substituted by v. Values of any type can be bound to names, that is, bindings also work for functions.

```
> let f=grade in f alice          > let late=alice-15 in grade late
Pass : Grade                      Fail : Grade
```

Note that in nested definitions, inner definitions hide (temporarily) outer definitions. This effect is also called *shadowing*. This means that the following expression should evaluate to 12.

```
let x=1 in x+(let x=5 in 2*x)+x
```

However, Elm actually does *not* accept that expression and complains about the shadowing of variables. The interpreter produces the error message "These variables cannot have the same name." This is a questionable design decision by the writer of the Elm compiler, since the above expression has a perfectly well-defined semantics. We can actually circumvent this restriction by placing the definition x = 1 into a module (say, ElmShadowing.elm) and then evaluating the body of the outermost let expression after importing the module.

```
> import ElmShadowing exposing (..)
> x+(let x=5 in 2*x)+x
12 : number
```

In the following we ignore the idiosyncratic Elm behavior and simply assume that nested let expressions can be compiled and evaluated as shown.

Now, how is the result actually obtained? An expression `let x=e in b` is evaluated by substituting `e` for all (non-shadowed) occurrences of `x` in `b`. In the last example, this means to substitute 1 for the first and last occurrence of x in `x+(let x=5 in 2*x)+x`, which results in the expression `1+(let x=5 in 2*x)+1`. Note how the nested let expression shields the use of x in its body from the substitution. This inner let expression can be evaluated in the same way by substituting 5 for x in `2*x`, which yields `2*5`. Thus the overall expression simplifies to `1+2*5+1`, which then evaluates to 12.

The let construct also allows the definitions of multiple variables, either in parallel using tuples or in sequence over multiple lines. This latter form is primarily for use in program files. Note that in multi-line definitions all the definitions in one let block have to be indented by the same amount.

```
> let (x,y) = (1,2) in (y+1,x-1)          let x=2          let x=1
(3,0) : (number,number1)                      y=3              y=x+1
                                          in               in
                                              x*y              (x,y)
```

The type `(number,number1)` in the response to the first example says that 3 and 0 are both numbers, but they don't have to be of the same number type, that is, one could be an `Int` and the other a `Float`.

Finally, note that names can also be defined within the interpreter and then subsequently used repeatedly, like so.

```
> x=3
> x
3 : number
> x+1
4 : number
```

Since such definitions are lost when the interpreter session ends, it is generally advisable to keep definitions as part of an Elm program file that is loaded into the current interpreter session.

2.2.2 Tracing Evaluations

The behavior of functions and expressions can be explained by tracing the evaluation of expressions step by step. This is particularly useful when expressions involve names. Consider again the expression `let x=1 in x+(let x=5 in 2*x)+x`. The challenge in this example is to resolve the different bindings for x correctly.

Exercise 2.2

What is the result of evaluating the following expressions?

(a) `let x=1 in let x=2 in x+x`

(b) `let x=1 in (let x=2 in x)+x`

(c) `let x=1 in (let y=x in (let x=y+1 in x))+x`

(d) `let x=let y=1 in y+1 in 2*x`

To test the first three examples in Elm, place the definition x = 1 into a file, load the file into the interpreter, and then evaluate the respective bodies of the let expressions, `let x=2 in x+x`, `(let x=2 in x)+x`, and `(let y=x in (let x=y+1 in x))+x`.

```
    let x=1 in x+(let x=5 in 2*x)+x
=> let x=1 in x+2*5+x
=> 1+2*5+1
=> 12
```

In many cases, it is possible to obtain different traces by simplifying subexpressions in a different order.

Since Elm expressions don't have any side effects,[5] the order of evaluation does not change the final result. For example, we could have just as well evaluated the outermost subexpression first.

```
    let x=1 in x+(let x=5 in 2*x)+x
=> 1+(let x=5 in 2*x)+1
=> 1+2*5+1
=> 12
```

Tracing expression evaluation is particularly useful in understanding the behavior of recursively defined functions and functions defined on data types such as lists. As an example, consider the following definition of the function rev for reversing the elements of a list.

```
rev : List Int -> List Int
rev l = case l of
    []     -> []
    x::xs -> rev xs ++ [x]
```

In addition to the type signature that says that rev takes a list of integers and produces a list of integers, the definition consists of a case expression that inspects the argument list l to consider the two possible cases of a list. The result of each

---

[5] A side effect is a change to the underlying program state made by an expression.

case is the expression to the right of the -> symbol. If the argument list is empty (that is, []), the resulting list is as well. The second case says that reversing a non-empty list, that is, a list that starts with some element x and is followed by a remainder list (or tail) xs, can be achieved by reversing xs and appending x at the end.[6]

We will discuss recursion in Section 2.4 and lists and pattern matching in Section 2.5. At this point, we want to understand how rev works, and we can do that by tracing example computations. Here is the first step in the trace for the evaluation of the expression rev [1,2,3].

```
    rev [1,2,3]
=> rev [2,3] ++ [1]
```

Note that the expression in the second line is parsed as (rev [2,3]) ++ [1], since function application has a higher syntactic precedence than infix operations.

Each step in a trace is obtained by substituting a function application by its result. For functions defined by case expressions this means to select the case that matches the argument. In our example, since rev is applied to a non-empty list, the second case must be used.

To determine the result expression of the case, we must first match the argument list [1,2,3] against the pattern x::xs. A pattern is an expression that may contain variables. In this example, the pattern x::xs denotes a list with first element x and tail xs. Matching a pattern against a value means to create bindings for the variables in the pattern, using the values from the argument. In this case, since the argument list [1,2,3] is just a nicer representation[7] of 1::[2,3], x will be bound to 1, and xs will be bound to [2,3].

Once the pattern on the left side of the arrow has been successfully matched against the argument, the result expression can be produced using the just-created bindings to substitute the variables. In our example this means to replace rev [1,2,3] by rev xs ++ [x] while substituting x by 1 and xs by [2,3]. This step can be made precise by using the trace notation: we first perform a substitution step, followed by a simplification of the let expression.

```
    rev [1,2,3]
=> let x=1 in let xs=[2,3] in rev xs ++ [x]
=> rev [2,3] ++ [1]
```

The intermediate step that makes the variable bindings explicit is usually omitted, but there is nothing wrong with including it if it is helpful in explaining how the bindings are handled.

---

[6]Here x::xs denotes a pattern of a non-empty list with first element x and tail xs, [x] creates a singleton list consisting of the element x, and ++ is a function that appends two lists.

[7]Sometimes called *syntactic sugar*.

The next step in the trace is obtained in exactly the same way, except that pattern matching now yields different variable bindings, that is, we replace the application rev [2,3] as follows.

```
   rev [2,3]
=> let x=2 in let xs=[3] in rev xs ++ [x]
=> rev [3] ++ [2]
```

The resulting expression is placed in the context of rev [2,3] of the trace, which leads to the following step in the trace.

```
   rev [2,3] ++ [1]
=> rev [3] ++ [2] ++ [1]
```

At this point we[8] have a choice to either continue with evaluating rev [3] or evaluating the rightmost application of ++ (which is allowed because the function ++ is associative). This is often a matter of taste. In the interest of keeping the traces small, let's evaluate the subexpression [2] ++ [1] next, which leads to the following step in the trace.

```
   rev [3] ++ [2] ++ [1]
=> rev [3] ++ [2,1]
```

We have treated ++ here as an atomic operation that concatenates two lists, which makes sense, since this effect is easy to show in a trace. However, ++ is actually itself a recursively defined function, and we could thus inspect the details of this computation by constructing a trace (see Exercise 2.3).

The next step in the trace is to evaluate rev [3]. Since [3] is syntactic sugar for the list constructed by 3::[], this leads to the following steps.

```
   rev [3]
=> let x=3 in let xs=[] in rev xs ++ [x]
=> rev [] ++ [3]
```

We can integrate this simplification into the trace and then again evaluate another application of ++.

```
   rev [3] ++ [2,1]
=> rev [] ++ [3] ++ [2,1]
=> rev [] ++ [3,2,1]
```

At this point, rev is applied to the empty list, which triggers the first case and yields []. By evaluating another append operation we get our final result.

---

[8]While the Elm interpreter will always evaluate in a specific order, humans who want to make sense of evaluations through traces can very well exploit algebraic laws about operations to explore different orderings.

```
   rev [] ++ [3,2,1]
=> [] ++ [3,2,1]
=> [3,2,1]
```

As a summary, here is the complete trace we just discussed, plus an alternative that results when we always evaluate recursive calls before ++.

```
     rev [1,2,3]                          rev [1,2,3]
=> rev [2,3] ++ [1]                  => rev [2,3] ++ [1]
=> rev [3] ++ [2] ++ [1]             => rev [3] ++ [2] ++ [1]
=> rev [3] ++ [2,1]                  => rev [] ++ [3] ++ [2] ++ [1]
=> rev [] ++ [3] ++ [2,1]            => [] ++ [3] ++ [2] ++ [1]
=> rev [] ++ [3,2,1]                 => [3] ++ [2] ++ [1]
=> [] ++ [3,2,1]                     => [3,2] ++ [1]
=> [3,2,1]                           => [3,2,1]
```

The tracing examples highlight the simplicity of functional programming: any computation happens by repeatedly replacing function applications by the function's definition in which all parameters are substituted by the arguments of the application (plus evaluation of basic operations, such as arithmetic). This observation is reflected by the fact that lambda calculus, the computational model that underlies functional programming, consists of only a single rule for computation (called β-reduction for historical reasons).

Exercise 2.3

Consider the following definition of the function ++ for appending two lists (see Section 2.5).[a]

```
(++) : List Int -> List Int -> List Int
(++) l1 l2 = case l1 of
    []     -> l2
    x::xs -> x::(xs ++ l2)
```

Create a trace for the evaluation of the expression [1,2] ++ [5] ++ [8].

---

[a]Note that in version 0.19 Elm has removed the ability to define infix operators, so we can't actually define the function ourselves in this way. But Elm does provide ++ as a built-in operator, which acts exactly according to the shown definition.

2.2.3   Tuples

A tuple is a data structure for representing aggregate data. A tuple can have two or more components,[9] which can be of potentially different types.

```
> (2.5,3.0+1)                        > (2==3,'a',[])
(2.5,4) : (Float,Float)              (False,'a',[]) : (Bool,Char,List a)
```

Tuples can also be nested.

```
> (2==3,(5/5,'a'))
(False,(1,'a')) : (Bool,(Float,Char))
```

The type of a tuple is a tuple type, which has the types of its components as argument types.

As indicated above, the type variable number indicates that a value can be either of type Int or Float. Consider the following example.

```
> (1,2)
(1,2) : (number,number1)
```

The fact that the type of the result uses two different type variables, number and number1, allows both tuple components to be of different number types (one could be an integer while the other one could be a float). This is why the following example works: at the time of definition, both tuple components have an unspecified number type, which allows the later use of the first component as an integer and the second one as a float.

```
> let (x,y) = (3,2) in (modBy 2 x,sqrt y)
(1,1.4142135623730951) : (Int,Float)
```

Note also that the nesting structure of tuples matters and is part of the tuple type, which means that, for example, the values (1,(2,3)), ((1,2),3), and (1,2,3) all have different types and can't even be compared.

The components of a tuple are accessed by position, which is typically done using pattern matching (as shown in the previous example and to be discussed in more detail in Section 2.6). For pairs, the two predefined functions first and second can access the first and second components, respectively.[10]

```
> Tuple.first (2+1,'a')        > Tuple.first (Tuple.second (True,("Hello",3)))
3 : number                     "Hello" : String
```

---

[9]A one-tuple is indistinguishable from a single value; the null-tuple value () is also called *unit*; it's the only value of type () (also called *unit*). Elm accepts only pairs or triples; tuples with more components have to be represented by records (which we won't discuss here).

[10]The functions are defined in the Tuple module and thus have to be either imported or used as qualified names.

2.3   Functions

Functional programming is centered around the definition and use of functions. A function takes an argument of some type T and transforms it into a result of some type U. The function has then the function type T -> U. We also say that T is the functions's *argument type* and U is the functions's *result type*. The transformation performed by a function is defined by an expression. Functions also typically have a name that allows them to be used many times, but this isn't strictly necessary as we will see.

2.3.1   Function Application

The syntax for applying a function f to an argument expression e is f e, that is, it uses plain prefix notation, that is, the function name[11] followed by its argument.[12] Note that e needs to be in parentheses only if it is not a name or value but another expression built through function application. This means that parentheses in an application such as f(3) are redundant and are conveniently omitted in Elm.

```
> sqrt 4        │  > sqrt(4)       │  > sqrt (4+5)    │  > sqrt 4+5
2 : Float       │  2 : Float       │  3 : Float       │  7 : Float
```

As can be seen in the last example, function application binds most strongly, that is, the expression is parsed as (sqrt 4)+5; to compute the square root of 4+5, the argument must be put into parentheses, as shown in the third example.

How do we apply functions that take more than one argument? We have seen that some binary operations are written using infix notation in between their arguments, but that doesn't work for functions with three or more arguments. One possibility is to group all arguments into a tuple and apply the function to the tuple. We have seen this already with the functions first and second. In functional languages, however, the general approach is to simply list the arguments following the function, again adding parentheses only when necessary. For example, to compute the smaller of 7 and 5*2 we write the following.[13]

```
> min 7 (5*2)
7 : number
```

---

[11]In general, the function to be applied need not be a name or symbol; it can itself be an expression, as long as it evaluates to a function.

[12]When the function has several arguments, say e1, e2, and e3, the prefix notation for function application is f e1 e2 e3. And, as already mentioned, binary operations with symbols as names such as + are written using infix notation.

[13]Quick test: what's the result of min 7 5*2?

2.3.2 Currying and Partial Function Application

What is the type of the function `min`? It can't be `(Int,Int) -> Int`, because in that case, we would have to apply the function to a pair, as in `min (7,5*2)`. It turns out that the type of the `min` function[14] is actually as follows.

```
min : Int -> Int -> Int
```

You can read and understand this type simply as saying that `min` takes two integer arguments (separated by space) and returns an integer. But still the notation may look peculiar. In particular, one may wonder what the purpose of the two function arrows is. The function arrow associates to the right, which means the above type is syntactic sugar for the following fully parenthesized type.

```
min :: Int -> (Int -> Int)
```

Now this type says that `min` is a function that takes a value of type `Int` and returns a (unary) function of type `Int -> Int`. The `min` function therefore takes an integer *n* and returns a function that computes the minimum of any value compared to *n*. Specifically, this means we can apply `min` to only one integer, bind the resulting function to a name, and then use that name to apply the function repeatedly.[15]

```
> let sofa = min 4 in (sofa 3,sofa 4,sofa 5)
(3,4,4) : (number,number1,number2)
```

Applying a function to only some of its arguments is called *partial function application*. It is a convenient feature that supports creating specialized instances of functions "on the fly." These kinds of function definitions that support partial function application are called *curried*[16] *function definitions*.

The fact that curried function definitions return functions as results can be made clear by considering an alternative way of defining functions. In Elm, we can write down a function value using so-called *lambda abstraction*. For example, the square function can be written as follows.

```
\x->x*x
```

Since this function has not been given a name, it's also called an *anonymous function*.

---

[14]As already mentioned, many functions in Elm are overloaded. And `min` is no different; its most general type is actually `min :: comparable -> comparable -> comparable`, which means that it can compute the smaller of two values for any type that has a `<=` operation defined, which includes numbers, characters, and strings, as well as lists and tuples of comparable types. For example, `min 'b' 'y' = 'b'` and `min [1,2,3] [1,2] = [1,2]`.

[15]Here `sofa` is meant to be read as "compute the *smaller of four and ...*".

[16]Name so after the logician Haskell B. Curry.

We can directly apply anonymous functions, put them into a data structure, or give them a name and then use them through the name.

```
> (\x->x*x) 4  | > Tuple.first (\x->x*x,abs) 5  | > let sqr = \x->x*x in sqr 6
16 : number    | 25 : number                     | 36 : number
```

In general, any equation f x = e can be also written as f = \x->e. For a function such as min this means we can either define it by listing all parameters on the left of the = sign, like so ...

```
min x y = if x<y then x else y
```

... or we can move arguments over to the right of the = sign and turn the expression into a lambda abstraction, which leads to the following.

```
min x = \y->if x<y then x else y
```

Both definitions are equivalent, but the latter emphasizes the fact that min is a function that takes a value *a* (that will be bound to the parameter named x) and then returns a function that will take another value *b* (that will be bound to the parameter named y) and returns *a* if *a* is smaller than *b* or otherwise returns *b*. More generally, this means that a function of *n* arguments can be viewed as a function of 1 argument that returns a function of *n* − 1 arguments.

We can also nest lambda abstractions. In the case for min that means we can also move the first argument to the right of the = sign and obtain as another equivalent definition the following.

```
min = \x->\y->if x<y then x else y
```

Partial function application also works for binary operations that are written in infix notation by placing the operation in parentheses and then applying it only to its first argument. Here are some examples.

```
succ = (+) 1  |  triple = (*) 3  |  twoToThe = (^) 2  |  oneOver = (/) 1
```

All these functions can then be applied to single values.

```
> succ 5      | > triple 6      | > twoToThe 7      | > oneOver 8
6 : number    | 18 : number     | 128 : number      | 0.125 : Float
```

Partial function application works in these cases because putting an infix operation into parentheses turns it into a prefix-notation function, that is, we can write 3+5 also as (+) 3 5.

```
> (+)
<function> : number -> number -> number
```

For the partially applied function `(+) 1` we then have the following type.

```
> (+) 1
<function> : number -> number
```

Note that partial function application is not tied to numeric functions; it works for functions of any type.

```
> isZero = (==) 0                    > greet = (++) "Hello "
<function> : number -> Bool          <function> : String -> String
```

Again, the resulting functions take one less argument. In this case, we again have obtained unary functions.

```
> isZero 0        > isZero 1              > greet "Kitty"
True : Bool       False : Bool            "Hello Kitty" : String
```

Partial function application is possible in languages that have so-called *higher-order functions*. Specifically, it must be possible for functions to return functions as a result. See Section 2.7 for more details.

Exercise 2.4

Similar to the function `isZero`, define the function `isPositive` using partial function application. *Note*: The solution is less obvious than you might think. If your first attempt fails, think about the fact that a definition `isPositive = f a`, when applied to an argument `b`, will result in the computation of `f a b` and what the order of arguments means for the choice of `f`.

2.3.3 Function Definitions

A function definition consists of a name, a type, and a defining expression. Consider the function `min3` that computes the smallest of three numbers. Since the function takes three arguments and returns one result, its type signature should be as follows.

```
min3 : Int -> Int -> Int -> Int
```

Strictly speaking, a definition doesn't always need a type signature, since the type can in most cases be inferred from the definition itself. However, starting any (non-trivial) function definition by giving a type signature is a good idea because types describe functions and programs more abstractly on a high level. A type acts as documentation and gives programmers the opportunity to express their intention about the function. The implementation of the function can then be checked against this intention by the type checker, and potential errors in the implementation can often be identified by the compiler.

Before reading any further, think about how you would define a function min3 that computes the smallest of three numbers. An implementation that uses a nested if-then-else with multiple comparisons should aim to describe three conditions that have to be true for each argument to be the result.

Here is a possible implementation that uses Elm's logical *and* operation &&.

```
min3 x y z = if x<=y && x<=z then x else
                if y<=x && y<=z then y else z
```

This definition is not so easy to read. One could use line breaks and indentation, but that makes the definition needlessly longer.

Nevertheless, we can improve the definition for min3. When implementing a function, you should always think about possibly reusing functions that have already been defined and that could be reused. For this example, we can profitably put the function min to work to obtain the following succinct implementation of min3.

```
min3 : Int -> Int -> Int -> Int
min3 x y z = min x (min y z)
```

Such a definition is preferable in most situations, since it is shorter and (in this case) requires less effort to understand. Being more succinct offers fewer opportunities for making mistakes (it's very easy to swap variable names in the conditions, which might lead to an error that might be difficult to detect). But the main benefit comes from the reduction of the definition to something already understood.

Exercise 2.5

Define a function sign that takes an integer and returns -1 if the argument is negative, 1 if the argument is positive, and 0 otherwise. First, define the function using two if-then-else expressions. Then think of a definition that needs only one if-then-else expression. (*Hint*: // is integer division, and abs computes absolute values.)

2.4   Iteration and Recursion

Consider the following excerpt from a C program for computing the factorial of 6. The while loop iterates over the values of n (downwards to 1) and accumulates the result in the variable f.

```
int f = 1;
int n = 6;
while (n>1) {
  f = f*n;
  n = n-1;
}
printf("%d\n",f);
```

The while loop effectively works like a conditional plus a jump,[17] that is, if the loop condition is true, the statements in the body of the loop are executed, followed by jump to the beginning of the loop. If the loop condition is false, the computation continues with the first statement after the loop. To concretely illustrate this fact, we can rewrite the program snippet into the following equivalent C code.[18] (The changed parts in the program are highlighted.)

```
int f = 1;
int n = 6;
fac:
if (n>1) {
  f = f*n;
  n = n-1;
  goto fac; }
else
  printf("%d\n",f);
```

Any while loop works by manipulating some part of the program state. In this example the state changes affect the two integer variables f and n. Specifically, f is updated to be f*n, and n is updated to be n-1.

If we had a mechanism to make this state explicit in the name for the loop (represented by the label fac) through, say, a list of parameters, then we could pass the updates directly to the parameters in the jump, and we could also initialize the loop in the same way. If we do that and also drop the goto keyword, we obtain the following program fragment.

```
fac(1,6);

fac (int f,int n) {
if (n>1)
   fac (f*n,n-1) ;
else
   printf("%d\n",f);
}
```

---

[17]That's actually what while loops are compiled into on most architectures.
[18]Labels and goto statements are indeed part of the C programming language.

You may already have noticed that this is actually valid C code for the definition and use of a recursive function fac.

The point of this example is that a recursive function definition can act as a description of a while loop. In fact, it could arguably be considered a better notation for loops than the while syntax because:

- it makes the type of state and its initialization explicit,
- it treats updates as transactions (that is, performs them independently of one another) and thus simplifies code understanding by avoiding state dependencies, and
- it makes the loop reusable by giving it a name.

In Elm we can define the same function as follows. The major conceptual difference is that the Elm function returns a value, whereas the C function performs an output side effect.

```
fac : (Int,Int) -> Int
fac (f,n) = if n>1 then
                 fac (f*n,n-1)
            else
                 f
```

The use of a pair for the two arguments and the multi-line conditional illustrate the similarity to the C notation. In particular, the loop has to be called in the same way by explicitly passing both arguments for f and n to fac. In Elm we would probably define the function in curried form, without a pair as argument.

```
fac : Int -> Int -> Int
fac f n = if n>1 then fac (f*n) (n-1) else f
```

In any case, this definition requires the initialization of the f parameter, that is, the loop has to be called as fac 1 6. However, we can put the curried function definition to good use here and partially apply fac to the initial value of the accumulator f to define the following function.

```
factorial : Int -> Int
factorial = fac 1
```

We can now compute the factorial of 6 through the call factorial 6.

We can observe that the accumulated factorial value does not have to be carried around explicitly in the state, since the intermediate values can be computed by the recursive function itself. This is often the case for problems that are by their very nature recursive, that is, the definition of the function tracks the inductive definition of the input. In the case of the factorial, the definition consists of two cases: one for the base case 1, and one for the general case *n* that

RECURSIVE FUNCTION DEFINITIONS

Any recursive definition always consists of at least a *base case* and an *inductive case*.

An effective approach for the definition of a recursive function is therefore to first identify the base case(s) by asking, *For which argument is the function definition trivial?* and, *What is the result in this case?* In some instances, there might be multiple different base cases with possibly different results. In any case, the argument pattern (*p*) and result (*r*) for a base case can in most cases be directly written as a pair *p -> r*.

The next step is to identify the inductive step by asking, *How can the definition for the general case be reduced to, or be expressed in terms of, a solution for a simpler argument?* This step actually requires figuring out two parts. First, we ask, *How is the argument simplified toward the base case?* For numbers, this often means to express the result of f n in terms of f (n-1) (as in the case of fac), and for lists this often means to express the result of f (x::xs) in terms of f xs (as in the case of rev). Second, we ask *How can the result be obtained from the result for a simpler argument?* Here, you should be guided by the result type of the function. For example, the result type of fac is Int, which means the result of the recursive call must be part of an Int operation (which is * in the case of fac).

When the function has multiple parameters, you also have to decide what parameter the recursion should be defined on. In some cases the recursion is on just one argument (think of defining a function plus recursively using only succ), while in other situations the recursion works in parallel on two arguments (think of defining a function merge for merging two sorted lists into one sorted list).

is based on the factorial for the simpler value $n - 1$. Accordingly, the standard recursive implementation of the factorial function needs only one parameter and can be directly implemented as follows.

```
fac : Int -> Int
fac n = if n>1 then n * fac (n-1) else 1
```

Finally, this definition can be simplified yet a little bit more by using pattern matching. We have seen an example of pattern matching earlier with the definition of the function rev, and we will look into pattern matching in more detail in Section 2.5 when we talk about lists, but the basic idea can also be illustrated with numbers. Specifically, we can use number values instead of variables in case expressions to select different cases. For example, we can rewrite the factorial function as follows.[19]

---

[19]Note that the definitions are not equivalent: the last definition of fac does not terminate for arguments that are smaller than 1.

```
fac : Int -> Int
fac x = case x of
    1 -> 1
    n -> n * fac (n-1)
```

When `fac` is applied to a number, the case expression will scrutinize the value and compare it with 1, and the result 1 is returned only if the argument is 1. Otherwise, the second case is examined, and since any number matches a variable, that case is then executed.

Some general strategies for creating recursive function definitions are briefly described in the box *Recursive Function Definitions* on page 33.

Exercise 2.6

Remember to approach the definition of a recursive function by first identifying the base case(s) and then the inductive/recursive case.

(a) Define a function `ld : Int -> Int` that computes base-2 logarithms of integers as (rounded down) integers. For example, `ld 512 = ld 513 = 9` while `ld 511 = 8`.

(b) Define a function `isEven : Int -> Bool` that yields `True` for even positive numbers and `False` for odd positive numbers. Don't use the functions `modBy` or `remainderBy`. (Hint: You should use a `case` expression with three cases: one for the base case 0, one for the base case 1, and one case for all other numbers n, which requires a recursive definition.)

(c) Define a function `fib : Int -> Int` for computing Fibonacci numbers.

2.5   Lists and Pattern Matching

Lists are the most important data structure in Elm and any functional language. Lists are a specific example of a *data type*. Each data type has one or more so-called *constructors* (also called *data constructors*), each of which carries zero or more arguments of potentially different types to represent the information for that particular case of the data type. Lists have the following two constructors.

> `[]` to represent an empty list, and
> `::` to add an element at the front of a list
> (The constructor `::` is called *cons* for historical reasons.)

Specifically, the syntax for adding e at the beginning of list 1 is e::1. Thus, to construct a list of the number 3 followed by the number 5, we can write the following.

```
> 3::5::[]              |   > [3,5]               |   > 3::[5]
[3,5] : List number     |   [3,5] : List number   |   [3,5] : List number
```

On the left we can observe that Elm prints lists by simply listing the elements in square brackets, and since lists are so important, this syntax is also offered as a more convenient way to write lists with a specific number of elements, as shown in the second example. The third example shows how we can combine the different notations.

We can also construct integer lists from elements within a specified range.

```
> List.range 3 5
[3,4,5] : List Int
```

The range function lives in the List module that contains many other useful functions on lists. If we don't import the function, we can still use it using the module name List as a qualifier for the function name.

Lists are a *polymorphic* (or *parameterized*) data type, that is, lists can store elements of arbitrary types, so we can have lists of Booleans, lists of characters, lists of lists of numbers, and even lists of functions.

```
> [1==2,True]              |   > [[1,2],[],[3]]
[False,True] : List Bool   |   [[1,2],[],[3]] : List (List number)

> ['H','i']                |   > [(*) 2,fac]
['H','i'] : List Char      |   [<function>,<function>] : List (Int -> Int)
```

Since we can build lists of different types, the type of the two list constructors is described using *type variables*.

```
> []                       |   > (::)
[] : List a                |   <function> : a -> List a -> List a
```

These two type signatures say that the empty list [] can be of any list type and that :: can add an individual element of any type at the beginning of a list of elements *of the same type*. This constraint is expressed by using the same type variable a for the type of the single element and the type of the elements in the list.

This constraint also means that while lists are polymorphic and thus can carry data of any type, they are also *homogeneous*, that is, all the elements in a list must have the same type, that is, lists such as [2,True] or [2,[3,4]] cannot be built.

Why is the latter example incorrect? It only contains numbers, and we said that lists can contain other lists. The problem is that the elements of the list do not have the same type. While the list [2,3,4] has the type List Int (that is, the elements in the list all have the type Int), and the list [[1,2],[],[3]] has the type List (List Int) (that is, the elements in the list all have the type List Int), the first element in the list [2,[3,4]] is of type Int whereas the second element is of type List Int. These are different types, and thus the list is not homogeneous.

Why is it important that all elements in a list have the same type? This is because Elm is a so-called *statically typed* language (see Section 5.5), which means that no program will be run that could lead to a runtime type error. If we allowed the construction of lists with elements of different types, the type checker could not ensure, without running a program, that the program would not lead to a type error.

To append two lists, you can use the predefined function ++, which we have seen before. Again, the use of the same type variable for both argument lists and the result list ensures that we can only append lists of the same type. If we look at the type of ++ in Elm, we notice that the type does not mention lists but curiously mentions the type variable appendable.

```
> (++)
<function> : appendable -> appendable -> appendable
```

The type variable appendable stands for lists of any type or strings, that is, we can think of (++) as an overloaded symbol for two functions of the following types.

```
(++) : List a -> List a -> List a
(++) : String -> String -> String
```

Note the slight but important difference between the types of ++ and ::. You have to remember that :: requires a single element as its first argument, whereas ++ takes a list.

Building lists is nice but gets boring quickly. What we really want to do is to compute with lists. So what can we do with lists? Since lists are constructed inductively, the most basic operation on lists is to inspect their structure, that is, using a case expression with *pattern matching* we can check whether a list is empty, and we can access the first element and tail of any non-empty list. For example, we can define the function isEmpty as follows.

```
isEmpty : List a -> Bool
isEmpty l = case l of
    []    -> True
    x::xs -> False
```

Similarly, since pattern matching gives us access to the components of a non-empty list, we can try to define functions head and tail for extracting the first element and remainder of a list, respectively. Let's start with head. We can start the following definition.

```
head : List a -> a
head l = case l of
    []    -> ...      -- Which value to return?
    x::xs -> x
```

But here we notice a problem: what value should we return in the case of an empty list? Since an empty list doesn't contain any values, we can't return one. Picking some default value is not an option, since there is no single value that is an element of every type. Since Elm requires pattern matching to be complete, that is, Elm requires a case for each constructor of the data type analyzed by the case expression, we cannot simply omit the [] case, and thus we are unable to complete this definition.

Another option would be to avoid a polymorphic definition and define head only for, say, integers, that is, with type List Int -> Int. In this case, we could return 0 or -9999 or some other arbitrary value, but this would not be a good idea, since this would let the function successfully indicate the computation of the head of a list that does not exit, which is bound to lead to difficult-to-spot programming errors down the road. Moreover, by giving up polymorphism we would have to define a separate head function for each different list type, which is not an attractive prospect.

Another idea is to return some kind of error value, but Elm doesn't offer this as a possibility.

Our predicament is caused by the fact that head is a *partial* function, that is, it is only defined for some elements of its argument type. We can acknowledge the partiality of head in its return type by using the Maybe type, which is specifically designed for such situations. The Maybe type has two constructors, Just for carrying "ordinary," non-error values and Nothing for representing error situations. The Maybe type is defined as follows.

```
type Maybe a = Just a | Nothing
```

With Maybe we can implement the head function by representing the success or failure in the return type. Specifically, we use the Just constructor to indicate that the function was successful and the Nothing constructor to represent an error in the case of empty lists.

```
head : List a -> Maybe a
head l = case l of
    []    -> Nothing
    x::xs -> Just x
```

Using Maybe in the result type has turned head into a total function that can never fail. The price for this guarantee is that we have to work with a more complex return type. Specifically, further operations on elements returned by head have to distinguish between the two cases represented by the two constructors Just and Nothing. For example, suppose we are given an integer list l and want to multiply its first element by 5. If we try to evaluate the expression head l * 5, we encounter a type error that tells us that head produces a Maybe Int and that * only works with Int (and Float).

Similar to head, the function List.tail also distinguishes in its return type between empty and non-empty lists.[20]

```
> List.tail
<function> : List a -> Maybe (List a)
```

With isEmpty, head, and tail we can inspect lists and extract parts as follows.

```
> isEmpty []                          > head [5,6,7]
True : Bool                           Just 5 : Maybe number

> isEmpty [2,3]                       > tail [5,6,7]
False : Bool                          Just [6,7] : Maybe (List number)
```

These three basic access functions are actually sufficient to implement any function on lists. Consider, for example, a function for computing the sum of a list of numbers. For an empty list, the sum is 0, and for a non-empty list, the sum is obtained by adding the first element to the sum of the list tail. We may be tempted to start a definition using the predicate isEmpty to distinguish between the two cases of a list and to extract the head of the list in the non-empty case using head, like so.

```
sum : List Int -> Int
sum l = if isEmpty l then 0 else head xs + ...   -- head returns Maybe Int
```

However, we are now faced with the problem that head returns a value of type Maybe Int, which cannot be used as an argument for +. The solution is to distinguish between the two cases of a list with a case expression, which provides direct access to the head and tail of non-empty lists. This leads to the following definition.

```
sum : List Int -> Int
sum l = case l of
    []    -> 0
    x::xs -> x + sum xs
```

---

[20]We can save ourselves the typing of qualified function names by importing all list functions from the module List with import List exposing (..).

Notably, the structure of the definition for sum is identical to that of head, tail, and isEmpty. This is no surprise. Since lists are inductively defined by the two constructors [] and ::, functions for processing lists will generally have to inspect the structure of lists and perform different computations based on the encountered structure.

It should be noted that case expressions with pattern matching are a convenient programming tool. For example, the pattern x::xs for the non-empty lists has two important effects:

- First, it matches only non-empty lists and directs a case expression to the appropriate case.
- Second, when matched against a non-empty list, the head of that list will be bound to x, and the tail will be bound to xs. These bindings can then be used on the right side of the arrow in the result expression.

It is this double-duty of pattern matching (discriminating between different cases of a data type and binding variables to the arguments of the constructor) that makes it such a convenient tool for function definitions.

In general, a pattern is an expression built from constructors, values, and variables, which means we can construct nested patterns, as in the following function that extracts the second element from a list.

```
snd : List a -> Maybe a
snd l = case l of
    x::y::ys -> Just y
    _        -> Nothing
```

The pattern x::y::ys matches a list that contains at least two elements, which are bound to the variables x and y, respectively. The variable ys will be bound to the remainder of the list, that is, the list without the first two elements. This pattern fails to match empty lists as well as lists that contain only one element. Since in both of these cases the function snd would be undefined, we can combine them into the so-called *wildcard pattern* _, which matches anything.

We can use the wildcard for all arguments of a pattern that are not needed in the function body, which means we could replace x and ys in the definition of snd by _. The use of wildcards is generally good programming practice, since it already indicates in the pattern that the corresponding parts of the data structure will be discarded. And it also helps prevent certain programming errors, since you can't accidentally use the wrong part of a data structure.

Note that a pattern must not contain function names, that is, we cannot write case expressions such as this one.

```
case l of
    xs++ys = ...                    -- INVALID PATTERN
```

In other words, case expressions cannot detect which function was used to construct a value: they can only inspect constructors.

Note also that a pattern must not contain repeated variables. For example, the following attempt to identify duplicate elements at the beginning of a list does *not* work.

```
rmDup : List a -> List a
rmDup l = case l of
    x::x::xs -> rmDup (x::xs)          -- INVALID PATTERN
    ...
```

However, it is easy to express the intended constraint through a condition.

```
rmDup l = case l of
    x::y::xs -> (if x==y then [] else [x]) ++ rmDup (y::xs)
    ...
```

The function sum illustrates how to consume lists of arbitrary length through recursion. We should also examine at least one function that constructs lists of varying length through recursion. As an example, consider the definition of the function range that constructs a list of integers in the range between two given numbers n and m. The key, as always, is to identify the base and inductive cases for the recursion. When the function to be defined builds a list, one can identify the base case by asking under which condition the result list is empty. This happens when $n > m$ because no numbers exist between n and m in this case. Otherwise, n will be part of the constructed list. Specifically, n precedes the elements of the list in the range $n + 1$ to m, which is obtained through a recursive call.

```
range : Int -> Int -> List Int
range n m = if n>m then [] else n::range (n+1) m
```

2.6   Data Types

In Elm, data structures are built with data types.[21] As already mentioned in Section 2.5, a data type provides *constructors* (also called *data constructors*) that may carry arguments of specific types. In addition to lists, we have already encountered two other data types, namely Maybe and Boolean values. The type Bool is actually not built into Elm but is defined by the following type definition.

---

[21]These are also sometimes called *algebraic* data types, since types are constructed with operations from sums (expressing alternatives or variants) and products (expressing tuples or records). The resulting types are correspondingly often called *sum types* (or *variant types*) and *product types*, respectively.

> **Exercise 2.7**
>
> (a) Define the function nth : `Int -> List a -> Maybe` a that selects an element from a list by its position. As is common practice, the index for the first element is defined to be 0. The function definition needs two arguments: the index and the list to be selected from. Since the definition is inductive on the number argument, you can apply the same strategy as for `fac` and write a case expression for the base case 0 and the general, inductive case *n*.
>
> (b) Reimplement the function nth using pattern matching for the list argument.
>
> (c) Give a definition of head that is based on nth.
>
> (d) Define the function length : `List a -> Int`.
>
> (e) Give a definition of isEmpty that is based on length.
>
> (f) What pattern matches any list of exactly one element? What pattern matches any list of exactly two elements?
>
> (g) Define the function member : `Int -> List Int -> Bool` that checks whether a particular number is contained in a list.
>
> (h) Define the function delete : `Int -> List Int -> List Int` that deletes all occurrences of the first argument from the list given as a second argument.
>
> (i) Define the function insert : `Int -> List Int -> List Int` that inserts an integer at the correct position into a sorted list of integers.

```
type Bool = True | False
```

This definition says that Bool consists of just two values, represented by the two constructors True and False, which carry no arguments. Data types whose constructors don't have arguments are also called *enumeration types*, and another example of an enumeration type can be found in the file Grading.elm, which defines the type Grade (see Figure 2.1).

Data constructors are similar to object constructors in C++ or Java. However, one important difference is that Elm constructors are immutable, that is, once you have called a constructor with an argument, that value is built and stays in memory until it is not referenced anymore and can be garbage-collected. This means that to replace an element in a data structure we have to actually rebuild (part of) the data structure with constructors that contain the replacement values while the old values still exist. To see what happens, consider the following function that takes a value x and a list and replaces the first element in the list by x.

```
replFst : a -> List a -> List a
replFst x l = case l of
    []     -> []
    _::xs -> x::xs
```

The pattern _::xs for the list argument matches any non-empty list and binds the tail of that list to xs, that is, when replFst is applied to 99 and [1,2,3], x will be bound to 99, and xs will be bound to [2,3].[22] The result of the application will be the list [99,2,3], which is not surprising. However, we have constructed a new list, and the old list still exists, as can be seen from the following interaction in the Elm interpreter.

```
> ys = [1,2,3]
[1,2,3] : List number
> replFst 99 ys
[99,2,3] : List number
> ys
[1,2,3] : List number
```

As you can see, replFst has produced a new list, and the old list ys was not changed at all. In general, to change a value in a data structure we have to copy the path from the root of the data structure to the element that is to be changed. The other parts of the data structure will be reused and shared between the new and old versions.

The functional behavior of data structures is a good thing, since it prevents side effects. A potential downside is that it is more time- and space-consuming. The question of efficiency is an interesting topic in the context of functional data structures and compilers, but it is not relevant here, since we will use Elm primarily as a mathematical language to describe the syntax and semantics of programming languages.

As another example we consider a data type for binary trees that has two constructors.

```
type Tree = Node Int Tree Tree
          | Leaf
```

This definition introduces a constructor Node that takes an integer value *n* and two trees *l* and *r* and builds a new tree with root *n* and left and right subtrees *l* and *r*, respectively. The constructor Leaf represents an empty tree. Here are the definitions of two trees, lft and t, where lft has three nodes and is used as the left subtree of the root node of tree t.

---

[22]The first list element 1 will be matched against the wildcard without generating a binding.

Exercise 2.8

To change a value somewhere inside a list, we cannot overwrite a list element. Instead we have to construct a new list with the new element in it and copy all elements from the front part of the list.

(a) Define the function `replK :: Int -> a -> List a -> List a` that replaces the kth element of a list. The first `Int` argument indicates the position of the element to be replaced. If the position exceeds the length of the list, the function should do nothing. (*Hint*: You need to consider three cases, one for the empty list, one for non-empty lists and position 0, and one for non-empty lists and position *n*.)

(b) Give a simple definition of `replFst` in terms of `replK`.

(c) Consider the following definitions.

```
xs = range 1 10
ys = replK 3 99 xs
```

Given that the definition for `xs` creates 10 cells in main memory, how many new cells are created by the call `replK 3 xs`? How many elements of the list `xs` are shared with the list `ys`?

```
> lft = Node 3 (Node 1 Leaf Leaf) (Node 5 Leaf Leaf)
Node 3 (Node 1 Leaf Leaf) (Node 5 Leaf Leaf)
    : Tree

t = Node 6 lft (Node 9 Leaf (Node 8 Leaf Leaf))
Node 6 (Node 3 (Node 1 Leaf Leaf) (Node 5 Leaf Leaf))
       (Node 9 Leaf (Node 8 Leaf Leaf))
    : Tree
```

Functions on the `Tree` data type are defined in a similar way to functions on lists, namely by case expressions that use patterns for the different constructors. As an example, consider the following definition of the function `inorder` that produces a list of nodes obtained by an in-order traversal of a tree.

```
inorder : Tree -> List Int
inorder t = case t of
    Leaf      -> []
    Node x l r -> inorder l ++ [x] ++ inorder r
```

Since the `Node` constructor takes three arguments, the corresponding pattern has three variables to match the value in the node as well as the left and right subtrees.

The definition of a data type directs or even dictates, to a large degree, the structure of function definitions for that type: for each constructor the function will have a separate case with a corresponding pattern that defines how to deal with that case of the type. However, this is not always the case: as we have seen with the function snd, sometimes several cases can be combined utilizing the wildcard.

We will use data types specifically to represent the abstract syntax of languages in Chapter 3. We will then also learn more about further aspects of data types and pattern matching.

Exercise 2.9

(a) Define the function preorder : Tree -> List Int that produces a list of nodes obtained by a pre-order traversal of the tree.

(b) Define a function findBST : Int -> Tree -> Bool that determines whether a number is contained in a tree, assuming that the tree is a binary search tree.

(c) Define a function find : Int -> Tree -> Bool that determines whether a number is contained in a tree. Don't assume that the tree is a binary search tree!

2.7 Higher-Order Functions

In functional programming, functions are values much like numbers or lists. Of course, we can't multiply functions like numbers, but we can't do that with lists either. Values of a particular type always support a specific set of operations. For numbers it is arithmetic operations such as multiplication, for lists (and all other data types) it is constructing values with constructors and deconstructing values using pattern matching. The two operations allowed for functions are (lambda) *abstraction* and *application*.

Since functions are values, we should be able to treat them like other values, that is, store them in lists, pass them as arguments to functions, and return them as results from functions. Functional languages, such as Elm, that allow functions to be handled this way are said to treat functions as *first-class citizens*, and a function that takes functions as arguments and/or produces a function as a result is called a *higher-order function*.

The function map is such a higher-order function: it takes a function, applies it to all elements of a list, and yields the list of all the results. The definition is as follows.

```
map : (a -> b) -> List a -> List b
map f l = case l of
    []    -> []
    x::xs -> f x::map f xs
```

The type of map indicates its generality: it can be applied to lists containing any kind of elements, and it can return a list of a different type, depending on the type of the applied function.

The function map represents a control structure for traversing a list in a loop. Here are two example applications of map.

```
> map ((^) 2) (range 1 5)        > map isEven [1,2,3,4]
[2,4,8,16,32] : List Int         [False,True,False,True] : List Bool
```

The second example illustrates the generality of map's type, which allows the type of the resulting list to be different from that of the argument list. Note also that the element type of the argument list doesn't have to be a simple type. For example, map can be used to apply functions to lists of lists.

```
> map length [[1,2],[],[3]]      > map sum [[1,2,3],[],range 1 10]
[2,0,1] : List Int               [6,0,55] : List Int
```

And we can also apply a function to all elements in a nested list of lists, which then produces a list of result lists. The key to understanding the following example is to take a close look at the individual types. Since the type of succ is Int -> Int, the type of map succ is List Int -> List Int, that is, map succ is a function that maps integer lists into integer lists. We can use this function then as an argument to map to apply it to a list of integer lists, like so.

```
> succ = (+) 1
<function> : number -> number

> map (map succ) [[1,2,3],range 4 7]
[[2,3,4],[5,6,7,8]] : List (List Int)
```

The importance and wide applicability of map lies in the fact that it implements iteration over a number of values.

Yet, the iteration offered by map is somewhat limited, since the individual list elements are all processed independently of one another. For aggregating the elements of a list, we can employ another higher-order function, foldr, which combines the elements of a list with a binary function. The function is defined as follows.[23]

---

[23]The type of the function is actually more general, namely foldr :: (a -> b -> b) -> b -> List a -> b, but working with the simpler type makes it initially easier to understand the function. The more general type indicates that the elements of a list can be aggregated into a value of a different type.

```
foldr : (a -> a -> a) -> a -> List a -> a
foldr f u l = case l of
    []     -> u
    x::xs -> f x (foldr f u xs)
```

The second argument, u, is used as an initial value for the aggregation. The effect of foldr can be best understood by looking at some examples. Let's start with expressing the sum function as an application of foldr.[24]

```
> sum = foldr (+) 0
<function> : List number -> number

> sum (range 1 10)
55 : Int
```

We can also use foldr to obtain the following succinct implementation of the factorial function.

```
fac : Int -> Int
fac n = foldr (*) 1 (range 2 n)
```

In case you wondered: the r in the name foldr indicates that the elements in the list are consumed from the right, and yes, there is also a function foldl that consumes elements from the left.

Finally, the third higher-order function that can be employed in many situations is function composition, which is written in Elm using the infix operator <<. The function can be thought of as defined as follows.

```
(<<) : (b -> c) -> (a -> b) -> a -> c
f << g = \x -> f (g x)
```

The notation indicates that values flow through the composed functions from right to left, that is, when the function f << g is applied to an argument x, first g x is computed, and the result of that application is then fed into f.

Here are a few example applications for function composition. If you need a function for adding 2 to a number, you can compose the successor function with itself. If you have defined the function isEven, you can obtain the isOdd predicate by composing it with not.

```
add2  = succ << succ          add2 x  = succ (succ x)
isOdd = not << isEven         isOdd x = not (isEven x)
```

---

[24] Remember that putting parentheses around an infix operation turns it into a prefix function. In the example we need to use the parentheses because otherwise, by writing foldr + 0, the Elm parser would assume that we want to apply + to foldr and 0, which is not the case.

As the equivalent definitions on the right illustrate, one can always rewrite the definitions using variables (and parentheses).

The composition of partial functions is a bit more tricky, since we have to deal with the fact that the intermediate values are wrapped in a Maybe type. For example, if we want to extract the second element of a list, we could do this in principle by first taking the tail of the list and then the head of the result. However, the result of the first tail operation is a value of type Maybe (List a), whereas the head operation requires an argument of type List a. What we need to do now is to apply head when the result of tail is a Just value and pass through the Nothing constructor otherwise. The function onJust allows us to do just that. It is one of several higher-order functions that help make programming with Maybe values less cumbersome.

```
onJust : (a -> Maybe b) -> Maybe a -> Maybe b
onJust f m = case m of
    Nothing -> Nothing
    Just x  -> f x
```

With onJust we can now compose head and tail using <<.

```
ht : List a -> Maybe a
ht = onJust head << tail
```

Similarly, if we want to define a function for dropping the first two elements from a list, we can achieve this by composing tail with itself, again using onJust.

```
tt : List a -> Maybe (List a)
tt = onJust tail << tail
```

Higher-order functions are the control structures of functional programming. Notably, none of the functions map, foldr, or << are built-in primitives of Elm; they are all defined as functions. The nice thing is that whenever we need a new specialized control structure, we can define it ourselves. By being able to define our own control structures, we can capture specific patterns of computation, make them explicit, and then use them. We will see examples later in Section 4.2.

Exercise 2.10

(a) Consider the following function definition.

```
th = onJust tail . head
```

Is this function well defined? If so, what is its type, and what does it do?

(b) What does the function `map f << map g` do? How could it be rewritten?

(c) Define the function `last : List a -> Maybe a` as a composition of a list function and the function `rev`.

(d) Consider the following two lists `xs` and `ys`. Note that `ys` is a nested list of lists.

```
xs = [1,2,3]
ys = [xs,[7]]
```

Which of the following expressions are type correct? What values do they evaluate to?

```
map sum xs
map sum ys
last ys
map last ys
last (last ys)
onJust last (last ys)
```

3

Syntax

Chapter Summary

An introduction to the syntax of programming languages. How context-free grammars are used to describe concrete syntax. Parse trees for representing sentence structure. The need for abstract syntax and its relationship to concrete syntax. Abstract syntax trees and how to represent them with Elm data types. Identifying recurring patterns in abstract syntax and how to represent them concisely in Elm.

The syntax of a language serves two major purposes. First, it defines the set of all valid sentences in that language, that is, the syntax of a programming language defines what is a valid program in that language. Second, the syntax defines the *structure* of sentences and programs. Understanding the structure of a sentence is important for understanding its meaning. This becomes clear when we look at examples of ambiguous sentences such as the following.

Alice opened the box with a knife.

The sentence might say that Alice used a knife for opening the box or that she opened a box that contained a knife. Similarly, it is important to understand the syntactic structure of programs. Consider, for example, the following attempt to compute Alice's grade, taking into account a deduction for late submission (see Figure 2.1 on page 15).

```
grade alice-15
```

Programming Language Fundamentals: A Metalanguage Approach in Elm, First edition. Martin Erwig.
© 2024 Martin Erwig. Published 2024 by John Wiley & Sons Inc.
Companion website: www.wiley.com/go/ProgrammingLanguageFun

As we have briefly mentioned in Section 2.1, this expression cannot be evaluated, since it is not type correct. The reason is that the expression is *parsed* as (grade alice)-15, that is, the expression tries to subtract a number from a Grade value, which is not possible.

This example illustrates that the representation of a program's structure is an important step in understanding its meaning. We will therefore first briefly review in Section 3.1 context-free grammars as a metalanguage for describing textual, concrete syntax and in Section 3.2 the notion of parse trees to represent the structure of languages. We will then focus in Section 3.3 on the concept of *abstract syntax* and how to represent abstract syntax in Elm.

3.1   Context-Free Grammars

How can we describe the set of sentences that belong to a language? Trying to simply enumerate them is not viable for languages that contain an infinite number of sentences, which is the case for all non-trivial programming languages. What we need is a finite description for an infinite set. Grammars offer such a description formalism. In fact, the grammar formalism is a metalanguage for describing (the concrete syntax of) languages.

A *grammar* is a formal system that consists of a set of *productions* (or *rules*) that can be used to derive sentences from a start symbol. For example, here are two productions that can generate sequences of zeros followed by twice as many ones.

$$zoo \ ::= \ 0\,1\,1 \qquad \text{(P1)}$$
$$zoo \ ::= \ 0\,zoo\,1\,1 \qquad \text{(P2)}$$

Each production is of the form $L ::= R$ where L and R are sequences of symbols. Every such symbol is either a *non-terminal symbol* (or *non-terminal* for short), written in *italic font*, or a *terminal symbol* (or *terminal* for short), written in typewriter font. A production can be used to repeatedly replace occurrences of L (the left-hand side, or LHS) in a sequence of symbols by R (the right-hand side, or RHS). We sometimes assign names to productions, such as (P1) and (P2), to allow us later to illustrate which productions have been used in a derivation.

In the following we will consider only the restricted case of *context-free grammars*, in which L is always given by a single non-terminal.[1]

---

[1]If we allow the left-hand sides to be sequences of symbols, the productions can depend on the context of the symbol being replaced, which yields a more powerful grammar formalism but one that is more difficult for parsers to work with.

To see our grammar in action, we can apply the second production to replace the start symbol *zoo* by 0 *zoo* 1 1. Then we can apply the first production to replace the new occurrence of *zoo* by 0 1 1. Such a repeated application of productions that ends with a sequence of only terminal symbols is called a *derivation*. Here is the derivation of the sentence 0 0 1 1 1 1 from the non-terminal *zoo*. For each step we show which production was used.

> *zoo*
> ⇒ 0 *zoo* 1 1   (P2)
> ⇒ 0 0 1 1 1 1   (P1)

The final sequence of terminal symbols is called a *sentence*, and the intermediate sequences of the derivation that still contain non-terminal symbols are called *sentential forms*. Sentential forms can be thought of as incomplete sentences that have the potential of becoming a sentence once all their non-terminals have been replaced by terminals.

Formally, a grammar is defined as a four-tuple (N, Σ, P, S) where

(1) N is a set of *non-terminal symbols*,
(2) Σ is a set of *terminal symbols* with $N \cap \Sigma = \varnothing$,
(3) $P \subseteq N \times (N \cup \Sigma)^*$ is a set of *productions*, and
(4) $S \in N$ is the *start symbol*.

With this definition, a sentence is an element of Σ^*, and a sentential form is an element of $(N \cup \Sigma)^*$. Given two sentential forms $\alpha, \beta \in (N \cup \Sigma)^*$, β can be *derived in one step* from α if one of its non-terminals can be replaced using a production so that the resulting sentential form is β, that is, if

(1) $\alpha = \alpha_1 A \alpha_2$ (with $\alpha_1, \alpha_2 \in (N \cup \Sigma)^*$),
(2) $(A, \gamma) \in P$, and
(3) $\beta = \alpha_1 \gamma \alpha_2$.

This one-step derivation relationship between two sentential forms is written as $\alpha \Rightarrow \beta$. The generalization to multi-step derivations is given by the reflexive, transitive closure of the one-step derivation relationship, and we can say that a sentential form β can be *derived* from α (in several steps), written as $\alpha \Rightarrow^* \beta$, if either $\beta = \alpha$ or $\alpha \Rightarrow \alpha'$ and $\alpha' \Rightarrow^* \beta$.

Finally, the *language* $L(G)$ defined by the grammar $G = (N, \Sigma, P, S)$ is the set of all sentences that can be derived from its start symbol, that is,

$$L(G) = \{\sigma \in \Sigma^* \mid S \Rightarrow^* \sigma\}$$

Our previous example grammar is formally defined by the following four-tuple.

$$G_{zoo} = (\{zoo\}, \{0, 1\}, \{(zoo, 0\,1\,1), (zoo, 0\,zoo\,1\,1)\}, zoo)$$

We have previously shown the derivation for the fact $S \Rightarrow^* 001111$, and the language defined by G_{zoo} is $L(G_{zoo}) = \{\, 0^k 1^{2k} \mid k > 0 \,\}$.

The grammar G_{zoo} is quite simple: it has only one terminal symbol, and its two productions don't leave any choice in the derivation of any given sentence. In general, this is of course not the case. Consider the following productions for describing the language of binary digit sequences (BDS).

$$
\begin{array}{lll}
dig & ::= 0 & \text{(P1)} \\
dig & ::= 1 & \text{(P2)} \\
bin & ::= dig & \text{(P3)} \\
bin & ::= dig\, bin & \text{(P4)}
\end{array}
$$

We observe that we have two productions for each of the non-terminals *dig* and *bin*. One consequence in this particular case is that we can obtain different derivations for the same sentence. Consider, for example, the following derivations of the sentence 101 from the start symbol *bin*.

	bin			*bin*			*bin*	
$\Rightarrow$	*dig bin*	(P4)	$\Rightarrow$	*dig bin*	(P4)	$\Rightarrow$	*dig bin*	(P4)
$\Rightarrow$	*dig dig bin*	(P4)	$\Rightarrow$	*dig dig bin*	(P4)	$\Rightarrow$	1 *bin*	(P2)
$\Rightarrow$	*dig dig dig*	(P3)	$\Rightarrow$	*dig dig dig*	(P3)	$\Rightarrow$	1 *dig bin*	(P4)
$\Rightarrow$	1 *dig dig*	(P2)	$\Rightarrow$	*dig dig* 1	(P2)	$\Rightarrow$	10 *bin*	(P1)
$\Rightarrow$	10 *dig*	(P1)	$\Rightarrow$	*dig* 01	(P1)	$\Rightarrow$	10 *dig*	(P3)
$\Rightarrow$	101	(P2)	$\Rightarrow$	101	(P2)	$\Rightarrow$	101	(P2)

The first and second derivation both replace non-terminals by terminals in their last three steps. Notably, the second derivation in the middle column applies the same rules in the same order as the first one, but it does this to different non-terminals in the sentential form. The third derivation replaces non-terminals by terminals as soon as possible.

While grammars sometimes offer a choice in which order to apply productions, the order actually doesn't matter when the goal is to derive a sentence. Ultimately, we are interested in the structure of sentences, which is captured in *parse trees* (explained in Section 3.2) and (abstract) *syntax trees* (explained in Section 3.3). These trees provide representations of sentences that abstract from the order in which productions have been applied. (Again, two examples of abstraction.)

To write down productions more economically, it is common practice to combine productions with the same LHS non-terminal by listing the different RHSs separated by a pipe or bar symbol (|). For the BDS language this looks as follows.

$dig ::= \text{0} \mid \text{1}$
$bin ::= dig \mid dig\,bin$

To identify specific productions, we can use the LHS non-terminal and the position of the RHS in the list. For example, (P1) is (dig_1), and (P4) is (bin_2).

Exercise 3.1

(a) The BDS language allows sequences that start with zeros as sentences. Change the grammar so that it describes proper binary numbers in which all sequences of more than one digit start with a 1.

(b) Write a grammar for Boolean expressions that contain the constants True and False and the unary operation not.

(c) Using the grammar from part (b), create a derivation of the sentence not not True.

If you look closely at the formal definition of a grammar, you will notice that the RHS of a production can be empty. Instead of simply leaving the RHS empty, it is common practice to use the symbol ϵ instead to make this fact explicit. Productions with an empty RHS are therefore also sometimes called ϵ-productions. The use of ϵ-productions can be very convenient and help simplify grammars. For example, we can rewrite the productions for the BDS language using just one non-terminal and three rules as follows.

$bin ::= \text{0}\,bin \mid \text{1}\,bin \mid \epsilon$

Note, however, that the language defined by this grammar is slightly different, since it contains the empty word.

Since ϵ-productions essentially allow the removal of non-terminals from sentential forms during a derivation, derivations often become shorter as well. For example, here is the derivation of the sentence 101 from the start symbol bin using the new grammar.

bin
$\Rightarrow$ 1 bin (bin_2)
$\Rightarrow$ 10 bin (bin_1)
$\Rightarrow$ 101 bin (bin_2)
$\Rightarrow$ 101 (bin_3)

The concept of derivation explains how a sentence can be produced with a grammar. However, the internal structure of the sentence that is revealed through this process is lost.

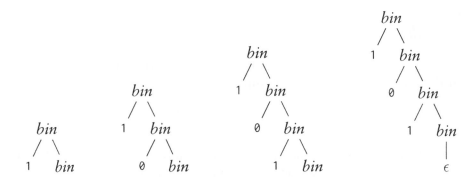

Figure 3.1 Creating a parse tree from the derivation $bin \Rightarrow 1\,bin \Rightarrow 10\,bin \Rightarrow$ $101\,bin \Rightarrow 101$. The leaves of each tree show the sentential form of the current step in the derivation. The leaves of the final tree contain only terminal symbols and thus show the derived sentence. (The ϵ can be regarded as a hidden terminal symbol.)

3.2   Parse Trees

A parse tree represents the structure of a sentence. We can think of a parse tree as a trace of a derivation. The internal nodes of a parse tree contain non-terminal symbols (with the start symbol in the root), and the leaves contain terminal symbols. A *parser* is a program, often part of a compiler or interpreter, that transforms text into parse trees for further processing.

A parse tree for a sentence can be obtained from a derivation for that sentence by following the steps of the derivation. Specifically, for each step in the derivation that applies a production $(A, \alpha_1 \ldots \alpha_n) \in P$ (where we assume $\alpha_1 \ldots \alpha_n \in N \cup \Sigma$) to replace a non-terminal $A \in N$ in the current sentential form, we add the symbols $\alpha_1 \ldots \alpha_n$ as children to the occurrence of A in the tree.

Let's see how we can produce a parse tree for the sentence 101 using the grammar for the BDS language with ϵ-productions. We start with *bin* as the root node and first apply production (bin_2), which means we have to add the symbols of the RHS of that production, 1 and *bin*, as children to the root. We repeat the same step twice, applying productions (bin_1) and (bin_2) to the non-terminal *bin* in the leaf of the tree. In a final step, we apply the ϵ-production. The process is illustrated in Figure 3.1.

The structure of a parse tree depends on the grammar of a language and not just the language. Let's take again a look at the grammar for the BDS language without the ϵ-production.

dig ::= 0 | 1
bin ::= dig | $dig\,bin$

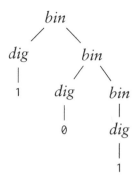

Figure 3.2 Parse tree for the sentence 101 based on the grammar without ϵ-productions.

The parse tree for the sentence 101 is shown in Figure 3.2; its structure is quite different from the parse tree in Figure 3.1.

A crucial property of parse trees is the following: while it does contain information about *which* productions have been applied, it does *not* tell us in which *order* they were applied. Specifically, if you recall the different derivations for the sentence 101 shown earlier, you will notice that they all produce the same parse tree.

The structure of either of the parse trees for 101 is admittedly not very interesting (as is the BDS language). However, for more complex languages parse trees contain important information about the structure of sentences, which can be exploited in the definition of the language's semantics.

As an example, let's consider the following grammar for a simple form of arithmetic expressions.

$$
\begin{aligned}
num &::= \texttt{0} \mid \texttt{1} \mid \texttt{2} \mid \texttt{3} \mid \ldots \\
expr &::= num \mid expr + expr \mid expr * expr
\end{aligned}
$$

Now consider the expression 1+2*3. It turns out that by switching the order in which we apply the productions $(expr_2)$ and $(expr_3)$ we get two derivations that produce different parse trees. We only have to look at the first two derivation steps to see what's going on. Since the sentential forms contain two occurrences of *expr*, I have underlined in the derivation the non-terminal that is going to be replaced in the next step.

	expr				*expr*	
⇒	*expr* + *expr*	$(expr_2)$		⇒	*expr* * *expr*	$(expr_3)$
⇒	*expr* + *expr* * *expr*	$(expr_3)$		⇒	*expr* + *expr* * *expr*	$(expr_2)$
	. . .				. . .	

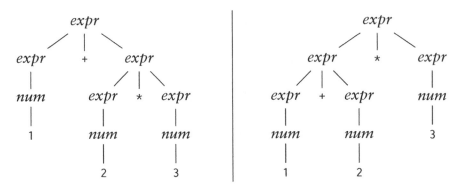

Figure 3.3 Two different parse trees for the expression 1+2*3. The tree on the left is obtained when production (*expr*$_2$) is applied first, followed by the application of production (*expr*$_3$) to the rightmost *expr* non-terminal. The tree on the right is obtained when the order is reversed and production (*expr*$_3$) is applied before production (*expr*$_2$), applied to the leftmost *expr* non-terminal.

As we can see in the third step, we have obtained the same sentential form through two different derivation sequences, and while the sentential forms are identical, the construction of the parse tree reflects the different order of applying the two *expr* productions in its internal structure, see Figure 3.3.

A grammar that allows the construction of two different parse trees for the same sentence is called *ambiguous*. Ambiguity is an undesirable property for grammars, since it makes predictions about the semantics of sentences difficult or impossible. For example, the left parse tree in Figure 3.3 groups the multiplication of 2 and 3 together, and an evaluation of the expression that follows this structure would correspondingly result in 7. In contrast, the right parse tree groups the addition of 1 and 2 together, which means that the evaluation of the expression would result in 9.

Ambiguity in grammars can be resolved by adding extra rules about operator precedences or by refactoring the grammar. The details are not important here.

What you should remember is that programs that are supplied in a linear form of text must be transformed into a representation that reveals the structure of the program.

3.3 Abstract Syntax

We have seen how grammars can describe languages, but the linear form of sentences is limited and often leaves questions about the intended meaning unanswered. Remember that a major reason for formalizing the syntax of a language is to facilitate the definition of its semantics. Consider again the expression

Exercise 3.2

(a) Draw the syntax tree for the sentence not not True based on the following grammar.

$bool$ ::= True | False | not *bool*

(b) Extend the grammar from part (a) so that it is possible to derive the sentence not (True or False) and draw a parse tree for it.

(c) Show that the following grammar is ambiguous by drawing two different parse trees for the sentence 0 1 0 1.

bins ::= 0 *bins* 1 *bins* | 1 *bins* 0 *bins* | ϵ

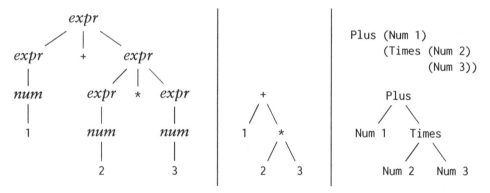

Figure 3.4 A parse tree for the expression 1+2*3 (on the left) and its corresponding abstract syntax tree (in the middle). The AST is more succinct: it eschews all non-terminal symbols and instead keeps operations in internal nodes. On the right: how the abstract syntax tree can be written as a value of an Elm data type. Elm data constructors are in fact operations for constructing trees.

1+2*3. Does it denote (1+2)*3 or 1+(2*3)? Parse trees make the structure of an expression explicit, but since they contain information that is not relevant for the definition of semantics (and other analyses one might want to perform on a program), the structure of a program is usually transformed from parse trees into a more succinct form, a so-called (*abstract*) *syntax tree*, or AST.

An example is shown in Figure 3.4, which presents the left parse tree from Figure 3.3 and its corresponding abstract syntax tree.

While a parse tree keeps vestiges of the derivation, the AST retains only the information necessary to understand the structure of the sentence. (As ever-so-subtly suggested by the name, abstract syntax is again an example of abstraction.) To distinguish the two forms of syntax, the set-of-sentences syntax defined

	Concrete syntax	Abstract syntax
Descriptive formalism	Context-free grammars	Elm data types
Structure representation	Parse trees	(Abstract) syntax trees
Denoted language	Set of sentences	Set of syntax trees
Ambiguity	Can be a problem	Cannot occur

Table 3.1   Comparison of concrete and abstract syntax.

by grammars is called *concrete syntax*, while a set-of-ASTs is called *abstract syntax*. The two forms of syntax are compared in Table 3.1.

The visual representation of trees is quite useful in illustrating concepts and explaining specific examples, but it is not well suited for use in formalizing operations on trees. Therefore, to effectively work with ASTs, we need a notation that allows us to do two things:

(1) Denote trees in a linear, text-based form.
(2) Denote tree patterns in definitions.

It turns out that Elm data types satisfy exactly these two requirements, which is why we use Elm data types as a metalanguage for describing abstract syntax. To represent the abstract syntax of a grammar in Elm, we define, as a rule of thumb, a separate data type for each non-terminal with a constructor for each of its productions. Exception to this rule are non-terminals that represent basic lexical units that are best represented by Elm built-in types, such as *num*, which we always represent by `Int`, or *name*, which we always represent by `String`. There are several other simplifications and special cases that can lead to more concise definitions, and we will discuss them all in due course.

As an example, consider again the very simple grammar for arithmetic expressions.

$$num ::= 0 \mid 1 \mid 2 \mid 3 \mid \ldots$$
$$expr ::= num \mid expr + expr \mid expr * expr$$

An abstract syntax representation is given by the following Elm data type.

```
type Expr = Num Int | Plus Expr Expr | Times Expr Expr
```

The *expr* non-terminal is represented by the data type `Expr`, and each *expr* production is represented by one constructor. In general, the argument types for each constructor are given by the types that represent the non-terminals that occur in the RHS of the corresponding production. For example, the RHS of the second *expr* production, *expr + expr*, contains two occurrences of *expr*. Therefore, the corresponding constructor Plus has two Expr arguments. The same applies to the third *expr* production and the corresponding Times constructor.

Since the first *expr* production contains the "basic" non-terminal *num*, we use the corresponding built-in type Int as an argument type for the constructor Num. Note that we have to invent a name for the constructor, since numbers are not accompanied by a terminal symbol. But why do we need a constructor at all and not just use Int as one case of the data type definition? Maybe we could do something like this.

```
type Expr = Int | Plus Expr Expr | Times Expr Expr    -- INCORRECT!
```

This definition would actually define Int as one constructor of Expr without any arguments, but that is not what we want. To view integers as expressions we need a constructor, such as Num, that injects them as one variant into the data type.

With the Elm data type definition for Expr, the AST shown in Figure 3.4 can be represented as follows.

```
> Plus (Num 1) (Times (Num 2) (Num 3))
Plus (Num 1) (Times (Num 2) (Num 3)) : Expr
```

At this point, constructing trees doesn't seem very useful, but the AST representation puts us in a position to implement syntactic transformations in a succinct way.

As another example, take a look at the following grammar for a toy imperative language. Before reading further, please try to define the abstract syntax for this grammar via two data types Cond and Stmt yourself. Note that & is a terminal symbol of the concrete syntax that represents a logical *and* operation.

$$cond ::= \text{true} \mid cond \& cond \mid \text{not } cond \mid (cond)$$
$$stmt ::= \text{while } cond \{ stmt \} \mid \text{skip}$$

It is important to remember that constructors and type names in Elm must start with a capital letter. Here is one possible representation of the grammar.

```
type Cond = T | And Cond Cond | Not Cond
type Stmt = While Cond Stmt | Skip
```

Three things deserve to be noted here. First, I have used T and not True as the name of the constructor for representing the terminal true. The reason is that True is already a defined constructor in Elm and cannot be defined again. The names of the constructors don't carry an intrinsic meaning, and the choice actually doesn't matter. We can represent *cond* just as well through the following definition.

Exercise 3.3

(a) Implement a simple optimizer for the Expr data type that replaces a (sub)expression such as 0 + 5 by 5. You will probably need to employ patterns such as the following that match 0 constants as parts of Plus expressions.

```
optimize : Expr -> Expr
optimize e = case e of
    ...
    Plus (Num 0) e2 -> e2
```

Note that you then need other cases for Plus, since Elm checks and enforces the completeness of patterns.

If this exercise is too easy, add simplifications that can also simplify the following expressions: 1 * 7 → 7 and 0 * 5 → 0. Note that by adding the last simplification, the order in which the different replacements happen matters. To see this, consider the expression 2+(0*3), which should be simplified to 2.

(b) Implement a pretty printer for Expr, that is, a function pp of type Expr -> String that converts expression ASTs into their textual representation. For example, pp should produce the following.

```
> pp (Plus (Num 1) (Times (Num 2) (Num 3)))
"1+2*3" : String
```

(You may want to use the function String.fromInt to convert integers to strings.) The basic structure of the function definition is straightforward. However, you have to be careful to create parentheses around Plus expressions that occur as arguments of Times without creating any unnecessary parentheses. For example, we expect pp to produce the following.

```
> pp (Plus (Num 0) (Plus (Times (Plus (Num 1) (Num 2)) (Num 3)) (Num 4)))
"0+(1+2)*3+4" : String
```

```
type Conditio = Verum | Et Conditio Conditio | Non Conditio
```

Or even this one:

```
type A = B | C A A | D A
```

What matters is that the constructors can accurately represent the information from the grammar productions. Of course, it's always a good idea to choose names wisely to support the writing and understanding of definitions that use these names.

Second, Cond doesn't have a constructor to represent the last *cond* production. The reason is that it is not needed, since it doesn't introduce any new operation on conditions or any new way of building conditions. Parentheses are used in linear representation to express the grouping of different parts. We do not need parentheses in trees, because the grouping happens through the hierarchical tree structure and the fact that children are associated with their parent. This resolves any ambiguity that could arise in a linear notation. The need for parentheses in the concrete syntax can be seen in the following sentence.

```
not true & true
```

What exactly are the arguments to the operations not and &? Since the grammar is ambiguous (the expression can be parsed either as (not true) & true or not (true & true)), no matter what disambiguating rule we pick, one or the other expression *cannot* be expressed without parentheses. In contrast, we can readily represent both expression in the abstract syntax.

```
And (Not T) T      -- represents (not true) & true
Not (And T T)      -- represents not (true & true)
```

This works because we can use the parentheses of the metalanguage (Elm) to express the grouping of subexpressions in the represented object language (*cond*).

Third, the curly braces in the first *stmt* production do not occur in the abstract syntax, again because they are not needed: the production is identified in the abstract syntax by the constructor While, and both non-terminal arguments of the production are represented by the corresponding argument types Cond and Stmt. The same applies to other "filler" terminal symbols such as do, begin, or end, which are often included in concrete syntax as key words to avoid ambiguity and aid the parser.

As in the case of Expr, we can use the abstract syntax to represent programs in Elm. Consider the following program in concrete syntax.

```
while not (true & true) {
    while true {
        skip
    }
}
```

The abstract syntax for this program is given by the following value of type Stmt.

```
While (Not (And T T)) (While T Skip)
```

Abstract and concrete syntax are two sides of the same coin. They both describe languages and their structure, but they have different purposes.

Concrete syntax is meant to be read and understood by programmers and is thus generally more readable than abstract syntax. But this also makes concrete syntax more verbose, especially through the use of key words and white

> ### ABSTRACT SYNTAX
>
> The abstract syntax of a language is a set of syntax trees. Using Elm data types to represent abstract syntax means that an abstract syntax tree is given by a value of an Elm data type, which facilitates the realization of program analyses and transformations as Elm functions.
>
> The concrete syntax of a language defined by a context-free grammar is the set of sentences that can be derived from the start symbol of that grammar. Correspondingly, an Elm data type defines the language of ASTs as the set of values that can be built using the data type's constructors.

space. Moreover, despite the availability of structure editors and visual program representations, programmers today still edit programs with text editors, which means the concrete program representation has to be a linear sequence of symbols. The corresponding grammar therefore often includes filler symbols for expressing grouping.

Abstract syntax, on the other hand, is generally more parsimonious than concrete syntax. Its major purpose is to present the structure of programs to compilers and mathematical formalisms. Abstract syntax is not meant to be read and edited by programmers.[2] The abstract syntax representation lays the foundation for defining the semantics of language constructs, and it facilitates different kinds of analyses of programs, including type checking and optimization. By being more concise, abstract syntax representations consume less space and reveal essential language structures more directly than concrete syntax.

3.4   Abstract Syntax Idioms

The simple standard approach described in Section 3.3 requires us to define a separate data type for each non-terminal and to introduce a constructor for each production. We have already seen an exception to the last rule and can simply ignore productions that introduce non-terminals for expressing grouping. In addition, several other patterns that occur quite frequently in grammars can be represented more succinctly in abstract syntax.

---

[2]Although computer science researchers use it extensively.

Exercise 3.4

(a) Define the abstract syntax for the following grammar as an Elm data type, and represent the abstract syntax tree for the sentence `flip flip on` as a value.

switch ::= on | off | flip *switch*

(b) Assume we add the following production to the grammar for *expr*.

expr ::= ... | (*expr*)

Do we need to change the abstract syntax, that is, do we have to add a constructor to the data type definition for `Expr`? If so, how? If not, why not?

(c) Assume we add the following *stmt* production to represent sequential composition of statements.

stmt ::= ... | *stmt*; *stmt*

Extend the abstract syntax by adding a constructor to the data type `Stmt`.

(d) The extension of *stmt* in part (c) seems to have added effectively a binary operation ; on two statements. Does this extension make the grammar ambiguous? If so, do we need to introduce a construct for grouping statements? If you think the grammar is ambiguous but we don't need syntax for grouping statements, explain why.

3.4.1   Factoring

Reusing existing constructors and embedding them into a new data type helps with managing names and also makes relationships between different types explicit. Consider, for example, the following definition of the `Cond` data type.

```
type Cond = T | F | And Cond Cond | Not Cond
```

We have already discussed the need to use `T` instead of `True`, since the latter is predefined. But instead of introducing new constructors for something that already exists, we could also reuse the type `Bool` and embed it into the definition of `Cond` as follows.

```
type Cond = Const Bool | And Cond Cond | Not Cond
```

Note that we need to introduce the constructor `Const` to inject Boolean values into the type `Cond`. (This is basically the same situation that we've seen before when we used `Num` to inject `Int` values into the data type `Expr`.) The use of `Bool` instead of `T` and `F` amounts to factoring the two constructors into a separate data type. The advantage of this representation is that we can reuse `Bool`; the disadvantage is that we need to use an additional constructor for Boolean constants when constructing `Cond` expressions. For example, instead of `And (Not T) T`, we now have to write the more verbose

```
And (Not (Const True)) (Const True)
```

This not a huge problem in practice, since (i) we construct such expressions rarely (often only once for creating test cases) and (ii) we can always introduce so-called *smart constructors*, that is, we can introduce abbreviations such as the following.

```
true = Const True
```

This allows us to write expressions again in a more readable way.

```
And (Not true) true
```

However, the additional constructors introduced through factoring still often make pattern matching more cumbersome.

Factoring is not limited to constructs that are pre-defined in the metalanguage, and it is not limited to constants either. For example, suppose the `Cond` data type contains several other binary operations, such as `Or`, `Xor`, and `Nand`. Instead of introducing each operation separately as a constructor of `Cond` we can combine all binary operations into one generalized constructor that takes the operation as an additional parameter and define the operations in a separate enumeration type `Op`.

```
type Op = And | Or | Xor | Nand
type Cond = Const Bool | Bin Op Cond Cond | Not Cond
```

This generalization captures the common structure of all binary operations in a single constructor `Bin`.

This last definition looks more economical from the perspective of the type definition. Having fewer constructors can be an advantage for later function definitions, since we have fewer cases to consider. However, expressions get bigger and more nested, and the added levels of indirection through constructors might be less attractive in other parts of the code. There's no general rule of which approach is better. The point is that it is possible, and that the metalanguage provides the language designer with options to choose from.

Finally, we can also factor the argument types of operations. For example, we could introduce a type definition for pairs of conditions and use that type as the argument type for binary operations. Combining this idea with the previous one would lead to the following definitions.

```
type alias CondPair = (Cond,Cond)
type Op = And | Or | Xor | Nand
type Cond = Const Bool | Bin Op CondPair | Not Cond
```

Note that `CondPair` is not a new type, that is, it doesn't introduce any new values. It's simply a name for an already existing type, and it is therefore defined as a type alias. The factoring of argument types is less common, and in this specific example it doesn't seem to enhance the abstract syntax definition, if only because `CondPair` is just used once.

3.4.2 Replacing Grammar Recursion by Lists

Most languages contain repetitions of specific syntactic categories, and programming languages are no exception. For example, a function can have zero or more parameters, a procedure may have an arbitrary number of local variable declarations, or a statement in an imperative language can itself be a sequence of one or more statements.

The repetition of syntactic structures is often represented in grammars through recursion. In many cases, we can simplify the abstract syntax representation by using Elm built-in lists to represent repetition more directly. Suppose we want to define the syntax for function definitions so that a function definition consists of a name, a sequence of zero or more parameters, and an expression defining its return value. Here is a possible definition.

$$\textit{fundef} ::= \textit{name params = expr}$$
$$\textit{params} ::= \textit{name params} \mid \epsilon$$

What is important to note is the two *params* productions for defining a list of parameter names. The only purpose of the non-terminal *params* is to be able to generate an arbitrary number of *name* non-terminals as parameter names for the function definition. This recursive pattern for defining a list is so common that many grammars have adopted a special notation for it: the repetition of a non-terminal can be expressed by simply attaching a * to it. With this notational extension, we can simplify the grammar as follows.

$$\textit{fundef} ::= \textit{name name}^* = \textit{expr}$$

The star notation is an abbreviation for the extended definition and can be used to refactor grammar definitions: First, identify (groups of) productions that define repeating syntactic structures. Then simplify them using the star. The star notation allows us to express repetition directly without having to invent an additional non-terminal. It's another example of an abstraction, in this case an abstraction that is part of a metalanguage.

If we translated the original grammar into abstract syntax using our standard method, we would obtain something like the following.[3]

```
type alias Name = String
type FunDef = Fun Name Params Expr
type Params = Param Name Params | Empty
```

This definition is fine, but it can be quite inconvenient to work with. Consider the following function definition in concrete syntax.

```
f m x y = m*x + y
```

The initial part of the AST for it looks as follows.[4]

```
Fun "f" (Param "m" (Param "x" (Param "y" Empty))) (Plus (Times ...) ...)
```

The need for the nested application of the Param constructor is quite annoying. It is difficult to look at and work with. Especially, the need to take care of the correct matching of parentheses is a frequent source of syntax errors. Fortunately, we can simplify the definition considerably, using a mechanism that mimics the star notation of the concrete syntax. Recognizing that Params is simply defining a list of Names, we can use Elm's list data type to express this type more directly.

```
type FunDef = Fun Name (List Name) Expr
```

Just as the use of the star notation obviates the need for the *params* non-terminal and its productions in the grammar for the concrete syntax, the use of Elm built-in lists saves us the definition of the Params data type and, most importantly, facilitates the use of the built-in list notation in the definition of ASTs. The AST for the program can now be written as follows.

```
Fun "f" ["m","x","y"] (Plus (Times ...) ...)
```

In addition to the star notation, grammars also sometimes attach a $^+$ to indicate a repetition of non-terminals that must occur at least once, that is, while A^* stands for *zero* or more occurrences of A, A^+ stands for *one* or more occurrences of A. Thus, if the language required a function definition to have at least one parameter, we would change the original grammar by replacing the ϵ-production for *params* by *name*, or we could use the plus notation.

fundef ::= *name name$^+$* = *expr*

---

[3]Since this example has only one production for function definitions, we could also use a type alias for FunDef, that is, type alias FunDef = (Name,Params,Expr).

[4]To try this example in the Elm interpreter, you need to add a constructor such as Var to the Expr data type for representing variables in expressions such as Times (Var "m") (Var "x").

How should we address the change in the abstract syntax? Since lists can be empty, the use of List Name as an argument type of the Fun constructor does not exactly reflect the grammar anymore. We could enforce the presence of at least one name by using a pair of a single name and a potentially empty list, like so.

```
type FunDef = Fun Name (Name,List Name) Expr
```

While this is technically an accurate representation of the syntax, the more permissive but simpler List Name is usually an acceptable or even better representation, in particular in contexts where we can assume that a parser ensures that the lists are not empty. In other words, we ignore the difference between empty and non-empty lists in the abstract syntax representation and would use the following definition.

```
type FunDef = Fun Name (List Name) Expr
```

The star or plus notation can also be applied to groups of syntactic elements. Suppose that the concrete syntax for function definitions requires parentheses around the parameters, which also must be separated by commas, that is, the definition of f would have to have the following form.

```
f (m,x,y) = m*x + y
```

The corresponding change in the grammar productions is as follows.

$$
\begin{aligned}
fundef &::= name \ (params) = expr \\
params &::= name, \ params \ | \ name
\end{aligned}
$$

Note that this definition requires the parameter list to be non-empty. To replace the use of *params* by the star notation we have to be a bit careful, since a list of n variables is accompanied by only $n - 1$ commas. In particular, we *cannot* use the plus notation in this situation. Instead, we have to express the syntax as a potentially empty list of names followed by a comma, which is then followed by a name. Note the two different types of parentheses in the definition: those set in typewriter font, which are part of the concrete syntax to indicate the beginning and end of the parameter list, and those set in math font, which are part of the grammar, that is, metalanguage, notation.

$$
fundef ::= name \ ((name,)^* \ name) = expr
$$

Applying the star to the group of two symbols "*name*" and "," means to repeat this group zero or more times. Notably, the representation of the abstract syntax doesn't change, since the comma is a filler symbol that doesn't add any information and is thus to be ignored in the abstract syntax.

To see how the use of lists for expressing repetition can be combined with tuples to express grouping, we examine the syntax of let expressions. A typical concrete syntax introduces the construct with the keyword let, followed by a list of name/expression pairs, which are separated by =, followed by the keyword in and the body of the let expression.

$$expr ::= \ldots \mid \text{let } (name = expr)^* \text{ in } expr$$

With the star notation, we can conveniently express the repetition of the "*name = expr*" group within the let production. On the abstract syntax level, we can express the grouping of the types Name and Expr as a pair and the repetition, again, using a list type.

```
type Expr = ... | Let (List (Name,Expr)) Expr
```

This syntax allows a let expression to have an empty list of definitions.

3.4.3   Grouping Associative Operations Using Lists

Consider again the definition of Cond from page 59. The & operator is meant to denote the logical *and* operation, which is an associative operation. Therefore, the grouping of nested applications of & doesn't matter, that is, a & (b & c) denotes the same value as (a & b) & c. Thus, instead of defining And with two arguments, we could alternatively define it with a list of arguments.

```
type Cond = ... | And (List Cond)
```

With this definition we can avoid nested applications of And and represent both of the previous expressions as follows.

```
And [a,b,c]
```

As another example consider the extension of *stmt* by a production for sequential composition (cf. Exercise 3.4(c)).

$$stmt ::= \ldots \mid stmt; stmt$$

The abstract syntax using a binary constructor would be defined as follows.

```
type Stmt = ... | Seq Stmt Stmt
```

And again, based on this representation, a sequence of three statements, say, s1, s2, and s3, needs to be built using two Seq constructors, that is, either as Seq s1 (Seq s2 s3) or Seq (Seq s1 s2) s3. That's exactly same situation as with the & operator.

Now suppose that we have to implement a syntax analysis that checks whether a property p holds for any kind of statement. Having Seq defined as a binary operation requires a recursive definition for that case, something like the following.

```
check : (Stmt -> Bool) -> Stmt -> Bool
check p s = case s of
    ...
    Seq s1 s2 -> check p s1 && check p s2
```

This doesn't seem too bad. However, the shown definition essentially implements a control structure for iterating over statements using recursion, whereas a list-based representation facilitates the reuse of control structures for lists that we already have. To illustrate this idea, consider the following alternative definition of the Seq constructor.

```
type Stmt = ... | Seq (List Stmt)
```

With this definition, the sequential composition of s1, s2, and s3 is written as Seq [s1,s2,s3]. Now for lists we have a function all that tests whether a predicate holds for all elements of a list.

```
> List.all
<function> : (a -> Bool) -> List a -> Bool
```

Using List.all we can implement the Seq-case for check as follows.

```
check : (Stmt -> Bool) -> Stmt -> Bool
check p s = case s of
    ...
    Seq ss -> List.all (check p) ss
```

Maybe this example doesn't make a compelling enough case yet for reusing list control structures. But consider the task of removing statements from a sequence of statements until a statement is reached that satisfies a specific property. We will see a concrete example that will need this kind of operation in Chapter 4, Exercise 4.1(a). Concretely, we are seeking a function removeUntil of type (Stmt -> Bool) -> Stmt -> Stmt . An implementation that works for binary trees built using Seq is not at all obvious (try it!). In contrast, we can relatively easily compose a solution using list functions by working on the reverse of a list. (The function rev was defined in Section 2.2.2; alternatively, we could also use List.reverse.)

```
keepUntil : (Stmt -> Bool) -> List Stmt -> List Stmt
keepUntil p stmts = case stmts of
    []    -> []
    s::ss -> if p s then [] else s::keepUntil p ss

removeUntil : (Stmt -> Bool) -> Stmt -> Stmt
removeUntil p stmt = case stmt of
    Seq ss -> (Seq << rev << keepUntil p << rev) ss
    ...
```

The same strategy is not so easy to realize for the alternative representation.

3.4.4   Representing Optional Syntax Elements

Language syntax often contains optional elements. Consider, for example, the definition of numbers that may be preceded by a + or - sign.

   sign ::= + | -
   snum ::= *num* | *sign num*

The fact that the sign is optional is expressed in the grammar definition by having two alternative productions for the non-terminal *snum*. Therefore, the definition of the corresponding abstract syntax gets two constructors for the type SNum.

```
type Sign = Plus | Minus
type SNum = Signed Sign Int | Unsigned Int
```

This way of representing optional elements is unsatisfactory, since it requires the duplication of identical type information in two constructors. In this example it is simply the type Int, but in general it may involve more elaborate types (see, for example, Exercise 3.5(c)).

Such redundancy is a well-known source of errors (known as *update anomalies* in the field of databases): when two (or more) definitions need to be changed in the same way, it is easy to change just one occurrence while forgetting the other one or performing the second change inconsistently. Therefore, to avoid duplicate RHSs, some grammar formalisms allow the definition of optional syntax elements by enclosing them in square brackets. With the square-bracket notation the two *snum* productions can be combined into a single one.

   snum ::= [*sign*] *num*

In the abstract syntax, optional elements can be represented by using the Maybe data type, which was introduced in Section 2.5 on page 37. With the Maybe type the abstract syntax for *snum* can be defined more succinctly as follows.

TRANSLATING GRAMMARS INTO DATA TYPES

The following table shows the correspondence between different elements of the grammar formalism for concrete syntax and data types for abstract syntax. non-terminals, which can generally be expanded to many different sequences of terminals, correspond to types, which contain many different values. Sequences of terminal symbols correspond to abstract syntax trees, and terminal symbols that represent operations (and are not just helpers for the parser to indicate grouping) correspond to tree constructors.

Grammar		Data type	
Basic non-terminal	*num, name, . . .*	Predefined type	Int, String, . . .
Non-basic non-terminal	*expr, stmt, . . .*	Data type	Expr, Stmt, . . .
Terminal for operation	+, while, . . .	Constructor	Plus, While, . . .
Grouping/filler terminal	begin, (,), do, . . .	–	–

The translation of a context-free grammar into an abstract syntax representation given by data types follows four basic rules.

(1) Represent each *basic non-terminal* by a *built-in type*.
(2) For each *other non-terminal*, define a separate *data type*.
(3) For each *production*, define a *constructor*.
(4) The *non-terminals* in a production determine the *argument types* of its constructor.

This simple method is refined by employing the different strategies for capturing specific syntactic patterns more succinctly, including factoring, representing repetition of syntactic elements using List, and using Maybe for optional material.

```
type SNum = Num (Maybe Sign) Int
```

Note that since we are left with only one production, we could also use a simple type alias.

In this particular example, we can observe another representational alternative. Since the argument type of Maybe is an enumeration type, we can list all potential values of SNum, namely, Just Plus, Just Minus, and Nothing. This observation suggests extending its argument type by a new value instead of using a Maybe type. In our example this could look as follows.

```
type Sign = Plus | Minus | NoSign
type SNum = Num Sign Int
```

Again, a simple type alias for SNum would be sufficient in this case as well.

To conclude this chapter, the box *Translating Grammars into Data Types* gives a summary of how to generate an abstract syntax definition from a concrete syntax. While the general method for obtaining abstract syntax is not complex, careful analysis can in many cases improve the representation significantly with great benefit to all operations that have to use it.

Exercise 3.5

(a) Consider the following grammar defining the syntax of a simple assembly language.

> *reg* ::= A | B | C
> *op* ::= MOV *num* TO *reg* | MOV *reg* TO *reg* | INC *reg* BY *num* | INC *reg* BY *reg*
> *prog* ::= *op* | *op* ; *prog*

Define the abstract syntax for this grammar through Elm data types.

(b) Does your solution to (a) contain a data type Op with four constructors, corresponding to the four *op* productions? Such a definition can be factored further by capturing the choice between a *num* and *reg* argument in a separate non-terminal (in the grammar) or data type (in the abstract syntax).

Define the refactored grammar and abstract syntax.

(c) Consider the following language for describing movements in the two-dimensional plane.

> *point* ::= (*num*, *num*)
> *move* ::= [from *point*] (via *point*)* to *point*

Define different versions of abstract syntax for *move*: First define abstract syntax not using either List or Maybe. Then define two more versions, one using only Maybe and one using only List. Finally, define a version that uses both Maybe and List.

(d) Consider again the final version of the abstract syntax for the movement language from part (c) (the representation that uses both Maybe and List). Can you optimize the representation even further? (*Hint*: Consider the type (Maybe Int, List Int) and all the values that can be represented with it. Try to identify an equivalent type that can represent basically the same information.)

4

Denotational Semantics

Chapter Summary

What is semantics and why it is important. Steps for defining denotational semantics. How to implement denotational semantics in Elm. Semantic domains for a variety of language features plus the systematic construction of advanced domains with type constructors.

Syntax is about the *form* and *structure* of languages. Semantics is about the *meaning* of languages, which is what ultimately matters. Speaking a language effectively does not merely mean being able to form syntactically correct sentences. To communicate ideas through a language, sentences must also represent coherent ideas or concepts. While it is of course obvious that you have to understand the semantics of a language before you can effectively use it, the question remains, *Why is semantics, and especially formal semantics, such an important topic for programming languages?*

Why Semantics?

Language semantics provides a number of important benefits.

First and foremost, the semantics of a programming language defines *precisely* the *meaning of individual programming constructs* and helps us understand what the constructs of the language do. In particular, a formal definition cannot leave any corner case uncovered and resolves any uncertainty about how a specific construct behaves in any situation.

Programming Language Fundamentals: A Metalanguage Approach in Elm, First edition. Martin Erwig.
© 2024 Martin Erwig. Published 2024 by John Wiley & Sons Inc.
Companion website: www.wiley.com/go/ProgrammingLanguageFun

Second, semantics allows us to *judge the correctness of a program* and compare expected with observed behavior. Based on an understanding of individual language constructs, we can understand what a whole program is doing and thus make sense of unexpected program behavior and correct mistakes in the program.

Third, a semantics definition for a language enables us to *prove properties about the language*. One such important property is the so-called *type soundness*, that is, the fact that the absence of type errors in a program guarantees the absence of a large class of runtime errors. We will look at this aspect in more detail in Chapter 5. The fact that a type checker can automatically prove the absence of a large class of errors is an extremely important language feature because it effectively delivers a partial correctness proof for programs. But type soundness can only be established for a language that has a semantics definition.

Fourth, semantics definitions help with *comparing languages*. For example, the way a language realizes parameter passing (for example, call-by-value or lazy evaluation) has implications for its expressiveness and efficiency and is thus an important consideration in picking a language for a particular project. The parameter passing style of a language is part of its semantics.

Finally, semantics definitions can *guide the design of languages*, which is particularly helpful for domain-specific languages. Ultimately, semantics can serve as a *specification for language implementations*.

What Is Semantics?

Having established that semantics plays an important role in many aspects of programming, the next questions are:

- *What actually is the semantics of a program?*
- *What is the semantics of a programming language?*

It turns out that the answers depend on the language. For example, the meaning of an arithmetic expression is a number, that is, the meaning of an individual program from the language of arithmetic expression is a number. In other words, the semantics of an arithmetic expression is a value of a particular type ($\mathbb{Z}$ or Int). In contrast, the meaning of a Boolean expression (see page 59) is either true or false, that is, the semantics of a Boolean expression is a value of type $\mathbb{B}$ or Bool.

These two languages are quite simple. What about a fully-fledged general-purpose programming language such as C or Java? What is the meaning of programs in these languages? Since a program in an imperative language works by manipulating state through assignment operations, its semantics can be described as the final state it produces when starting with a particular initial state. This effect can be described as a function that maps an input state to an output state. In other words, given a type $\mathbb{S}$ (or State) capturing all possible states, the semantics of an imperative language is a function of type $\mathbb{S} \to \mathbb{S}$ (or State -> State).

The sets $\mathbb{Z}$, $\mathbb{B}$, and $\mathbb{S} \to \mathbb{S}$ (as well as the corresponding Elm types Int, Bool, and State -> State) are called *semantic domains*; they capture the range of all possible program meanings for a specific programming language. Thus the semantics of an individual program is given by a value of its language's semantic domain. More generally, the semantics of a programming language is then given by a function, called its *semantic function*, that maps each program to a corresponding semantic value.

This approach of identifying and formally defining the semantic domain of a language and then defining a mapping from sentences or ASTs to elements of the semantic domain is called *denotational semantics*. We will look into how this works in more detail in this chapter. There are also other styles of defining semantics, notably *operational semantics* in which the semantics of programs is described by transformation rules that simplify a program into some resulting value, and *axiomatic semantics* in which the effect of programs (or parts of programs) are described by pairs of pre- and post-conditions.

It may seem that a language definition starts with the definition of the syntax and is then followed by the identification of the semantic domain. However, that is not really the case. The semantic domain for a language must actually be known (at least informally) before the syntax of the language can be defined. For example, if you decide to define a new imperative programming language, then you already have chosen $\mathbb{S} \to \mathbb{S}$ as the domain, and your decision on the syntax for an assignment operation presumes this domain because without state transformation as the underlying semantic domain for the language, an assignment operation makes no sense and can't even be defined. Here is another example to make this point clear. Consider the language of chemical formulae, which are used to describe the proportions of atoms in chemical substances. Using H_2O to denote water makes sense to us now, but would not have made any sense before 1661 when Robert Boyle proposed a model of chemical substances of atomic particles.

About This Chapter

In Section 4.1 I will illustrate the three basic steps to defining denotational semantics with the simple example language of arithmetic expressions. In Section 4.2 I will describe a few general constructions for semantic domains that capture

---

DENOTATIONAL SEMANTICS DEFINITION

The denotational semantics of a language consists of three components.

(1) *Syntax* (a set S)
(2) *Semantic domain* (a CPO D)
(3) *Semantic function* (a function $[\![\cdot]\!] : S \to D$)

Performing a denotational semantics definition in Elm means to define the representation of the three components and involves the following three steps.

(1) Define a type S of ASTs.
(2) Define a type D of semantic values.
(3) Define the function sem : S -> D that maps ASTs to semantic values.

Note: While it seems natural to define the semantic domain in step 2, it must be known, even if only implicitly, before the definition of the syntax in step 1.

---

some prototypical structures that occur frequently in programming languages. These examples demonstrate that a significant part of the effort in defining semantics is devoted to the design of semantic domains.

4.1 Defining Semantics in Three Steps

Since we represent abstract syntax as Elm data types, the semantics function will be given by an Elm function and, consequently, the semantic domain will be given by an Elm type.

In the formal, mathematical version of denotational semantics, domains are defined as so-called *complete partial orders*, or *CPOs*, which are sets plus a partial order relation $\sqsubseteq$ and a least or bottom element $\bot$. The need for CPOs arises from recursion (or iteration). To give proper definitions of the meaning of arbitrary programs, we need to account for non-termination and assign different values from the domain to terminating and non-terminating functions. For lack of space we will not pursue this any further and instead focus mostly on how to define denotational semantics directly in Elm. The process is summarized in the box *Denotational Semantics Definition*.

Let's consider as an example the language of arithmetic expression from Chapter 3. We already have a type for the abstract syntax.

```
type Expr = Num Int | Plus Expr Expr | Times Expr Expr
```

The next step is to determine the semantic domain, which is the type of all values that can be denoted by an expression of type Expr. In this example, the answer is fairly obvious: we consider arithmetic expressions to denote the integers they evaluate to. The semantic domain is thus given by the type Int.

Finally, we map ASTs (represented by values of type Expr) to semantics values (that is, integers) by defining a function sem. (The function name is, of course, arbitrary.)

```
sem : Expr -> Int
sem e = case e of
    Num i        -> i
    Plus e1 e2   -> sem e1 + sem e2
    Times e1 e2 -> sem e1 * sem e2
```

The function definition is mostly self-explanatory: First, an integer (injected into the type Expr with the constructor Num) denotes itself. Second, a plus expression, represented by an AST with a Plus constructor as its root, denotes the integer that is obtained by adding (using the integer operation +) the integers that are denoted by the expressions represented by the two argument ASTs of Plus. These integers can be obtained by recursively applying sem to the argument ASTs. Third, the semantics of a times expression is obtained in the same way as a plus expression, except that the integers resulting from the argument ASTs are multiplied.

The mathematical version of this definition looks very similar. Instead of an AST representation as a data type, the syntax is typically defined by a context-free grammar. In this example, we use the grammar given on page 58. In the context of semantics definitions, the grammar notation is typically extended to introduce so-called *metavariables*, which can stand for sentences that can be derived from a particular non-terminal. For our example, we write $n \in num$ to express that n stands for (or "ranges over") terminal symbols representing numbers, and we write $e_1, e_2 \in expr$ to express that e_1 and e_2 range over expression sentences.[1] Those metavariables are then used in defining the semantics, but they can also be used in place of non-terminals in productions. The expression grammar using this extended notation looks as follows.

$$n \in num ::= 0 \mid 1 \mid 2 \mid 3 \mid \ldots$$
$$e_1, e_2 \in expr ::= n \mid e_1 + e_2 \mid e_1 * e_2$$

The semantic domain D would in this case be the CPO $\mathbb{Z}_\perp = (\mathbb{Z} \cup \{\perp\}, \sqsubseteq)$, which is the set of integers $\mathbb{Z}$, extended by a so-called *bottom element* $\perp$ to represent an "undefined" value plus the partial order $\sqsubseteq = \{(\perp, x) \mid x \in \mathbb{Z}\}$.

The semantic function is defined by an equation for each *expr* production, much like sem is defined by a case rule for each Expr constructor. In the first equation, we employ the notation $\underline{n}$ that maps a *num* terminal to the integer it

---

[1] We essentially use a non-terminal A as a shorthand for the set $L(A)$.

represents. Even though this is a trivial mapping ($\underline{0} = 0$, $\underline{1} = 1$, $\underline{2} = 2$, etc.), it is nevertheless important because the syntax of a number is different from the number it stands for.[2] With this mapping we can finally give the equations for the denotational semantics.

$$
\begin{aligned}
[\![\cdot]\!] &: expr \to \mathbb{Z}_\perp \\
[\![n]\!] &= \underline{n} \\
[\![e_1{+}e_2]\!] &= [\![e_1]\!] + [\![e_2]\!] \\
[\![e_1{*}e_2]\!] &= [\![e_1]\!] \cdot [\![e_2]\!]
\end{aligned}
$$

The hollow square brackets assist in parsing the notation: everything within the brackets belongs to the syntax; everything outside belongs to the semantic domain (which also means that the results produced by the function $[\![\cdot]\!]$ are semantic values). Note some of the subtleties of the notation; for example, on the left-hand side of the second equation, the + symbol inside the brackets is part of the syntax; it's the terminal that stands for the plus operation. In contrast, the + symbol on the right-hand side of the equation denotes the plus operation on integers (the semantic domain); it is applied to $[\![e_1]\!]$ and $[\![e_2]\!]$, the integers denoted by the syntactic expressions e_1 and e_2, respectively.

In the Elm definition, the distinction between the syntax and semantic domains is clearly expressed through the different types: syntactic objects, that is, ASTs, are values of type Expr, whereas semantic values are of type Int. Specifically, the syntax for addition is expressed by the constructor Plus, whereas the addition operation on semantic values is the Elm function denoted by +, defined on Int values, and the syntax for numbers is delineated from the semantic values by the constructor Num.

You may have noticed that for the current limited set of expressions, which only contain a plus and times operation, the bottom element is not needed, and the simpler set $\mathbb{Z}$ would suffice as semantic domain. However, consider what happens if we add an operation for division.

$$
e_1, e_2 \in expr ::= \ldots \mid e_1/e_2
$$

Now the situation changes because the semantics of an expression such as 5/0 cannot be a value from the set $\mathbb{Z}$. To capture this case we can amend the semantic function as follows.

$$
[\![e_1/e_2]\!] = \begin{cases} [\![e_1]\!] \div [\![e_2]\!] & \text{if } [\![e_2]\!] \neq 0 \\ \perp & \text{otherwise} \end{cases}
$$

---

[2]Formally, we are using a function $\underline{\cdot} : num \to \mathbb{Z}$. If we were to use, for example, roman numerals as the syntax for numbers, the need for the mapping would be more obvious. For example, we then would have $\underline{\text{III}} = 3$, $\underline{\text{IV}} = 4$, or $\underline{\text{CCCLXXXI}} = 381$.

In a corresponding extension of the Elm definition, we could add simply continue to work with `Int` and use integer division in the definition of `sem`. First, we extend the abstract syntax by a constructor.

```
type Expr = ... | Div Expr Expr
```

And then we add a corresponding case to the semantic function.

```
sem e = case e of
    ...
    Div e1 e2 -> sem e1 // sem e2
```

However, if we try to determine the semantics of an expression such as $5/0$, we encounter a surprising result.

```
> sem (Div (Num 5) (Num 0))
0 : Int
```

This behavior does not agree with the mathematical view that division by 0 is undefined. The decision to define integer division like this in Elm is probably motivated by the goal of eliminating runtime errors as much as possible, but as a general strategy for defining the semantics of partial functions, this approach is not acceptable. Since Elm types are not CPOs, we need to deal with this situation in a different way, which we will do in Section 4.2.1.

The need for the partial order arises when the semantic domain includes partial functions, which are needed to represent the semantics of recursive function definitions in a language. In the following, we will not go into the details of the mathematical foundations of the formalization and accept the fact that recursive function definitions can be given a mathematical meaning. Table 4.1 compares the concepts that are used in math with those used in Elm for expressing denotational semantics.

	Math	Elm
Syntax	Context-free grammar	Data type
Semantic domain	CPO	Type
Semantic function	Function	Function
Undefined	$\perp$	Nothing (or other constructor)

Table 4.1 Comparing Math and Elm as a metalanguage for describing denotational semantics.

Exercise 4.1

The goal of this exercise is to define the language of Boolean expressions. The syntax is given by the following grammar.

$$b, b_1, b_2 \in bexpr ::= \text{T} \mid \text{F} \mid b_1 \vee b_2 \mid b_1 \wedge b_2 \mid \neg b$$

(a) Give the abstract syntax for *bexpr* by defining a data type BExpr.

(b) Identify the type D for the semantic domain.

(c) Define the semantic function sem : BExpr -> D in Elm.

(d) Define the semantic function $[\![\cdot]\!] : bexpr \to \mathbb{B}$ in math notation.

Much, if not most, of the work in defining denotational semantics is devoted to the identification and definition of the semantic domains. This observation is consistent with computer science more generally, namely, that finding the right representation for a problem is often the key to a solution. For the Elm-based approach to denotational semantics this means that a key step in defining denotational semantics is the definition of types for the semantic domains. We will look at this aspect next.

4.2   Systematic Construction of Semantic Domains

The languages considered in the previous section had very simple semantic domains such as Int or Bool (or (Int,Int) in the case of Exercise 4.2). To define the semantics of more realistic languages we need to express more advanced domains, describing a richer set of semantic values. It turns out that semantic domains can often be built systematically, employing only a few basic principles. When defining semantic domains within Elm, these principles essentially correspond to specific *type constructors*, which are operators on types that build new types from existing ones.

Table 4.2 provides a brief overview of language features and how to incorporate them through type constructors into semantic domains of languages. Note that designing semantic domains is still not a trivial exercise, because the question of how to combine multiple features requires careful thought about how to compose the corresponding type constructors. Consider, for example, adding errors to a simple product domain (D1,D2). This task already presents a choice of seven possible combinations.

Exercise 4.2

The following grammar describes a language for controlling the moves of a robot in the two-dimensional plane. In the productions for *move*, we use the metavariable $n \in num$.

$$m_1, m_2 \in move ::= \text{go up}\, n \mid \text{go right}\, n \mid m_1; m_2$$

(a) Define the abstract syntax for *move* as a data type Move. (Remember to choose constructor names that are not already predefined.)

(b) The semantics of a *move* program m is the point in the plane the robot ends up after performing all the steps in m, starting at the home position $(0, 0)$. Identify the type D for the semantic domain.

(c) Define the semantic function sem : Move -> D.

Hint 1: First, think about what the final position of the robot is when the program contains only a single move, say, go up 3. This will tell you the definition for sem for this case. Then do the same for the operation go right. Finally, think about what effect the sequencing of two moves has on their respective positions. This will tell you how to define sem for this case.

Hint 2: Consider defining an auxiliary function for combining values of D that you could use here.

```
(Maybe D1,D2)              Maybe (D1,D2)
(D1,Maybe D2)              Maybe (Maybe D1,D2)
(Maybe D1,Maybe D2)        Maybe (D1,Maybe D2)
                           Maybe (Maybe D1,Maybe D2)
```

Which of these types provides the correct definition of the semantic domain depends on where errors can occur, how they are propagated, and whether or not they should be distinguished.

Domain construction	Type representation
Adding errors	Use Maybe (or Either)
Product of domains	Use tuple types
Union of domains	Define data type (or use Either)
Adding state	Use function types

Table 4.2 Domain constructions and corresponding type representation.

Exercise 4.3

Assume that we add a move home to the robot-move language from Exercise 4.2 that has the effect of bringing the robot back to the home position.

move ::= ... | go home

(a) Extend the language definition to account for this new operation. The definition is not as easy as it might seem at first. Think about what the correct values of all of the following programs should be.

```
go up 4; go home
go home; go up 3
go up 4; go home; go up 3
go up 4; go home; go up 3; go home; go right 2
```

Hint 1: What effect does the go home move have on all the preceding moves?

Hint 2: Employ a helper function simplify : Move -> Move to simplify a Move program without changing its semantics.

Hint 3: The simplification should try to get rid of go home moves.

(b) If you have represented ; as a binary operation, try the list-based representation described in Section 3.4.3.

4.2.1 Error Domains

When a program execution goes wrong and can't continue, this situation is often resolved by aborting the computation while reporting a runtime error. From the denotational semantics point of view, this means two things.

First, a computation that can't continue amounts to a case in the semantic function definition that can't be assigned a proper semantic value from the semantic domain. Second, to capture this information we need to add a special value to the semantic domain that can be clearly distinguished from all other values.

In the mathematical formulation of denotational semantics, the undefined value $\perp$ plays the role of this special value. It is already part of any domain because in the mathematical approach, domains are CPOs that contain $\perp$ as their least value. Thus when the semantic function ordinarily returns values of some type D, we can have it return $\perp$ from the domain $D_\perp$ in undefined cases when an ordinary D value can't be given. We have seen this earlier with handling division by zero in the semantics for *expr*.

Since Elm types don't have an undefined value to fall back on, we have to add such a value explicitly when needed. We can do this conveniently using the Maybe data type, which we already discussed in Section 2.5.

```
type Maybe a = Nothing | Just a
```

The Just constructor represents "regular" values, and the Nothing constructor represents an "undefined" value that is to be used in error situations. Like Elm lists, Maybe is parameterized and thus is a type constructor, that is, Maybe D represents the type of values of type D, extended by the value Nothing.

The Maybe type constructor provides a means to define the denotational semantics for the Expr type extended by a constructor Div for representing a division operation. First of all, we change the semantic domain to be Maybe Int so that we have access to the constructor Nothing to represent an error (or undefined) situation. While this seems like an innocent change, it affects the definition of sem all over the place. Most annoyingly, we cannot use the results of sem as arguments to integer operations anymore, since sem returns values of type Maybe Int instead of Int. Consider the definition in the case of Plus.

```
sem e = case e of
    Plus e1 e2 -> sem e1 + sem e2
    ...
```

This is a simple definition that captures the meaning of Plus clearly. But since sem e1 and sem e2 can either return an integer (wrapped in a Just constructor) or undefined (represented by the Nothing constructor), we have four possible cases to deal with. Only in the case when both sem e1 and sem e2 return an integer can we apply + and return a Maybe Int value built using Just. In all three other cases we have to return Nothing.

There are several ways to implement the definition, and it's instructive to take a closer look at the different options because it provides more practice in functional programming specifically and illustrates strategies for building type-based abstractions more generally. We will use these strategies again later, and they are good software engineering practices as well.

The first approach is to scrutinize the results of the two sem calls by distinguishing between the two cases of the Maybe Int. We can use two case expressions to scrutinize the results of sem e1 and sem e2 and define sem for Plus as follows. Note that we compute and analyze sem e2 only if sem e1 is not Nothing because in the latter case we know that the overall result has to be Nothing.

```
sem e = case e of
    Plus e1 e2 -> case sem e1 of
                     Just i -> case sem e2 of
                                  Just j -> Just (i+j)
                                  _      -> Nothing
                     _      -> Nothing
```

The definition shows that only if both sem e1 and sem e2 return an integer can we apply + and return a new integer. While this definition is not difficult to understand, it is quite verbose: one line of code has ballooned into five. This is particularly annoying considering that we have to repeat the same code for other binary operations such as Times, when the only thing that changes is the integer operation (replace + by *).

Since we only have to distinguish between two of the four possible cases, we can simplify the definition somewhat by scrutinizing the result of the pair (sem e1,sem e2) in the case expression, which leads to the following code.

```
sem e = case e of
    Plus e1 e2 -> case (sem e1,sem e2) of
                     (Just i,Just j) -> Just (i+j)
                     _               -> Nothing
```

This is much better, but still not ideal, since we are forced to repeat the boiler-plate code for the case expression. But since our metalanguage Elm is a fully-fledged functional programming language, we can capture this programming pattern easily in a function definition. Remember that one of the features of functional programming is its ability to define customized control structures, and this particular way of computing with Maybe values occurs frequently enough that it deserves its own control structure.

And as it turns out, Elm already provides a function map2 in the Maybe library that does exactly what we want: it takes a binary function f and two Maybe values m1 and m2 and applies f to the arguments of m1 and m2 if both of them are Just values. Otherwise, it returns Nothing.

```
map2 : (a -> b -> c) -> Maybe a -> Maybe b -> Maybe c
map2 f m1 m2 = case (m1,m2) of
    (Just x,Just y) -> Just (f x y)
    _               -> Nothing
```

From a denotational semantics point of view, map2 ensures that the function f is applied only if both of its arguments are defined and otherwise propagates undefined. The type of the function also explains its name: like map on lists, which applies a function to all elements contained in a list, the function map : (a -> b) -> Maybe a -> Maybe b in the module Maybe applies a function to all elements contained in a Maybe value, which can be at most one. Similarly, map2 extends this behavior to a binary function and two Maybe values. With map2 we can define the semantics for Expr with division as follows.

```
sem : Expr -> Maybe Int
sem e = case e of
    Num i        -> Just i
    Plus e1 e2  -> map2 (+) (sem e1) (sem e2)
    Times e1 e2 -> map2 (*) (sem e1) (sem e2)
    Div e1 e2    -> if sem e2==Just 0 then Nothing
                                else map2 (//) (sem e1) (sem e2)
```

In case you are wondering: the recomputing of the divisor sem e2 in the case for Div can be avoided by using a let expression.

```
    Div e1 e2    -> let d=sem e2 in
                        if d==Just 0 then Nothing
                                else map2 (//) (sem e1) d
```

But since efficiency is not a concern in the context of defining semantics, the previous definition is acceptable and maybe even preferable because it is simpler.

Note that instead of using a separate data type such as Maybe, errors can also be represented more directly if the semantic domain is already given by a data type (as discussed in Section 4.2.3). In that case, we can extend the domain by a constructor to represent the undefined/error case, or we may even decide to have multiple constructors to distinguish between the different error situations.

Exercise 4.4

(a) Consider again the Move language introduced in Exercise 4.3.

$$m_1, m_2 \in move ::= \text{go up}\, n \mid \text{go right}\, n \mid m_1 ; m_2$$

Adapt the semantics so that the arguments of go up moves can be at most 9.

(b) Instead of just returning an undefined value, we can also provide an error message that explains the reason for failure. To this end, we can use the following data type as a substitute for Maybe.

```
type Result a = OK a | Error String
```

Change the semantics definitions for Expr and Move to use Error instead of Maybe for the semantic domain.

4.2.2 Product Domains

Product domains correspond to the cartesian product of sets. They can appear in two different situations.

First, a semantic domain is given as the cartesian product of simpler domains. Again, the Move language introduced in Exercise 4.3 provides an example: a position is given by a pair of integers, that is, an element of the type (Int, Int), which corresponds to the cartesian product of Int with itself. More generally, any aggregation of semantic information into tuples asks for a corresponding semantic product domain, which is represented by Elm tuple types.

Second, if we have two different semantics for a language, we can combine them into one semantics that produces pairs of values, taken from the product domain of the individual domains. To illustrate this idea, let's assume we have defined a so-called *count semantics* that determines for an expression how many operations need to be evaluated to determine its value: no operation is needed for evaluating constants, and any expression using a binary operation requires one step plus the steps needed for evaluating the arguments.

```
type alias Count = Int

semCount : Expr -> Count
semCount e = case e of
    Num i       -> 0
    Plus e1 e2  -> 1 + semCount e1 + semCount e2
    Times e1 e2 -> 1 + semCount e1 + semCount e2
```

This count semantics could be regarded as a simple cost model for expressions. If we want to create a new semantics that combines the value semantics and the cost semantics, we need to combine the domains and the semantic functions. The semantic domain for the combined semantics would be (Int, Count), and we could define a new semantic function, say semVC :: Expr -> (Int, Count), by combining the expressions from both definitions for each case of the syntax. But we could also use the function both that applies two functions to a value and returns the pair of results to combine the two semantics. It is defined as follows.

```
both : (a -> b) -> (a -> c) -> (a -> (b,c))
both f g x = (f x,g x)
```

With the help of both we can compose the combined semantics simply as follows.

```
semVC : Expr -> (Int,Count)
semVC = both sem semCount
```

4.2.3 Union Domains

When the constructs of a language can produce values of different types, such as integers, Booleans, or strings, the semantic domain must be able to represent values of these types. The obvious approach in Elm is to define a data type with a constructor for each different value domain.

To consider a concrete example, let's extend the Expr language with an operation to compare values for equality, which returns Boolean values, as well as an operation for negating logical values.

```
type Expr = Num Int | Plus Expr Expr | Equal Expr Expr | Not Expr
```

Since an arbitrary expression may denote either an integer or a Boolean, the semantic domain must be a data type with constructors for integers and Booleans. In a first attempt, we can use the following definition.

```
type Val = I Int | B Bool
```

We can tag integers with I and Booleans with B and thus join both types Int and Bool in the *union domain* Val. Since the integers and Booleans are tagged by the respective constructors I and B, a value of type Val is always different from an Int or Bool value.

If we now tried to define the semantic function with type sem : Expr -> Val, we would soon run into a problem defining the semantics for some of the expressions. For example, what value should the expression Not (Num 3) denote?

With multiple types we have suddenly introduced the possibility of *type errors* in expressions, and the semantics should reflect the fact that the meaning of type-incorrect expressions is undefined. Therefore, we either have to change the semantic domain to Maybe Val, or we integrate the undefined value directly into the union type Val through a separate constructor, as shown in the following definition.

```
type Val = I Int | B Bool | Undefined
```

When adopting this extended version of Val, the definition of the semantic function has to make sure that the arguments of operations are of the correct type; only then can a result be computed. Otherwise, the value Undefined must be returned. This situation is similar to the one in Section 4.2.1 where we had to deal with potential division-by-zero errors, except that now every operation can potentially introduce an error.

As before, we can employ different strategies for defining the semantic function. Instead of nesting case expressions, we can again group the semantics of arguments of binary operations into pairs for pattern matching, which is more concise, but still somewhat repetitive.

```
sem : Expr -> Val
sem e = case e of
    Num i        -> I i
    Plus e1 e2  -> case (sem e1,sem e2) of
                        (I i,I j) -> I (i+j)
                                  -> Undefined
    Equal e1 e2 -> case (sem e1,sem e2) of
                        (I i,I j) -> B (i==j)
                                  -> Undefined
    Not e1       -> case sem e1 of
                        B b -> B (not b)
                          -> Undefined
```

The repeated pattern of testing for a particular subtype of Val (that is, checking for the I and B constructors) is striking and calls for refactoring. In this example we can introduce different auxiliary functions that depend on the type of the function to be applied. For example, the function mapIII lifts a binary integer function to the Val type by ensuring through pattern matching against the I constructor that both arguments are integers and injecting the integer result again with the I constructor back into the Val type. If one of the arguments is not an integer, the result is Undefined. Thus the mapIII function effectively realizes dynamic type checking[3] for binary integer functions; it is similar to the function map2, which we have used in Section 4.2.1.

```
mapIII : (Int -> Int -> Int) -> Val -> Val -> Val
mapIII f v1 v2 = case (v1,v2) of
    (I x,I y) -> I (f x y)
               -> Undefined
```

We can define similar functions for differently typed binary functions (see Exercise 4.5(a)). With the help of these auxiliary lifting/type checking functions we can define the semantic function more concisely.

```
sem : Expr -> Val
sem e = case e of
    Num i        -> I i
    Plus e1 e2  -> mapIII (+)  (sem e1) (sem e2)
    Equal e1 e2 -> mapIIB (==) (sem e1) (sem e2)
    Not e1       -> mapBB  not  (sem e1)
```

---

[3]A topic we will address in more detail in Chapter 5.

Exercise 4.5

(a) Implement the following type checking functions.

```
mapIIB : (Int -> Int -> Bool) -> Val -> Val -> Val
mapBB  : (Bool -> Bool)        -> Val -> Val
```

(b) Extend the semantics for Expr so that two Boolean values can also be successfully compared by Equal. Note that you can't use the mapIIB function for this. But you can go back to using the case expression approach and provide two success cases (one for two integers and one for two Booleans).

4.2.4 Domains for Modeling Stateful Computation

The essential idea behind denotational semantics is that a program denotes a value from a suitably chosen semantic domain, where the semantic function defines this mapping from programs to semantic values precisely. How do imperative languages fit into this picture?

The essence of an imperative program is to manipulate an underlying state and not to produce a value like a functional program. By accumulating the effects of individual statements on an initial state into a final state, the meaning of an imperative program can be described as a function that maps input states to output states.

To illustrate this basic idea, let's consider a very simple imperative language with operations to store and retrieve integers. The abstract syntax consists of two parts: (1) a language of expressions and (2) a language of statements.

```
type alias Name = String
type Expr = Num Int | Plus Expr Expr | Var Name
type Stmt = Assign Name Expr | Seq Stmt Stmt
```

The Var constructor of the Expr type represents the use of a variable name in an expression. The following program (given in some fictitious concrete syntax) would map an empty start state into a state in which x is bound to 3 and y is bound to 5.

```
x := 3;
y := x+2
```

This program can be represented in our abstract syntax as a value of type Stmt as follows.

```
Seq (Assign "x" (Num 3))
    (Assign "y" (Plus (Var "x") (Num 2)))
```

To define the semantics `sem : Stmt -> D` we next need to identify the semantic domain `D`. Since the semantics of an imperative program can be described as a mapping from a start to a result state, the appropriate type for `D` would be a function type `State -> State`, where `State` is a mapping from names (that is, strings) to integers.

To represent this mapping, we employ Elm's dictionary type `Dict`, which is parameterized by *two* types, the type of keys `k` and the type `v` of values to be stored with the keys. To represent a program state we use `Dict` with names as the keys and integers as the values.

```
type alias State = Dict Name Int
type alias D = State -> State
```

The dictionary type is defined in the module `Dict`. We can import this type together with the three functions that we need for our purposes as follows.

```
import Dict exposing (Dict,empty,insert,get)
```

Here are the types of these functions, specialized to our use here to emphasize the role they play in defining the semantics.

```
empty  : Dict Name Int
insert : Name -> Int -> State -> State
get    : Name -> State -> Maybe Int
```

The value `empty` denotes an empty state, and `insert x i s` updates the state s so that name x is mapped to the integer value i. If an entry for x already exists in s, it will be updated to i, while a new entry is created if x does not exist in s.

Note that as with any data structure in a functional language, the state value s is not changed at all, and instead a new state is created and returned as a value by `insert`. We can verify this fact easily in the Elm interpreter.[4]

```
> s = insert "x" 3 empty
Dict.fromList [("x",3)] : Dict String number

> t = insert "x" 5 s
Dict.fromList [("x",5)] : Dict String number

> s
Dict.fromList [("x",3)] : Dict String number
```

---

[4]To use the `Dict` functions without the module name as a qualifier, you can import `Dict` in the interpreter. The `Dict.fromList` prefix in the interpreter response can be read as, *The dictionary you are looking at is the same that you get when you apply* `fromList` *to the shown list*. In fact, `fromList` is a function in the `Dict` module that allows the construction of a map from a list of pairs, and evaluating `s == fromList [("x",3)]` actually yields `True`.

As we can see, the update of x to 5 is only visible in the map t; the old map s is unchanged and still carries the old value for x. In other words, any update to a dictionary s creates a new dictionary and does *not* perform a side effect on s.

When we try to define sem, we quickly notice that we actually need to define *two* semantic functions, one for statements, of course, but also one for expressions, since we need to determine the values denoted by expressions as part of defining the semantics of the assignment operation. What should the semantic domain for Expr be? One may be tempted to pick Int, but what then would be the semantics of an expression such as Var "x"? The value of x depends on the state, and it is a hallmark of imperative languages that the value of x can change over the course of a program execution. In other words, the semantics of a variable (lookup) is *not* an integer, but rather something like a "state-dependent integer."

The state dependence of variables (and thus expressions in general) can be expressed through a function type, that is, the semantic domain for expressions should be the function type State -> Int, and the semantic function for expressions then maps Expr values to values of this type.

But wait. What is the semantics of a variable that is not defined? To account for undefined variables we should define the semantic domain to be State -> Maybe Int. With that final adjustment we obtain the following types.

```
type E = State -> Maybe Int

semE : Expr -> E
```

Before we define semE, we should take a moment to understand the types that are at play here.

First, when we substitute the definition of E in the type for semE, we notice that semE looks like a function that takes two arguments.[5]

```
semE : Expr -> State -> Maybe Int
```

Doesn't this violate the general schema for semantic functions sem : S -> D, which demands that a semantic function be always a unary function that maps ASTs of some type S to semantic values of type D (or E in this case)?

No, it doesn't. We can actually look at the type of semE in two ways. On the one hand, we can understand semE as a function that takes *two* arguments, an AST and a state, and potentially returns an integer (that is, a value of type Maybe Int). On the other hand, we can also view semE as a higher-order function (see Section 2.7), that is, semE takes an AST and returns a function from states

---

[5]Remember that since the function arrow type constructor is right-associative, the type Expr -> (State -> Maybe Int) is the same as Expr -> State -> Maybe Int.

to potential integers, and it is this function type that represents the semantic domain for Expr.

For defining semE the first view is often preferred, since it treats the state as an auxiliary argument that can be consulted to yield the denotation of variables. The definition of semE consists of three cases, one for each constructor of Expr. The definition under the "two-argument view" looks as follows.

```
semE : Expr -> State -> Maybe Int
semE e s = case e of
    Num i      -> Just i
    Plus e1 e2 -> map2 (+) (semE e1 s) (semE e2 s)
    Var x      -> get x s
```

We can see that the state is not needed for determining the value of an integer constant, which always denotes itself. The value of a Plus expression is obtained by determining the values of its arguments where the current state is passed to the recursive semE calls. The third case finally makes use of the state when a variable's value needs to be retrieved from the state argument s, which is done using the Dict function get.

The definition of semE looks and reads like the definition of a binary function because the definition for semE has two arguments, e and s. But we can rewrite the definitions using lambda abstractions (see Section 2.3.2) to illustrate that we are actually defining a unary function that returns function values.

```
semE e = case e of
    Num i      -> \_ -> Just i
    Plus e1 e2 -> \s -> map2 (+) (semE e1 s) (semE e2 s)
    Var x      -> \s -> get x s
```

Here semE has only one argument, and each case returns a function, as indicated by the lambda abstraction. For example, the second case can now be read as, *The semantics of a* Plus *expression is a function that maps a state* s *to an integer that is obtained by adding the denotations of the two arguments in the context of the state* s.

With semE we can define the semantics of programs. Again, the function domain D allows the definition to be read in two different ways. Here is the definition of sem in the standard form that treats the state as a second argument.

```
sem : Stmt -> State -> State
sem stmt s = case stmt of
    Assign x e -> case (semE e s) of
                     Just i  -> insert x i s
                     Nothing -> s
    Seq s1 s2  -> sem s2 (sem s1 s)
```

Exercise 4.6

The goal of this exercise is to define the semantics of a language for controlling a one-register machine. Programs in this language are given by element of type `Prog`, which is defined as follows.

```
type Op = LD Int | INC | DBL
type alias Prog = List Op
```

The operation `LD` loads an integer into the register, `INC` increases the value in the register by 1, and `DBL` doubles the value in the register. For example, assuming that the register is initially set to 0, the program `[LD 2,INC,DBL]` would leave the number 6 in the register.

(a) Define the semantic domain `D`.

(b) Define the semantic function `sem : Prog -> D`. Note that it might be helpful to define an auxiliary function `semOp : Op -> D` to capture the semantics of individual operations.

The semantics of assigning an expression `e` to a variable `x` is obtained by first determining the value of `e` in the current state `s` using the semantic function `semE` and then binding the resulting integer (if it exists) to `x` in the state `s`, using the `Dict` function `insert`. The meaning of a sequence of statements `s1` followed by `s2` is the state that is obtained by first determining the state (say, `s'`) that results from performing `s1` in the current state `s` and then determining the meaning of `s2` in the state `s'`. Again, we could rewrite the definition using lambda abstraction to emphasize that the meaning of a statement is a function. In particular, the definition for `Seq` is instructive, since it reveals an interesting fundamental relationship between imperative and functional programming.

```
sem stmt = case stmt of
    Seq s1 s2 -> \s -> sem s2 (sem s1 s)
```

If you look at the definition closely, you might recognize that the definition of `sem (Seq s1 s2)` is the composition of the functions `sem s1` and `sem s2` (recall the definition of function composition from Section 2.7). This means we can rewrite the definition as follows.

```
sem stmt = case stmt of
    Seq s1 s2 -> sem s2 << sem s1
```

This definition says that the meaning of sequential composition of imperative programs is given by the composition of their state changes. This also shows that the basic control structure of sequential composition in imperative languages corresponds to function composition in functional languages.

With sem and semE we can now determine the meaning of imperative programs such as x := 3; y := x+2.

```
> sem (Seq (Assign "x" (Num 3)) (Assign "y" (Plus (Var "x") (Num 2)))) empty
Dict.fromList [("x",3),("y",5)] : State
```

Exercise 4.7

Assume the register machine from Exercise 4.6 is extended to work with two registers, and the language adds a corresponding register parameter to its operations.

```
type Reg = A | B
type Op = LD Reg Int | INC Reg | DBL Reg
type alias Prog = List Op
```

(a) Define the semantic domain D for the two-register machine language.

(b) Define the semantic function sem : Prog -> D for the two-register machine language.

So far we have looked at an absolute minimal version of an imperative language to illustrate the need for two semantic functions and, in particular, function domains. It is not difficult to extend the language in many different directions (multiple types plus type checking, returning an error for undefined variables, etc.). Here we should contemplate at least one other extension, namely the addition of loops. To add, say, while loops, we need to add a constructor to Stmt with an Expr argument to represent the loop's condition and a Stmt argument to represent the loop's body.

```
type Stmt = ... | While Expr Stmt
```

Since our language lacks comparison operators and Boolean values, we let any non-zero integer correspond to the Boolean value True, that is, a while loop will execute its body as long as the condition doesn't evaluate to zero.

Is this a good design? Not at all! This representation is really just a temporary, rather ugly hack; it is *not* recommended for the design of any language. I'm using it here only, since it allows me to keep the following definition of the while semantics simple.

In any case, with this convention we can extend the definition of sem as follows.

```
sem stmt s = case stmt of
    While c b  -> case semE c s of
                    Just 0 -> s
                    _      -> sem (While c b) (sem b s)
```

The definition can best be understood operationally. It says that when the condition c is false (that is, c denotes Just 0 in the current state s), the loop will not be executed and has no effect, that is, the current state s is the result. Otherwise, the body of the loop, b, is executed once, which produces a new intermediate state, say s'. Then the loop is executed again in this intermediate state s', which will end the loop if c evaluates in s' to zero or continue it otherwise.

Note that the definition treats the case when semE c s yields Nothing (a runtime error) in the same way as when it produces Just 0 (the representation of False), which will often lead to an infinite loop (when the undefined variables that cause Nothing aren't assigned values in b). Proper error handling would demand making the result state also into a Maybe value, but that definition complicates the structure and buries the handling of state in the error handling.

If we add a Times constructor to Expr, we can now represent a program for computing factorials in our language. Here is a function that creates a factorial program for any given number m.

```
fac : Int -> Stmt
fac m = Seq (Seq
         (Assign "f" (Num m))
         (Assign "n" (Num (m-1))))
         (While (Var "n")
           (Seq
             (Assign "f" (Times (Var "f") (Var "n")))
             (Assign "n" (Plus (Var "n") (Num (-1)))))))
```

The type of fac indicates that it is a *program generator* that creates for a given integer a program in the language Stmt that computes the factorial for that number. With fac we can easily test our semantics on different factorial programs.

```
> sem (fac 3) empty
Dict.fromList [("f",6),("n",0)] : State

> sem (fac 6) empty
Dict.fromList [("f",720),("n",0)] : State
```

Exercise 4.8

Extend the imperative language by an if-then-else construct.

(a) Extend the abstract syntax of Stmt.

(b) Extend the definition of sem.

5

Types

Chapter Summary

The role of types in programming languages. What a type is and why types are so beneficial. Inference rules and how they can be used to define type systems. Type checking as a process to enforce typing rules. The representation of types and type checkers in Elm. The notion of type safety and the difference between static and dynamic typing.

Types can be a real nuisance because type checkers often complain about what seem to be minor things. Programming can quickly turn into a frustrating endeavor when you can't make it past the type checker. A type checker sometimes seems like a very strict and unforgiving teacher that instead of encouraging you with a "Good Job!" or "This is a good start," often harshly tells you that your program is simply incorrect. But whenever the type checker tells you that your program is not correct, your program is not correct.[1] Thus, while potentially quite annoying, the type checker is really your best friend in your struggle to write correct programs – albeit maybe ill-mannered.

Types and type systems enhance programming languages and offer a number of concrete benefits for programmers.

- Types *summarize* a program on an abstract level and thus provide *precise documentation* of programs.
- Type correctness means *partial correctness* of programs. In other words, a type checker delivers *partial correctness proofs* for programs.

---

[1]For a static type checker this is, in fact, not always the case, as we will soon discuss.

Programming Language Fundamentals: A Metalanguage Approach in Elm, First edition. Martin Erwig.
© 2024 Martin Erwig. Published 2024 by John Wiley & Sons Inc.
Companion website: www.wiley.com/go/ProgrammingLanguageFun

- Type systems can *prevent runtime errors* and can thus save a lot of debugging effort.
- Type information can be exploited in the generation of *efficient code*.

About This Chapter

In this chapter we will learn about types and how they are part of programming languages. Specifically, we will address the following questions in Section 5.2.

- What is a type?
- What is a type system?
- What are typing rules?
- What is a type error?

Since type systems are usually defined through typing rules, we start this chapter in Section 5.1 by learning about *inference rules*, which are the formal basis for expressing typing rules. How a type system described by typing rules can be turned into a type checking algorithm for spotting type errors will then be explained in Section 5.3, and in Section 5.4 we will discuss the notion of *type safety*.

Finally, we will look in Section 5.5 into the difference between two different approaches to type checking, *static typing* and *dynamic typing*, and point out the limitations and advantages of each approach. Unless explicitly stated otherwise, I will use the type names and rules as they exist in Elm (ignoring overloading). Later in Section 5.5, I will also present some types and typing rules of Python.

5.1 Inference Rules

Inference rules are a very general formalism for defining reasoning systems as well as inductive sets and relations. In general, an inference rule relates logical statements called *judgments* and has the following form.

$$\frac{\mathcal{P}_1 \quad \cdots \quad \mathcal{P}_n}{\mathcal{C}}$$

The judgments $\mathcal{P}_1, \ldots, \mathcal{P}_n$ above the horizontal line are called *premises*, and the judgment $\mathcal{C}$ is called the *conclusion* of the rule. The meaning of such a rule is that the conclusion $\mathcal{C}$ is true if all premises $\mathcal{P}_1, \ldots, \mathcal{P}_n$ are true.

Inference rules have a wide range of applications.[2] One of the most basic applications is the formulation of logical reasoning rules. For example, the reasoning rule called *modus ponens* says that if A implies B and if A is true, then we can conclude that B is true. This rule can be expressed as an inference rule as follows.

$$\frac{A \Rightarrow B \qquad A}{B}$$

In this example, the judgments are propositions represented by variables (A and B) that stand for arbitrary propositions and propositional formulas (such as $A \Rightarrow B$). Other reasoning rules can be defined in a similar way.

More generally, we can use inference rules to define arbitrary relations. The simplest case is unary relations, which are just plain sets, defined as subsets over some known set. Consider, for example, the set of non-negative even numbers. We can introduce a judgment $even(n)$ and define it through two rules.

$$\frac{}{even(0)} \qquad\qquad \frac{even(n)}{even(n+2)}$$

The first rule has no premises and establishes the base case that 0 is an even number. A rule without any premises is unconditionally true and is also called an *axiom*. The second rule says that we can get an even number by adding 2 to a number already known to be even. This example illustrates how inference rules can inductively – that is, through recursion – define infinite sets.

It is important to understand that a judgment is just a specific way of talking about a relation. For example, the *even* judgment defines a unary predicate on numbers and thus corresponds to a unary relation, which is simply a set. Therefore, any judgment such as $even(0)$ or $even(n+2)$ can always be written using set notation, such as $0 \in Even$ or $n + 2 \in Even$ (where $Even$ is the name of the set), and we can write rules as implications. For example, the second rule can also be written as follows.

$$n \in Even \implies n + 2 \in Even$$

As an example of a binary relation, consider the judgment $fac(n, m)$ that says that m is the factorial of n. In Section 2.4 we have already defined an Elm function for computing factorials, but we can also define this binary relation between numbers with inference rules.

$$\frac{}{fac(1, 1)} \qquad\qquad \frac{fac(n - 1, m)}{fac(n, n \cdot m)}$$

---

[2]In addition to describing typing rules, we will encounter them again in Chapter 8 as Prolog rules.

Again, we have an axiom defining a base case and an inductive rule that can be used to generate pairs of this relation building on prior, simpler examples. The second rule can be written in a variety of different ways. For example, we can use $n + 1$ in the conclusion instead of $n - 1$ in the premise, and we can also express the multiplication for the result as a separate premise.

$$\frac{fac(n, m)}{fac(n + 1, (n + 1) \cdot m)} \qquad \frac{fac(n - 1, k) \qquad k \cdot n = m}{fac(n, m)}$$

Note, again, that the prefix notation is just one way of writing a judgment, which in this case is binary. We could alternatively write the judgments using set notation, for example, $(1, 1) \in Fac$ or $(n, n \cdot m) \in Fac$, and we could write rules as implications.

$$(n - 1, m) \in Fac \implies (n, n \cdot m) \in Fac$$

Or we could invent special syntax and write the rules in the following way.

$$\frac{n! = m}{(n + 1)! = (n + 1) \cdot m} \qquad \frac{(n - 1)! = k \qquad k \cdot n = m}{n! = m}$$

One may think that inference rules are just a different notation for writing function definitions, but that's not the case. In fact, inference rules are more general, since they can be used to define relations that are not functions. As a simple example, consider the less-than relation on integers, which can be defined with two rules.

$$\frac{}{n < n + 1} \qquad \frac{n < k \qquad k < m}{n < m}$$

The axiom[3] says that any number is smaller than its immediate successor, and the rule defines the transitive closure of the successor relation.

The generative view of inference rules (that is, inductive rules produce complex examples from simpler ones) indicates that inference rules can also be used for the same purpose as grammars, namely defining the syntax of languages. Consider again the simplified grammar for arithmetic expressions used in Sections 3.2, 3.3, and 4.1.

$$n \in num ::= 0 \mid 1 \mid 2 \mid 3 \mid \cdots$$
$$e_1, e_2 \in expr ::= n \mid e_1 + e_2 \mid e_1 * e_2$$

---

[3]This rule is also called an *axiom schema*, since it describes, through the use of the variable n, an infinite set of axioms, one for each number.

We can define the set of expressions *expr* as a set membership judgment of the form $e \in expr$ by the following inference rules.[4]

$$\frac{\quad}{n \in expr} \; n \in \mathbb{Z} \qquad \frac{e_1 \in expr \qquad e_2 \in expr}{e_1 + e_2 \in expr} \qquad \frac{e_1 \in expr \qquad e_2 \in expr}{e_1 * e_2 \in expr}$$

The first rule says that any integer (that is, any element of the set $\mathbb{Z}$) is an expression. The other two rules say that if e_1 and e_2 are expressions, then so are, respectively, $e_1 + e_2$ and $e_1 * e_2$. The form "$e \in expr$" can be understood as applying a unary predicate "$\in expr$" in postfix notation on (potential) sentences e of the language of expressions. This example (and the next) illustrate that inference rules are also in fact another example of a metalanguage.

Since inference rules can be used to define arbitrary relations, it should not be too surprising that we can express denotational semantics through inference rules. Again, consider the mathematical definition from Section 4.1.

$$\begin{aligned}
\llbracket \cdot \rrbracket &: \; expr \to \mathbb{Z}_\perp \\
\llbracket n \rrbracket &= \; \underline{n} \\
\llbracket e_1 + e_2 \rrbracket &= \; \llbracket e_1 \rrbracket + \llbracket e_2 \rrbracket \\
\llbracket e_1 * e_2 \rrbracket &= \; \llbracket e_1 \rrbracket \cdot \llbracket e_2 \rrbracket
\end{aligned}$$

To define the semantics using inference rules, we first have to decide what form the judgments should have. We could adopt the notation from the semantic function definition and use judgments of the form $\llbracket e \rrbracket = n$, but that notation is a bit confusing, since $\llbracket \cdot \rrbracket$ denotes a function, but we want to define a relation between expressions and numbers. We can resort to using a name such as *sem* or *eval*, similar to the *even* and *fac* relations, but it is customary to express evaluation judgments using arrow symbols. Thus we use the judgment $e \Downarrow n$ to express that the expression e evaluates to the number n.

$$\frac{\quad}{n \Downarrow \underline{n}} \qquad \frac{e_1 \Downarrow n \qquad e_2 \Downarrow m}{e_1 + e_2 \Downarrow n + m} \qquad \frac{e_1 \Downarrow n \qquad e_2 \Downarrow m}{e_1 * e_2 \Downarrow n \cdot m}$$

Note how we have to use the notation $\underline{n}$ again in the axiom to map a number symbol (which is an element of *expr*) to its corresponding integer (an element of $\mathbb{Z}$). You may wonder why we use $\underline{n}$ in the first rule but not in the other rules.

It can be a bit tricky to parse and understand the notation correctly. It is always a good idea to be clear about the types of the relationships being defined. In this example, the $\Downarrow$ binary relationship has the type $\Downarrow \; \subseteq expr \times \mathbb{Z}$. For the notation in the rules, this means that when n occurs as part of the left argument

---

[4]We could also add a rule for a judgment $n \in num$, but it wouldn't add anything important.

of ⇓, it is a metavariable that ranges over syntactic *num* elements and thus has to be transformed into a value of $\mathbb{Z}$ when also used as part of the right argument. However, when used only as part of right arguments of ⇓, n is a variable that ranges over elements of $\mathbb{Z}$ and doesn't require any transformation.

Exercise 5.1

(a) Define the binary relation *fib*(n, m), which says that m is the nth Fibonacci number, with inference rules.

(b) Consider the grammar for statements (cf. page 59 and Exercise 3.4(c) on page 63).

$stmt$ ::= skip | while *cond* { *stmt* } | *stmt*; *stmt*

Define the judgment $s \in stmt$ with inference rules. (You can make use of the judgment $c \in cond$ as one of the premises.)

5.2   Type Systems

A *type system* defines (i) the types of all basic programming constructs (such as values and functions) and (ii) provides rules for what compositions of those constructs are valid and what the resulting types are.

To talk about the types of values, we need a language of types, discussed in Section 5.2.1. Equipped with such a type language, we can then describe the rules of a type system with so-called *typing rules*, which are explained in Section 5.2.2. Typing rules describe a type system on a very high level. A *type checker* is an algorithm that implements these rules with the specific purpose of identifying situations in which values and operations are used inconsistently with regard to their types, a situation called a *type error*. The process of executing a type checker is called *type checking*. I will explain this process in Section 5.3.

5.2.1   The Language of Types

A *type* is a collection of programming language elements that share a common behavior. While the extent of types varies with different programming languages, types are typically associated with values, functions (or procedures/methods/...), and control structures as well as their compositions.

Types often have a name. This is, in particular, the case for atomic, non-constructed programming language elements. For example, the type of integers is a collection of numbers that can be added, multiplied, compared, etc.; in Elm it has the name Int. But types don't necessarily have a name. Consider, for example, the type of pairs of integers. This type can be denoted by the *type expression* (Int,Int), but it doesn't have to have its own name, even though we can define a name for it using a type alias definition such as the following.

```
type alias IntPair = (Int,Int)
```

Note that a *type alias definition* is something very different from a *(data) type definition* (introduced in Section 2.6), which introduces constructors and their types. A type alias definition does not introduce any new values; it only defines a new name, a so-called *type synonym* or *type alias*, for a pre-existing type. The synonym and the type it stands for can be used interchangeably. Thus, while type synonyms are a convenient programming language feature, they are not an essential part of a type system.

Type expressions are built by applying *type constructors* to type names and other type expressions. Examples of type constructors are the list type constructor List (Section 2.5), the Maybe type constructor (Sections 2.5 and 4.2.1), and the function type constructor -> (Section 2.3).

Type constructors are functions on types that can have different arities (that is, different numbers of parameters), just like operators and functions on values. For example, List and Maybe are unary type constructors, that is, they take exactly one type as an argument. Examples of type expressions built using these constructors are List Int, Maybe Bool, List (Maybe Int), and Maybe (List String). In contrast, -> and (,) are binary type constructors that take two arguments. Examples of type expressions built using these constructors are Int -> Bool, (Int,Bool), and Int -> (Int -> Int).

Exercise 5.2

(a) Give example values that have the following types.

- List (Maybe Bool)
- Maybe (List Bool)
- (Int,List Bool)
- List (Int,Bool)
- Bool -> Int
- Int -> (Int,Int)

(b) What are the types of the following expressions?

- Just (Just True)
- 3/0
- [not]
- (+) 3::[]
- tail [3]
- Just even

A function definition typically has the following form: it consists of a name f, has one or more parameters (represented by variables x, y, etc.), and has an expression e that defines the value to be returned.

```
f x y = e
```

Viewing a type constructor as a function on types suggests a very similar pattern for a type constructor definition: it consists of a type name T, has one or more parameters (represented by type variables a, b, etc.), and has a type expression U that defines the type to be constructed.

```
type alias T a b = U
```

Here are two examples of type constructors and their use: Pair is a binary type constructor for building different pair types, and Property constructs function types that have Bool as a return type.

```
type alias Pair a b = (a,b)
type alias Property a = a -> Bool
```

A type expression that contains type variables is a *polymorphic type*, which means it actually represents many different types (in fact, infinitely many). More specifically, this kind of polymorphism is called *parametric polymorphism*, since the polymorphism is expressed by type parameters, that is, type variables. We have seen several examples already in Sections 2.5 (cf. the types of head or null) and 2.7 (cf. the types of map or foldr). Just as we can apply functions to values to return values, we can apply type constructors to denote new types, and just as we can use functions in expressions to define new functions, we can use type constructors in type expressions to define new type constructors.

```
type alias Pos = Pair Int Int
type alias ListProperty a = Property (List a)
```

We can then use these type constructors and types in the type signatures of the definition of values.

```
pos : Pos          isZero : Property Int        isOrigin : Property Pos
pos = (3,4)        isZero = (==) 0              isOrigin = (==) (0,0)
```

Exercise 5.3

Try to predict the polymorphic types of the following expressions. (Note that you may need to import the list functions using import List exposing (map,head,tail,reverse).)

- Just Nothing
- Just Just
- (Just,Nothing)

- []::[]
- (::) []
- (::) Just

- map head
- tail << reverse
- Just << Just

Then check in the Elm interpreter whether your predictions were correct.

5.2.2 Typing Rules

Typing rules express judgments about the types of expressions. It is also customary to say that typing rules *assign* types to expressions, but this has nothing to do with the assignment operation found in imperative languages.

In general, a typing rule assigns a type to an expression *e* based on the structure of *e* and on preconditions about the types of *e*'s parts. If the expression *e* is an atomic value or operation, that is, if *e* cannot be decomposed into further parts, then the typing rule for *e* universally assigns it a specific type without any precondition. As mentioned, such rules are also called *axioms*. For example, the integer constant 3 has type Int,[5] and the function even has type Int -> Bool.

On the other hand, the type of a non-atomic expression generally depends on the type of its parts. For example, the rule for the type of a function application, that is, an expression of the form *f e*, is as follows.

> **if** the function *f* has type $T \to U$ **and**
>   the expression *e* has type T
> **then**
>   the application *f e* is well defined and has type U

Here, the metavariables *f* and *e* range over expressions, and T and U range over types.

We can write such rules in a more concise way with the help of inference rules. The judgments are of the form $e : T$ (read as "*e has type T*"), where *e* is an expression of the language and T is a type, for example, 3 : Int and isEven : Int -> Bool. Thus the rule for function application can be rewritten as an inference rule as follows. (APP is the name given to the rule.)

$$\text{APP} \ \frac{f : T \to U \qquad e : T}{f e : U}$$

With this rule we can check that the type of isEven 3 is Bool by substituting for the metavariables *f* and *e*, *T*, and *U* as follows.

$$\text{APP} \ \frac{\text{isEven} : \text{Int} \ \text{->} \ \text{Bool} \qquad 3 : \text{Int}}{\text{isEven} \ 3 : \text{Bool}}$$

The binary typing judgment $e : T$ seems plain and simple, and it works well in many cases. However, it is somewhat limited, since it assumes that the type of

---

[5]In this chapter we assume that each symbol uniquely determines a value of a specific type. In particular, we disregard the overloading of symbols; cf. the discussion of overloading on page 18 in Section 2.2.

each name and symbol is globally defined (by axioms). Specifically, it is impossible to define the type of let expressions with the judgment $e : T$. Consider, for example, the following expressions, which are all well typed.

(a) `let x=3 in x+1`
(b) `let x=True in not x`
(c) `let x=True in if x then let x=3 in x+1 else 5`

The type of (a) is `Int`, while the type of (b) is `Bool`. To type the body of the let expressions, x has to be of type `Int` in (a) but needs to be of type `Bool` in (b). As expression (c) illustrates, it must be possible for one variable to have different types in different local contexts of an expression: here x is of type `Bool` in the outer let expression but of type `Int` in the inner let expression.[6]

Therefore, a type system must be able to flexibly assign types for variables depending on the context, which can't be achieved by using a global assignment. The solution is to extend the typing judgment into a ternary relation by adding a so-called *type environment* Γ, which is a set of so-called *type assumptions*, to keep track of locally introduced variable/type pairs. A type assumption consists of a variable and its type and is written like a plain type judgment, as in `x : Int`. Then $\Gamma = \{x : Int, f : Int \text{ -> } Bool\}$ is a set of two type assumptions. The *has-type* typing judgment now becomes $\Gamma \vdash e : T$, which says that expression e has type T in the context of the type assumptions Γ.[7] When e contains variables, their types are determined by the assumptions in Γ.[8] For example, we can have the following typing judgments.

$$\{x : Int\} \vdash x : Int$$
$$\{x : Int, y : Int\} \vdash x+y : Int$$
$$\{x : Bool, y : Int\} \vdash not\ x : Bool$$

As the last example shows, not all type assumptions have to be used in determining the type of an expression. On the other hand, we can't determine a type for an expression containing a variable that doesn't have a type assumption in Γ.

$$\{\} \vdash x+1 : \text{TYPE ERROR}$$

---

[6]Note that the Elm compiler actually doesn't accept (c) because of its restrictive shadowing rule (see the discussion on page 19 in Section 2.2.1).

[7]Note that the symbol $\vdash$ has no special meaning; it is part of the concrete syntax for the typing judgment, and its only purpose is to visibly separate the type assumptions from the *has-type* part of the typing judgment.

[8]Since Γ defines the context for determining the types of variables, it is also sometimes called a *typing context*.

The typing rule for variables simply looks up their type in the type environment.

$$\text{Var} \; \frac{x : T \in \Gamma}{\Gamma \vdash x : T}$$

This rule says that a variable has whatever type it has been assigned in the type environment.

To define the typing rule for let expressions, we need to be able to add or overwrite type assumptions in the type environment, which is done by simply adding an assumption separated by a comma. For example, $\Gamma, \text{x} : \text{Int}$ has the same assumptions as Γ, except for x whose type is now Int.

More generally, if Γ does not contain an assumption for v, the notation $\Gamma, v : T$ adds the type assumption $v : T$ to Γ. Otherwise, it changes the assumption for v in Γ to T, but only temporarily. One can think of Γ as a stack onto which assumptions can be pushed using the comma notation. The added assumption is valid only within the specific judgment within which it is added. Outside of it, the previous, original version of Γ is used.

With the ability to (temporarily) change the assumptions in the type environment, we can formulate the typing rule for let expressions as follows.

$$\text{Let} \; \frac{\Gamma \vdash e_1 : U \qquad \Gamma, x : U \vdash e_2 : T}{\Gamma \vdash \text{let } x{=}e_1 \text{ in } e_2 : T}$$

This rule says that the type of a let expression is given by the type of its body e_2, assuming that the bound variable x has the type of the expression e_1. By substituting x for x, 3 for e_1, x+1 for e_2, and Int for U and T, we can now see how the type for the expressions (a) is obtained.

$$\text{Let} \; \frac{\{\} \vdash 3 : \text{Int} \qquad \{\text{x} : \text{Int}\} \vdash \text{x+1} : \text{Int}}{\{\} \vdash \text{let } \text{x=3} \text{ in } \text{x+1} : \text{Int}}$$

In a similar way, we obtain the result for (b).

$$\text{Let} \; \frac{\{\} \vdash \text{True} : \text{Bool} \qquad \{\text{x} : \text{Bool}\} \vdash \text{not x} : \text{Bool}}{\{\} \vdash \text{let } \text{x=True} \text{ in } \text{not x} : \text{Bool}}$$

In both examples we are using $\{\}$ for Γ, which means that the typing does not employ any assumptions other than the one locally added for x in the second premise. More specifically, we can observe how Γ is only temporarily changed by an assumption for x (that is, x). The assumption is not needed for typing e_1 (that is, 3 or True), and notably, it is not needed for typing the complete let expressions (a) or (b) either.

In the example we rely on the following axioms for the types of 3, True, +, and not.

$$\frac{}{\Gamma \vdash 3 : \text{Int}} \qquad\qquad \frac{}{\Gamma \vdash \text{True} : \text{Bool}}$$

$$\frac{}{\Gamma \vdash + : \text{Int -> Int -> Int}} \qquad\qquad \frac{}{\Gamma \vdash \text{not} : \text{Bool -> Bool}}$$

Instead of using such axioms, we could also add type assumptions about predefined values and functions to a "standard" type environment Γ_0 to be used in all typing rules.

$$\Gamma_0 = \{ \ldots, 3 : \text{Int}, + : \text{Int -> Int -> Int}, \ldots, \text{True} : \text{Bool}, \text{not} : \text{Bool -> Bool}, \ldots \}$$

Both examples use a non-atomic judgment as the second premise, namely $\{x : \text{Int}\} \vdash x+1 : \text{Int}$ in the rule instance for (a), and $\{x : \text{Bool}\} \vdash \text{not } x : \text{Bool}$ in the rule instance for (b). These judgments have to be justified by applying corresponding typing rules. In the case of (b) this is a simple application of the APP rule, for which in turn we need an application of the VAR rule to determine the type of x. For (a) we could use an additional application rule for binary operations (see Exercise 5.4). But if we consider x+1 as syntactic sugar for (+) x 1,[9] then we can also derive the typing judgment for x+1 in two steps. First, we show with rule APP that + partially applied to x has the type Int -> Int.

$$\text{APP} \; \frac{\{x : \text{Int}\} \vdash (+) : \text{Int -> Int -> Int} \qquad \{x : \text{Int}\} \vdash x : \text{Int}}{\{x : \text{Int}\} \vdash (+) \; x : \text{Int -> Int}}$$

In a second step, we can use this result in another application of APP.

$$\text{APP} \; \frac{\{x : \text{Int}\} \vdash (+) \; x : \text{Int -> Int} \qquad \{x : \text{Int}\} \vdash 1 : \text{Int}}{\{x : \text{Int}\} \vdash (+) \; x \; 1 : \text{Int}}$$

You may have noticed that we could substitute the occurrence of a judgment $\mathcal{J}$ in a premise of a rule by a rule that has $\mathcal{J}$ as its conclusion and thus build whole trees of judgments (which are also called *derivations* or *proof trees*). However, we will not look into this aspect here.

Finally, how are type errors and type-incorrect expressions dealt with by typing rules? The simple answer is: they aren't. Any expression for which it is impossible to derive a type with the typing rules is considered to be type

---

[9]Remember that the parentheses turn an infix operation into a prefix operation, cf. Section 2.3.2.

> ### Exercise 5.4
>
> (a) Write a typing rule for applying arbitrary binary (infix) operations such as +. It might be a good idea to first create the rule for + and then generalize it to more general types.
>
> (b) Write a typing rule for the cons operation (::) and a rule for the empty list [].
>
> (c) Use the rules from part (b) to show that the expression [3,4] has type List Int.
>
> (d) Pick an appropriate type environment to formulate a typing judgment for the expression xs ++ ys. Then use the rule from part (a) to show that the judgment is true.

incorrect. Typical examples of type errors are the application of functions to values of the wrong type, as in not 3, or the use of undefined variables. But how can we be sure that an expression cannot be typed? For this we need to turn the descriptive typing rules into an algorithm for checking expressions and programs.

5.3 Type Checking

A *type checker* is an algorithm that uses *type declarations* of values and functions in a program to ensure that all functions and values are used according to the typing rules of the underlying programming language. A *type inference algorithm* does basically the same thing, but it generally doesn't need type declarations and instead automatically infers the most general types for any names being used.

We can operationalize typing rules, which are declarative statements, into a type checking algorithm in a systematic way by first identifying dedicated inputs and outputs of the typing relation and then transforming rules into function equations.

I'll explain this idea using the factorial rules as an example. First, $fac(n, m)$ is a binary relation, which means we want to turn it into a function $fac : \mathbb{N} \to \mathbb{N}$ that takes one argument and returns one result. Second, we probably want the first component to be the argument and the second component the result: since $fac(n, m)$ says that m is the factorial of n, we want to derive a function that computes m given n.[10] Third, we turn each rule into one case rule "p -> r" of a case expression starting with "case x of" where p is a pattern representing the specific form of the argument x and r is an expression computing the result. For an axiom the case rule is trivial, since the result does not depend on any premises. In our example, we can simply turn $fac(1, 1)$ into 1 -> 1. The inductive rule is more interesting, since it has two premises and a recursive occurrence of the judgment.

$$\frac{fac(n-1, k) \qquad k \cdot n = m}{fac(n, m)}$$

The argument of the conclusion $fac(n, m)$ determines the pattern of the case rule, that is, p is instantiated to a simple variable n in this example. Next we have to assemble the result expression r from the premises of the rule that define m. The second premise says that $m = k \cdot n$ (where n corresponds to the pattern variable n), and the first premise says that k is the result of fac for the argument $n - 1$, which corresponds to the recursive call of the function we are defining. In other words, the result expression r becomes (reversing the order of multiplication) n * fac (n-1). Altogether we therefore obtain the following function definition.

```
fac : Int -> Int
fac x = case x of
    1 -> 1
    n -> n * fac (n-1)
```

Now let's try the same transformation with the typing rules. The first step is to identify the input and output of the typing judgment $\Gamma \vdash e : T$. Since we want the type checker to determine the types of expressions, the third component of the relation should be the result, and consequently the first two components should be the arguments. As with denotational semantics, we want to define the type checker as an Elm function so that we can experiment with examples. This means we need type definitions for the argument and result types. Specifically, we need a type for the abstract syntax of the language and a type for the type expressions to be returned by the type checker. We start with the expression language from Section 4.2.3, which had expressions of two different types. To illustrate the use of the type environment in type checking, we add two constructors to represent let expressions and variable references.

```
type alias Name = String
type Expr = Num Int | Plus Expr Expr | Equal Expr Expr | Not Expr
         | Let Name Expr Expr | Var Name
```

---

[10]Note that we could, in principle, also do the opposite, that is, given a number m compute the number n of which m is a factorial. This would be some kind of "inverse factorial" function, and it would be a partial function that is undefined for many arguments m.

With the two added constructors we can represent an expression such as `let x=3 in x+1` as follows.

```
Let "x" (Num 3) (Plus (Var "x") (Num 1))
```

The type language in this example is quite simple: we only have expressions of type `Int` and `Bool` and no function types or type constructors yet. But we do need to represent the case when the type checker encounters a type error. As in Section 4.2.3, we have two possibilities for representing errors: we can define a type `Type` with only constructors for the two types and then use `Maybe Type` as the result type for the type checker, or we can integrate the error into the type definition for `Type`. While the latter approach may lead to simpler definitions in some parts, it is also less clear. In particular, we have to store types in type environments, and being able to store the type "type error" for a variable seems wrong. We therefore define `Type` without a constructor to represent type errors.

```
type Type = TyInt | TyBool
```

In addition to `Expr` and `Type`, we also need an Elm type definition to represent the type environment Γ. Since a type environment is essentially a mapping of variable names to types, we can represent it using the type `Dict`, much like we did in Section 4.2.4 where we represented state as a mapping of variables to values.[11]

```
type alias TyEnv = Dict Name Type
```

With these representations we can define the type signature for the type checking function. Note that we use the `Maybe` type constructor to distinguish between proper types of expressions and type errors (represented by the constructor `Nothing`).[12] This needs to happen whenever we turn a relation into a partial function.

```
tc : TyEnv -> Expr -> Maybe Type
```

Next we translate the typing rules into case rules for the type checking function `tc`.

The first two cases are simple: an integer always has type `Int`, and a variable has whatever type is stored for it in the type environment, where we can look it up using the `get` function.

---

[11]The relevant definitions can be imported by adding the statement `import Dict exposing (Dict,empty,insert,get)` at the top of the Elm file.

[12]A summary of how types and values in object- and metalanguage are related is provided in Table 5.1.

Type system concept	Elm representation	Example
Syntax of object language	Data type	Expr
Syntax of types/type language	Data type	Type
Type	Constructor	TyInt of type Type
Type error	Constructor	Nothing
Typing rule	Case rule	e -> t
Type checker	Function	tc

Table 5.1   Representing type system concepts using Elm as a metalanguage. Note that a *type* (name) in the object language is represented by a *value* (that is, constructor) in the metalanguage, and the set of all object language types (that is, the *type language* as described in Section 5.2.1) is represented as a *type* in the metalanguage (see also Table 4.1 on page 79).

```
tc g e = case e of
    Num i -> Just TyInt
    Var x -> get x g
```

If a variable's type is undefined, that is, if no type is stored in the type environment, the type checker has encountered a type error and must return the constructor Nothing. This is achieved directly by the get function, which itself has the following type (with instantiated type parameters Name and Type).

```
get : Name -> Dict Name Type -> Maybe Type
```

Next we define the case rule for the Not operation. The typing rule expresses the condition that the argument of Not must have type Bool employing a single premise.

$$\text{Not} \; \frac{\Gamma \vdash e : \texttt{Bool}}{\Gamma \vdash \texttt{not } e : \texttt{Bool}}$$

The sole purpose of the premise is to pose a constraint on the conclusion; the result type of a Not expression is always Bool. Therefore, we can express the resulting value for tc using a conditional.

```
Not e1 -> if tc g e1 == Just TyBool then Just TyBool else Nothing
```

Since this programming pattern if c then Just v else Nothing occurs several times in the definition of tc, it's a good idea to factor it into a reusable function. We therefore define the function check that takes the condition c and the value v to be returned in case the condition is true and returns Just v or Nothing, depending on c.

```
check : Bool -> a -> Maybe a
check c v = if c then Just v else Nothing
```

With `check` we can express this case rule more succinctly as follows.

```
Not e1 -> check (tc g e1 == Just TyBool) TyBool
```

We encounter a similar situation for binary operations such as `Plus`: The typing rule does not "compute" a result type in the premises; it only expresses constraints on the conclusion.

$$\text{PLUS} \frac{\Gamma \vdash e_1 : \text{Int} \qquad \Gamma \vdash e_2 : \text{Int}}{\Gamma \vdash e_1\text{+}e_2 : \text{Int}}$$

Correspondingly, the case rule for `tc` needs two conditions. Since we have the full expressive power of Elm available, we can introduce some auxiliary definitions to avoid redundancy in the definition. For example, we can use the function `both` to apply the type checker to both argument expressions "in parallel," returning a pair of results, and we can create a value for a pair of constructors representing `Int` types that we can then compare the results to.

```
both : (a -> b) -> (a, a) -> (b, b)
both f (x,y) = (f x,f y)

tc2 : TyEnv -> (Expr,Expr) -> (Maybe Type,Maybe Type)
tc2 g = both (tc g)

jTyInt2  = (Just TyInt,Just TyInt)
jTyBool2 = (Just TyBool,Just TyBool)
```

With `tc2` and `jTyInt2` we can express the PLUS rule using a case rule that combines both premises in one condition to be tested using `check`.

```
Plus e1 e2 -> check (tc2 g (e1,e2) == jTyInt2) TyInt
```

The typing rule for `Equal` is quite similar to that of `Plus`, except that we may want to allow the comparison of integers as well as Booleans. This can be achieved through two separate typing rules.

$$\text{EQUAL}_1 \qquad\qquad\qquad \text{EQUAL}_2$$
$$\frac{\Gamma \vdash e_1 : \text{Int} \qquad \Gamma \vdash e_2 : \text{Int}}{\Gamma \vdash e_1\text{==}e_2 : \text{Bool}} \qquad \frac{\Gamma \vdash e_1 : \text{Bool} \qquad \Gamma \vdash e_2 : \text{Bool}}{\Gamma \vdash e_1\text{==}e_2 : \text{Bool}}$$

To derive the type of a concrete expression, we can pick whichever rule is applicable depending on the context, that is, depending on whether the arguments have type `Int` or `Bool`. We can translate the rules into a case rule where `check` receives a disjunction of two conditions, one for `Int` arguments and one for `Bool` arguments.

```
tc : TyEnv -> Expr -> Maybe Type
tc g e = case e of
    Num i        -> Just TyInt
    Var x        -> get x g
    Not e1       -> check (tc g e1 == Just TyBool) TyBool
    Plus e1 e2   -> check (tc2 g (e1,e2) == jTyInt2) TyInt
    Equal e1 e2  -> check (tc2 g (e1,e2) == jTyInt2 ||
                           tc2 g (e1,e2) == jTyBool2) TyBool
    Let x e1 e2  -> case tc g e1 of
                        Just t -> tc (insert x t g) e2
                        _      -> Nothing
```

Figure 5.1   Complete definition of the type checker.

```
Equal e1 e2 -> check (tc2 g (e1,e2) == jTyInt2 ||
                      tc2 g (e1,e2) == jTyBool2) TyBool
```

Finally, the LET rule (see page 107) needs in the first premise to check the type of the definition e_1 and use that type U as an assumption for the bound variable x when determining the type of the body of the let expression e_2. We turn this rule into a case rule where we examine the result of type checking e1 and proceed with checking e2 only if e1 is well typed. Otherwise, we return a type error (that is, Nothing).

```
Let x e1 e2 -> case tc g e1 of
                   Just t -> tc (insert x t g) e2
                   _      -> Nothing
```

The complete definition of the function tc is shown in Figure 5.1.

Exercise 5.5

The goal of this exercise is to extend the Expr language with non-nested pairs of integers and extend the definition of the type checker accordingly.

(a) Extend the abstract syntax of the Expr language with an operation Pair for construct-ing non-nested pairs of integers, an operation Fst, which selects the first component of an integer pair, and Swap, which exchanges the two components of an integer pair.

(b) Extend the data type Type with a constructor to represent an integer pair type.

(c) Define the typing rules for the operations Pair, Fst, and Swap.

(d) Expand the definition of the type checker tc by equations for the operations Pair, Fst, and Swap.

> ### Exercise 5.6
>
> This exercise builds on Exercise 5.5. Now we want to extend the Expr language with *nested* pairs of any types and extend the definition of the type checker accordingly. The abstract syntax Expr can remain unchanged.
>
> (a) Change the data type Type so that the constructor for pair types can represent arbitrary pair types (including nested pairs).
>
> (b) Redefine the typing rules for the operations Pair, Fst, and Swap.
>
> (c) Change the definition of the type checker tc by equations for the operations Pair, Fst, and Swap to account for nested pairs.

5.4 Type Safety

After having spent so much effort in designing typing rules and transforming them into a type checking algorithm, the questions arise, *Why do we need all of this?* and, *What are the benefits of a type system and its "enforcer" the type checker?* The most important feature of a type system (and its implementation in a type checker) is *type safety*, which is a property of a programming language that guarantees the absence of a large class of programming errors.

Consider, for example, the expression not 3. What should the result of this expression be? In Section 4.2.3 we have defined the semantics to be undefined.

```
sem : Expr -> Val
sem e = case e of
    ...
    Not e1 -> case sem e1 of
                B b -> B (not b)
                _   -> Undefined
```

This definition is complicated by the fact that the type of the semantics of e1 must be checked before the operation not can be applied. The same is true for all other operations as well: for every application of an operation we must ensure that its arguments have the correct type. Obviously, such repeated tests are quite inefficient.

If we knew in advance that every operation is applied only to arguments of the correct type, we wouldn't need any of these tests and could generate more efficient code. A type checker provides exactly such an assurance.

A program that passes the type checker won't apply operations to arguments of the wrong type. We could therefore simplify the implementation of an interpreter or compiler accordingly and get rid of all such tests. Here is an *attempt* to define a simplified version of sem from Section 4.2.3. This definition assumes that all arguments have the correct type. Note that we can therefore remove the Undefined constructor from the data type Val.

```
type Val = I Int | B Bool

eval : Expr -> Val
eval e = case e of
    ...
    Plus e1 e2 -> case (eval e1,eval e2) of (I i,I j) -> I (i+j)
    Not e1     -> case eval e1 of B b -> B (not b)
```

Alas, the Elm compiler does not accept the above definition. The fact that eval can in principle return either an I or B value leads the Elm compiler to complain that the case expressions in the results expressions for Plus and Not do not cover all cases. Now *we* might know that when we apply eval to a type-correct expression, those other cases can never occur, but the Elm compiler doesn't, and we have no way to convince the compiler of that fact either. This means that we actually *cannot* implement this optimized version of eval in Elm. If we could, it would not be safe in general, that is, we could evaluate an expression with a type error, such as Not (Num 3), which would then lead to some kind of runtime error.

But assuming for the sake of argument that we could define the unsafe version in Elm, we nevertheless can then create a safe version of eval that uses tc to filter out expressions containing type errors.

```
evalSafe : Expr -> Maybe Val
evalSafe e = case tc empty e of
                Just _ -> Just (eval e)
                _      -> Nothing
```

With evalSafe we apply eval to an expression e only if the type checker tc has approved it, that is, if tc returns a proper type. Otherwise, we return Nothing.

```
> evalSafe (Not (Num 1))        | > evalSafe (Not (Equal (Num 1) (Num 2)))
Nothing : Maybe Val             | Just (B True) : Maybe Val
```

Note how Nothing is used for two different kinds of errors: the Nothing that may result from tc (which would be matched by the underscore in the last line of evalSafe) represents a type error, whereas the Nothing that is returned in that line represents an undefined value to indicate that the expression can't be evaluated.

We can simplify the implementation even further by using a single type as a representation for all values. This could save us the inspection of tags and the extraction of values from union types in patterns. We can use integers in this case and represent False by 0 and True by 1.

```
eval : Expr -> Int
eval e = case e of
    ...
    Plus e1 e2 -> eval e1 + eval e2
    Not e1     -> if eval e1==0 then 1 else 0
```

In the definition of evalSafe we only have to change the return type to Maybe
Int. Type checking works as before, but the returned values are, of course, only
integers.

```
> evalSafe (Not (Num 1))        |    > evalSafe (Not (Equal (Num 1) (Num 2)))
Nothing : Maybe Int             |    Just 1 : Maybe Int
```

The last implementation looks so simple. Why can't we just use it directly, without the type checker? Because the representation can lead to unexpected results:
The definition of eval for Not regards all non-zero integers as representations of
True, since applying Not to any non-zero number yields 0, which represents False.
But now we are in the strange situation where, while in most cases True + True
equals True, this is not always the case. Consider, for example, 3 and -3. Thus
this representation is inconsistent and makes reasoning about programs difficult.

Another example is this: we would expect Not (Not e) to be equal to e, but Not
(Not (Num 2)) evaluates to 1 and not 2. The concept of type safety is summarized
in the box *Type Safety* on page 118. The most important take-away is that
type-safe languages detect all type errors in programs and so can avoid a large
number of program execution failures as well as semantic errors.

5.5 Static and Dynamic Typing

The most obvious difference between static and dynamic typing is the time when
types are checked:

- *Static typing*: Types are checked *before* a program is run.
- *Dynamic typing*: Types are checked *while* a program is run.

If this were all, this section would be pretty short. However, the time of when
typing rules are checked has some important implications and leads to different
advantages for the two approaches. Consider the following expression. What
is the resulting value, and what is its type?

```
if 1<2 then 3 else "Hello"
```

The answer depends on the programming language. In Elm we get a type error,
since the two branches of the conditional have different types. Therefore, the

> ### TYPE SAFETY
>
> *Type correctness* is a property of individual programs. Each program can be deemed type correct or type incorrect by a type checker. In contrast, *type safety* is a property of a programming language and its type system: A programming language is said to be *type safe* if its type system detects all type errors. In a type-safe programming language no type errors go undetected, whereas unsafe languages generally allow operations to be performed on values for which they are not defined, leading to unpredictable results.
>
> Note that type safety is independent of the time when types are checked, that is, whether a programming language uses static or dynamic typing is not relevant for its type safety. Specifically, dynamically typed languages can be type safe, and statically typed languages are not necessarily type safe.
>
> Also note that most non-toy programming language that are considered type safe should probably better be called "mostly" type safe unless this property has been formally established. In particular, specific language implementations may contain "extra features" that allow type errors to escape the type checker.
>
> | | (Mostly) type safe | Unsafe |
> | ------------------ | ------------------ | ------ |
> | Statically typed | Elm, Java | C, C++ |
> | Dynamically typed | Python, Scheme | |

expression won't be evaluated and doesn't produce a result. In Python, on the other hand, the expression can be evaluated without a problem.[13]

```
>>> 3 if 1<2 else "Hello"
3
```

Correspondingly, the type of the Elm expression is undefined whereas the type of the Python expression is `<type 'int'>` (which corresponds to `Int`).

```
>>> type(3 if 1<2 else "Hello")
<type 'int'>
```

The Elm type checker requires both branches of a conditional expression to have the same type, while Python doesn't have that restriction. Elm refuses to evaluate a perfectly fine expression that doesn't lead to any runtime error. Why is that? To see the problem that the Elm type checker faces, consider the following function definition.

---

[13] I'm using the standard Python prompt >>> to distinguish interactions with the Python interpreter from those with Elm. Moreover, I'm using the Python single-line syntax for conditionals that inverts the usual order of the then/true-branch expression and the condition.

	Advantages	Disadvantages
Static typing	Smaller & faster code Early error detection (saves debugging)	Rejects some o.k. programs
Dynamic typing	Fewer programming restrictions Faster compilation	Slower execution More bugs in released programs

Table 5.2 Advantages and disadvantages of static and dynamic typing.

```
f x = if test x then x+1 else "Hello"
```

The argument type of f must be Int (because the expression x+1 requires x to be of type Int), and the result of the function depends on the result of the condition test x: If it evaluates to True, the result type of f is Int, otherwise it is String. Thus, to decide the return type of f we need to evaluate the expression test x, but since test can be an arbitrarily complicated function, this effectively amounts to executing a program, which would turn the Elm static type checker into a dynamic type checker.

A specific, thorny problem with trying to determine the outcome of conditions to decide between two competing types for a conditional is that the evaluation of the condition might not terminate. And since we require a static type checker to terminate, the prospect of potential non-termination is unacceptable.

Static typing avoids this problem by requiring that both branches have the same type because in that case it doesn't matter which branch is taken, and we don't need to evaluate the condition. The typing rule for the conditional expresses this constraint by using the same metavariable T in the typing judgment for both branches.

$$\text{COND} \ \frac{\Gamma \vdash e : \texttt{Bool} \qquad \Gamma \vdash e_1 : T \qquad \Gamma \vdash e_2 : T}{\Gamma \vdash \texttt{if } e \texttt{ then } e_1 \texttt{ else } e_2 : T}$$

Due to this rule, static type systems generally only *approximate* the types of conditional expressions. In particular, the COND rule cannot be used to assign a type to the examples shown above, which causes the type checker to report an error. As we have seen, this behavior is sometimes overly restrictive, since the rejected expression may very well evaluate without any problems. Thus while static type checking seems like a great idea, it also has its drawbacks. A summary comparison of the advantages and disadvantages of the two approaches is given in Table 5.2.

```
type Val = I Int | B Bool | Undefined

tc : Expr -> Maybe Type
tc e = case e of
    ...
    If e0 e1 e2 -> if tc e0==Just TyBool && tc e1==tc e2 then tc e1 else Nothing
```

```
eval : Expr -> Val                          dyn : Expr -> Val
eval e = case e of                          dyn e = case e of
    ...                                         ...
    If e0 e1 e2 -> case eval e0 of              If e0 e1 e2 -> case dyn e0 of
        B True -> eval e1                           B True  -> dyn e1
        _      -> eval e2                           B False -> dyn e2
                                                    _       -> Undefined
stat : Expr -> Maybe Val
stat e = case tc e of
          Just _ -> Just (eval e)
          _      -> Nothing
```

Figure 5.2 Comparing static and dynamic typing: eval does not check for type errors and relies on tc to ensure the first argument of If is of type Bool. In contrast, dyn has a third case for when a dynamic type error occurs. Moreover, dyn evaluates e1 or e2 irrespective of their types, whereas stat makes sure through tc that e1 and e2 have the same type before eval can evaluate.

Interestingly, while most typing rules have an equivalent representation in both the static type checker tc and in the semantics that employs dynamic type checks, this is not the case for the COND rule. This should not be too surprising, since the COND rule specifically expresses a constraint for static typing.

A technical comparison of static and dynamic typing is given in Figure 5.2 where we contrast excerpts from a dynamically typed interpreter dyn[14] with corresponding parts of a statically typed interpreter stat, which employs the already shown static type checker tc and an untyped evaluator eval, described earlier in Section 5.4.

We can now examine the different behavior of the dynamically and statically typed interpreters. First, we can observe that dyn works fine with conditionals using differently typed branches that are rejected by stat.

```
> one = Num 1
Num 1 : Expr
> true = Equal one one
Equal (Num 1) (Num 1) : Expr
```

---

[14]This is basically the semantic function sem described in Section 4.2.3.

```
> stat (If true one true)          > dyn (If true one true)
Nothing : Maybe Val                I 1
```

On the other hand, stat immediately rejects programs with obvious type errors, whereas dyn happily accepts them, only to abort with a runtime error later.

```
> stat (Plus one true)             > dyn (Plus one true)
Nothing : Maybe Val                Undefined : Val
```

The output reveals the difference in behavior: Undefined is a value that represents a runtime error, whereas Nothing represents a type error, which shows that stat never calls eval with the type-incorrect expression. Specifically, stat will never produce a result Just Undefined; such a value would point to an incorrectness in the type checker, which would have ok'ed an expression that nevertheless evaluates to a runtime error.

In summary, types are a powerful abstraction mechanism that is successfully employed as precise program documentation as well as effective guidance for avoiding errors in programs. While static type checking does not protect against *all* runtime errors (for example, type-safe languages can still abort with division-by-zero errors or stack overflows), it makes programs overall significantly more reliable. Whether the benefits of static typing outweigh the restrictions imposed by the typing rules on programs will probably remain a matter of discussion and disagreement among programmers for the foreseeable future.

Exercise 5.7

This exercise tests your understanding of static typing and the difference between static and dynamic typing. The expressions are given in some fictitious notation that is close, but not identical, to Elm syntax. For each of the following expressions, answer the following three questions.

(1) Is the expression well typed under static typing, and if so what is the type of the expression?

(2) What is the type or behavior of the expression under dynamic typing? If the answer depends on the type and/or value of the used variables, explain the dependency.

(3) What type(s) must the variables in the expression have to make the expression well typed/not lead to a runtime error?

For example, for the expression `if x=3 then x+1 else not x` we get:

(1) Type Error

(2) `Int` if x=3, otherwise Type Error

(3) `x : Int`

(a) `if x<2 then even x else x`

(b) `if head x then x else tail x`

(c) `if x then x+1 else x-1`

(d) `if False then "Hello" else x`

(e) `if x then x+1 else x`

(f) `if even x then x else even (x+1)`

(g) `if f(3) then 3 else f(True)`

6

Scope

Chapter Summary

Managing name spaces with blocks. How the concept of scope formalizes the relationship between the definitions of variables and their uses. Using the runtime stack to explain the scoping behavior of programs. The difference between static and dynamic scoping.

Names are one of the most fundamental language concepts: it seems anything that exists – and even things that don't exist – can be given a name to refer to it. A name also seems to be a fairly simple concept: a name is a word[1] that stands for something (an object, a person, and idea, a set, etc.), and we use names successfully all the time. It is therefore not surprising that names play an important part in programming languages as well. Names are used for variables, parameters, functions, types, and, depending on the language, many other programming abstractions (objects, modules, constructors, rules, etc.).

However, names are not as simple a concept as it may seem. Shakespeare's Juliet was on to something when she said:

> *What's in a name? That which we call a rose*
> *By any other name would smell as sweet.*

Juliet challenges the assumptions that names have intrinsic meaning, suggesting that names are rather arbitrary, a fact well known to every programmer.

---

[1]Symbols and non-textual representations can also be used for naming. But the form of names doesn't affect the discussion of scope.

Programming Language Fundamentals: A Metalanguage Approach in Elm, First edition. Martin Erwig.
© 2024 Martin Erwig. Published 2024 by John Wiley & Sons Inc.
Companion website: www.wiley.com/go/ProgrammingLanguageFun

The use of names is often complicated by the existence of so-called *synonyms* (when multiple names refer to one and the same thing) and *homonyms* (when one name refers to two or more different things). Synonyms can pose problems specifically in imperative languages when one data item can be accessed – and modified – through different names. This situation is a root cause of side effects, which make reasoning about imperative programs difficult and also complicate optimizations. Homonyms pose a different kind of challenge, one that universally applies to most programming languages, and that is the question, *What does a name at a specific location in a program refer to?* In the following we will consider the case of names for values, but most of the results for named values apply to other names as well. We also use the common term *variable* for names of values.

To motivate the contents of this chapter, here are some general observations. First, names have to be introduced through a mechanism that associates a name x with some value v. Such a name/value is called a *binding* and is written as $x=v$. Bindings are created, for example, through an assignment operation or a let expression, but they also result whenever a function is applied to an argument.

Second, since one and the same name can refer to different values at different places in a program, we need a way to identify and talk about places in a program. The notion of *blocks* explained in Section 6.1 serves this purpose.

And third, since even at one specific location a name can refer to different values at different times (think about a function parameter), we also need a way to track the dynamic behavior of programs, at least as far as the dynamic behavior of bindings is concerned. The notions of *runtime stack* and *activation record* are introduced in Section 6.2 to explain the dynamic behavior of bindings.

6.1 The Landscape of Programs: Blocks and Scope

A program is a static description of a computation. To define the visibility of names, we can partition a program into separate areas. When viewing a program as a tree (that is, an AST), a location or point in a program corresponds to a node in a tree. The region associated with any node n in the tree T is the set of n's descendants in T, for which we write $T[n]$. Thus the region for any syntactically correct part p of a program is given by $T[n]$, where T is the syntax tree of the program and n is the node representing p in T.

A *block* is a subtree of an AST, which itself has two subtrees: one (called the *declaration*) that introduces one or more names, and one (called the *body*) that represents the part of the program where the names are available for use. If n is

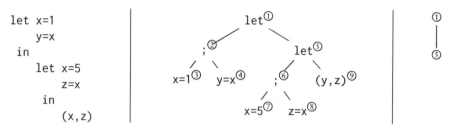

Figure 6.1 A nested let expression (left) and its corresponding (compressed)[3] AST (middle). Individual variable definitions and the innermost let body are shown as expressions instead of trees. The block structure that represents the nesting of blocks is shown as a tree on the right.

the root of a block, we write $D[n]$ for the region that contains the declarations and $B[n]$ for the region of the body. With this definition we have $T[n] = \{n\} \cup D[n] \cup B[n]$. (In the following we sometimes equate a block with its root node, that is, when we talk about "block n" we really mean the whole region $T[n]$.) For example, for the expression in Figure 6.1 we have $D[1] = \{2..4\}$ and $B[1] = \{5..9\}$.[2] The example expression actually contains another block at node 5, for which we have $D[5] = \{6..8\}$ and $B[5] = \{9\}$.

Two different blocks in a program, say $T[n]$ and $T[m]$, can stand in one of exactly two relationships to one another: they are either disjoint, that is, $T[n] \cap T[m] = \varnothing$, or one is included in the body of the other, that is, $T[n] \subseteq T[m] \vee T[m] \subseteq T[n]$. We can use block inclusion to define a partial order on AST nodes as follows.

$$n \vartriangleleft m :\Longleftrightarrow T[n] \supseteq T[m]$$

The relationship $n \vartriangleleft m$ can be read as "block n *includes* block m" or "block m is *nested* inside of block n." In the example, block 1 includes block 5, that is, $1 \vartriangleleft 5$, since $T[1] \supseteq T[5] = B[1]$. In general, one block can include several distinct blocks, and the inclusion of blocks is transitive, that is, one block can be included in a block that is itself included in another block, etc. Consider the following example.

```
> let x=1 in (x,let y=2 in let z=3 in (y,z),let y=4 in y)
(1,(2,3),4)
```

---

[2]We abbreviate sequences of consecutive nodes as intervals and write, for example, $\{2..4\}$ for $\{2,3,4\}$ and $\{2..4,6,8..9\}$ for $\{2,3,4,6,8,9\}$.

[3]For the purpose of discussing bindings and scope we employ an abbreviating notation of ASTs in which we allow whole subtrees to be represented as syntactic expressions.

If, for convenience, we identify each block with the number defined in its declaration, we see that $1 \triangleleft 2$, $1 \triangleleft 3$, $2 \triangleleft 3$, and $1 \triangleleft 4$. In particular, block 1 includes two non-overlapping blocks 2 and 4, and block 1 includes block 3 transitively.

This example suggests that the block structure of a program can be represented as a tree where the complete program is the block at the root. This tree determines for each node n a sequence of blocks from the root to the block that contains n, called the node's *block path* and denoted by $P[n]$. In Figure 6.1 we have $P[9] = 1, 5$ and $P[4] = 1$.

Each variable declaration with root n has a *scope*, written as $S[n]$, which is the set of nodes in which this variable is accessible (for reading and writing). The scope includes the body of the block, except for those nodes in which the declaration is hidden by a nested declaration for the same variable. Depending on the programming language, the scope of a variable may also include the definition part of the following declarations and even the declaration region itself. The expression in Figure 6.1 has variable declarations at nodes 3, 4, 7, and 8. As the use of x in node 4 indicates, the scope in a functional language like Elm *does* include later declarations of the same block. Therefore, the scopes of the four variable declarations appear to be as follows.

$$S[3] = \{4..6\} \qquad\qquad S[7] = \{8..9\}$$
$$S[4] = \{5..9\} \qquad\qquad S[8] = \{9\}$$

We can make two important observations.

First, $S[3]$ does *not* include nodes $\{7..9\}$, because the declaration in node 7 is for the same name and thus *shadows* the declaration from node 4. In this example the shadowing simply "shortens" the scope of the declaration at node 3. In general, shadowing can "poke holes" into what is otherwise a contiguous scope region, and this can happen multiple times. Consider, for example, the following expression.

```
> let x=1 in (x,let x=2 in x,x,let x=3 in x,x)
(1,2,1,3,1)
```

It is instructive to visualize the scope with the help of the abstract syntax tree for this expression.

Exercise 6.1

Draw the abstract syntax tree for the following expressions, and identify the sets D, B, and S. Also, draw the tree representing the block structure.

(a) `let x=1 in (x,let x=2 in x,x,let x=3 in x,x)`

(b) `let x=1 in (x,let x=2 in (x,let x=3 in x,x),x)`

Second, the shown scopes do not include the region of their own declaration, that is, $n \notin S[n]$. However, in some languages, including Elm, let expressions are recursive in the sense that in a definition let x=e in e' the expression e may contain a reference to x. Consider, for example, the following definition of the factorial function.

```
> let fac = \x -> if x==1 then 1 else x*fac(x-1)
> fac 6
720
```

Thus the scopes of the four variable declarations that use recursive let expressions is actually as follows.

$$S[3] = \{3..6\} \qquad S[7] = \{7..9\}$$
$$S[4] = \{4..9\} \qquad S[8] = \{8..9\}$$

Next we need to distinguish between two principally different occurrences of a variable, that is, its *definitions* and *uses*. In general, each variable can have zero or more definitions and uses. The example in Figure 6.1 contains the three variables x, y, and z, which have the following definitions (*d*) and uses (*u*).

$$d[x] = \{3, 7\} \qquad u[x] = \{4, 8\}$$
$$d[y] = \{4\} \qquad u[y] = \{9\}$$
$$d[z] = \{8\} \qquad u[z] = \{9\}$$

To determine the meaning of an expression, we need to figure out for each use of a variable which of its definitions is relevant and should be consulted to retrieve the variable's value. We write $R[x, n]$ for the location of the definition that is referenced by the use of a variable x at location n. In the example in Figure 6.1 we have the following reference information.

$$R[x, 4] = 3 \qquad R[x, 8] = 7 \qquad R[y, 9] = 4 \qquad R[z, 9] = 8$$

We can see that in this example each variable use has a definition and that each definition is used exactly once. But this is not always the case. In the following example the definition of x is not used at all, and y doesn't reference any definition, that is, $R[y, 3] = \bot$.

let x=1 in y

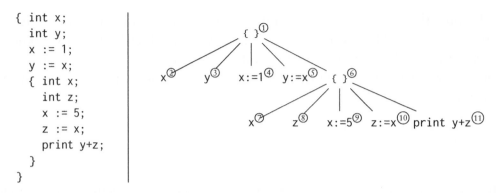

```
{ int x;
  int y;
  x := 1;
  y := x;
  { int x;
    int z;
    x := 5;
    z := x;
    print y+z;
  }
}
```

Figure 6.2 A nested block in an imperative programming language and its corresponding (compressed) AST.

In general, we can observe the following relationships between scope, definition, and use for defined variables.

$$u[x] \subseteq \bigcup_{n \in d[x]} S[n]$$

$$n \in u[x] \implies R[x, n] \in d[x]$$

The concepts of block, declaration, body, definition, use, and reference hold for other language constructs as well. For example, given the function definition f x = b, the application f e forms a block in which the function parameter x and the argument e constitute the definitions and b is the body. Moreover, the concepts are relevant for any language that provides some kind of block-based structuring mechanism. For example, the imperative program shown in Figure 6.2 has essentially the same block structure with the same definition and uses as the let expression from Figure 6.1.

Exercise 6.2

Give the definitions for D, B, S, d, u, and R for the AST shown in Figure 6.2.

Finally, we can distinguish between *local* and *non-local* uses of a variable: When a variable is used in the same block in which it is declared, its use is local. Otherwise, it is non-local, which means the declaration of the variable occurs in a block that contains the block where the use occurs. With the previous definitions we can make this idea more precise. Remember that $P[n]$ yields the block path for node n. For convenience we write $P^*[n]$ for the last element of $P[n]$, which gives the innermost block that contains n, and we write $P^+[n]$ for $P[n]$ *without* its last element, which gives the list of all enclosing blocks. The use of variable x at location n is:

```
nonlocal =
    let x=1      in
    let f y=x+y  in
    let x=2      in
        f 0

> nonlocal
1
```

Figure 6.3 A non-local variable use in a function. Under *static scoping* the declaration visible at the function definition is relevant.

- *local*   iff $d[x] \cap D[P^*[n]] \neq \varnothing$.
- *non-local* iff $d[x] \cap D[P^*[n]] = \varnothing \wedge \exists k \in P^+[n].d[x] \cap D[k] \neq \varnothing$.

In Figure 6.1 the uses of x in nodes 4 and 8 and z in node 9 are local, whereas the use of y in node 9 is non-local.

To determine the semantics of an expression or program we need to determine a value for each variable use. Since one variable can have multiple different definitions, the question is which one is relevant. For local uses of variables it seems obvious to pick the value as given by the corresponding local declaration of the same block. However, for non-local uses the situation is sometimes not so obvious.

In simple cases, the answer seems to be clear. For example, in the following expression the use of x is non-local, and while we have two declarations of enclosing blocks to choose from, it seems natural to choose the latest definition from the closest enclosing block because this is the one that is visible, since it shadows the other definition.

```
> let x=1 in let x=2 in let y=3 in x
2
```

We can find the relevant declaration by searching the block path $P[n]$ from the last element (which is the local block) to the front (which is the outermost block), which gives us the declaration that is visible for that use.

While the case seems to be clear for let expressions, other forms of bindings can be more complicated. Consider the example in Figure 6.3. Here the situation is similar, but also somewhat different. First, we can observe two declarations for x and one non-local use of x in the body of the function f. The evaluation of f 0 requires the value of x, which is obtained from block 1 and not from block 5. This behavior can indeed be predicted by the block structure: we have three scopes of definitions, one for f: $S[4] = \{4..7\}$, and two for x: $S[2] = \{2..5\}$ and $S[6] = \{6..7\}$. Since the use of x in node 4 is only in the scope $S[2]$, this is the definition to be used.

So far so good. But we can notice that the evaluation of f 0 also requires the value of y, and there is no block immediately discernible in the program where y is defined. So what's going on here? Indeed the binding for y is created dynamically at runtime. It cannot be directly inferred from the program.[4]

Thus the static block structure of a program is not enough to keep track of the creation and visibility of bindings. We need something else.

6.2   The Runtime Stack

Consider again the latest version of the Expr language with let expression (cf. Section 5.3, page 110). To simplify the following discussion, we omit the Equal and Not constructors.

```
type alias Name = String
type Expr = Num Int | Plus Expr Expr | Let Name Expr Expr | Var Name
```

As we have already discussed in Section 4.2.4, a function that determines a value for an expression needs as an additional argument a mapping of variable names to values. Otherwise, we couldn't say what the result of an expression such as Var "x" is. Instead of an abstract mapping type, however, we use here a simple list of name/value pairs to keep track of bindings that are created when evaluating let expressions. This list is effectively used as a stack: we add elements only at the front of the list (which represents the top of the stack), and we look up variable bindings also by searching the stack from top to bottom. This stack is called the *runtime stack*, since its existence is tied to the time of a program's execution.

The use of a stack causes newer declarations from nested blocks to effectively hide potential earlier declarations of the same variable and ensures that references to a variable that has multiple bindings will always be resolved in favor of the latest definition.

A very simple interpreter for Expr that uses a runtime stack for keeping bindings is shown in Figure 6.4.

The case for the Let constructor shows how the runtime stack evolves: the result i of the defining expression e1 (computed by eval s e1) is paired with the variable name v and then pushed onto the current stack s, and then the body e2 of the let expression is evaluated in the context of this expanded stack.

It seems that the stack only grows larger. Does it ever shrink? Yes. Consider what happens when we evaluate the expression (let x=1 in x+2)+4 in the context

---

[4]In this simple example it actually could be inferred, but consider the slight modification of the example where $B[5]$ is f (if test x then 0 else 9). Here we don't know what value is bound to y, since it depends on the result of test x, which will only be known at runtime.

```
type alias Val = Maybe Int
type alias Stack = List (Name,Int)

eval : Stack -> Expr -> Val
eval s e = case e of
  Num i         -> Just i                          getVar : Name -> Stack -> Val
  Plus e1 e2  -> map2 (+) (eval s e1) (eval s e2)  getVar n s = case s of
  Var v          -> getVar v s                     []              -> Nothing
  Let v e1 e2 -> case eval s e1 of                 (m,v)::s1 ->
                   Just i  -> eval ((v,i)::s) e2       if n==m then v
                   Nothing -> Nothing                  else getVar n s1
```

Figure 6.4   An evaluator for the Expr language that uses a runtime stack to keep track of bindings. Each entry on the stack is a single name/value binding.

of an empty stack. The evaluation of x+2 happens in the expanded stack [x=1], but the second argument of the addition, that is, 4, as well as the addition itself, is evaluated in the original, empty stack. Two traces of the computation are shown in Figure 6.5. We use a slightly extended version of the trace notation introduced in Section 2.2.2 where, in addition to the expression being evaluated, we also add the following representations:

(a) We show the current version of the stack.
(b) We show the results of the evaluation of subexpressions.
(c) We indent evaluations of subexpressions.

The detailed trace notation on the right of Figure 6.5 reads as follows. We start on the first line by showing the expression to be evaluated plus the empty stack in which it is evaluated (separated by a horizontal bar), which leads to (indicated by ⇒) the evaluation of the defining expression 1 in the context of the same stack. Since this expression is part of the let expression, its evaluation is indented. The third line shows the result of the evaluation, which is produced by the first case rule of eval.

The fourth line shows the evaluation of x+2, the body of the let expression, which happens in the stack that is extended by the binding x=1. Since this expression is a subexpression of the let expression, its evaluation is also indented. Since the expression is an application of +, it requires evaluation of its subexpressions first, which happens in lines 5 through 8 in the same way as explained before, now indented two levels. The result 3 is shown in line 9, again indented only one level, aligning with the expression from line 4 for which it is the result. We indicate this connection of a result to its originating expression by a dotted line.

At this point the evaluation of the let expression is complete, and the next step in line 10 is the evaluation of the top-level addition, in which the let expres-

```
          (let x=1 in x+2)+4  │  []              (let x=1 in x+2)+4  │  []
     ⇒        x+2             │  [x=1]      ⇒         1              │  []
              3                                      1
     ⇒ 3+4                    │  []          ⇒        x+2            │  [x=1]
         7                                   ⇒         x             │  [x=1]
                                                      1
                                             ⇒         2             │  [x=1]
                                                      2
                                                      3
                                             ⇒ 3+4                   │  []
                                             ⇒         3             │  []
                                                      3
                                             ⇒         4             │  []
                                                      4
                                                 7
```

Figure 6.5 Two traces of the evaluation of (let x=1 in x+2)+4. On the left: an abbreviated trace that omits evaluation steps for variables and constants. On the right: a complete version that includes all steps.

sion is replaced by its result. The evaluation happens with the original empty stack because the extended stack was only passed to, and thus was visible in, the evaluation of the let body.[5] The evaluation then continues and ends with the final result.

We can observe that the stack in the function eval from Figure 6.4 stores single name/value bindings. How can we deal with blocks that contain multiple declarations, as in the example in Figure 6.1? The representation for Stack was chosen to keep the implementation of eval simple. It is actually not difficult to extend it to work with groups of bindings, but that implementation is more verbose and doesn't contribute much to the understanding of scope. In any case, such a group of bindings is called an *activation record*,[6] and we write $\langle x_1=v_1, \ldots, x_n=v_n \rangle$ to denote an activation record with multiple bindings. Using this notation, the (abbreviated) trace for the let expression from Figure 6.1 looks as follows.[7] Note that we sometimes abbreviate traces further by not showing

---

[5]This is because the list cons operation is not an imperative update but creates a new list, cf. Section 2.6.

[6]The term *stack frame* is also sometimes used.

[7]The use of the semicolon to connect multiple bindings for a let expression in a single line is not valid Elm syntax; it is allowed in Haskell.

redundant results. In this example, the result of each let expressions is identical to the result of the innermost body.

```
    let x=1;y=x in let x=5;z=x in (x,z)   |  []
⇒      let x=5;z=x in (x,z)               |  [⟨x=1, y=1⟩]
⇒         (x,z)                           |  [⟨x=5, z=5⟩,⟨x=1, y=1⟩]
          (5,5)
```

On the other hand, we can always represent a let expression with multiple declarations by nested let expressions that each have only one declaration. The same applies to blocks in imperative languages. For the previous example this looks as follows.

```
    let x=1 in let y=x in let x=5 in let z=x in (x,z)  |  []
⇒      let y=x in let x=5 in let z=x in (x,z)          |  [x=1]
⇒         let x=5 in let z=x in (x,z)                  |  [y=1,x=1]
⇒            let z=x in (x,z)                          |  [x=5,y=1,x=1]
⇒               (x,z)                                  |  [z=5,x=5,y=1,x=1]
                (5,5)
```

The splitting of declarations into nested let expressions changes the order in which some of the declarations appear on the stack. However, this does not lead to unintended shadowing and a different behavior, since all declarations in one block must be for different variables.

The activation record notation sometimes leads to more succinct traces, and we use it whenever convenient. Otherwise, it is fine to assume and work with the simpler one-declaration-per-block model.

> ### Exercise 6.3
>
> Create evaluation traces for the following expressions.
>
> (a) let x=1 in (x,let x=2 in x)
>
> (b) let x=1 in (x,let x=2 in (x,let x=3 in x,x),x)

The example in Figure 6.5 shows the effect of block structure during program execution on the runtime stack. Specifically, *entering* a block has the effect of *pushing* an activation record (or single binding in the simplified model) onto the stack, and *leaving* a block causes the top element to be *popped off* the stack.

The trace notation works in a similar way for imperative languages. Figure 6.6 shows a slight variation of the example from Figure 6.2 to illustrate the push/pop behavior of the stack and local vs. non-local variable access.

```
{ int x;
    int y;        |   [⟨x=?, y=?⟩]           enter block ⇒ push
    x := 1;       |   [⟨x=1, y=?⟩]           local update
    { int x;      |   [⟨x=?⟩,⟨x=1, y=?⟩]     enter block ⇒ push
        x := 5;   |   [⟨x=5⟩,⟨x=1, y=?⟩]     local update
        y := x;   |   [⟨x=5⟩,⟨x=1, y=5⟩]     local lookup & non-local update
    };            |   [⟨x=1, y=5⟩]           leave block ⇒ pop
    { int z;      |   [⟨z=?⟩,⟨x=1, y=5⟩]     enter block ⇒ push
        y := x;   |   [⟨z=?⟩,⟨x=1, y=1⟩]     non-local lookup & update
    };            |   [⟨x=1, y=1⟩]           leave block ⇒ pop
};                |   []                     leave ⇒ pop
```

Figure 6.6   Execution trace for nested blocks in an imperative language.

With the runtime stack we are now in the position to trace examples in which the block structure changes dynamically during runtime. Consider again the example from Figure 6.3. In addition to the three nested blocks that result from the nested let expression, a fourth block is given by the body of the function f. This block is entered when the function is called with the argument 0. As with the static let blocks, entering the function body causes a new activation record with the single binding y=0 to be pushed onto the runtime stack. The following trace captures the evaluation up to the point where the interpreter is ready to evaluate the body of the function, x+y.

```
      let x=1 in let f y=x+y in let x=2 in f 0   |   []
⇒        let f y=x+y in let x=2 in f 0           |   [x=1]
⇒             let x=2 in f 0                     |   [f=\y->x+y,x=1]
⇒                  f 0                           |   [x=2,f=\y->x+y,x=1]
⇒                      x+y                       |   [y=0,x=2,f=\y->x+y,x=1]
```

But now we encounter a problem: searching for the bindings of y and x starting from the top of the stack would retrieve the binding x=2 and produce the result 2 instead of 1. What has gone wrong here?

6.3   Static vs. Dynamic Scoping

A closer look at the runtime stack for the previous example helps explain the problem: First, we can see that the declaration x=1 is hidden by the declaration x=2. This happened because f was called *after* the declaration x=2, and thus the non-local access to x in the block x+y created dynamically by the function call "sees" this later declaration.

In other words, the declaration x=2 is the one that's visible *dynamically*, when the program is executed, whereas prior to execution, that is, *statically*, when looking at the program text, the declaration x=1 is visible when the function f is declared.

A language definition (or implementor) has a choice: either select the dynamically visible binding (in this case x=2) or the statically visible binding (in this case x=1). The former strategy is called *dynamic scoping*, and the latter strategy is called *static scoping*. In other words, in a programming language with static scoping (semantics), a non-local name refers to the declaration that is visible (that is, "in scope") where the function is defined. In contrast, in a programming language with dynamic scoping (semantics), a non-local name refers to the declaration that is visible (that is, "in scope") where the function is used.

To continue the example trace from the previous section, we can now easily produce the result under dynamic scoping, using the nearest definition for x, and return 2, but how can we create the result for static scoping? It seems we somehow should "skip over" and ignore the second declaration in the runtime stack to find the statically visible one. Essentially, we should start searching the stack not from the top, but from the place where f is defined, that is, at the place in the stack that contains the activation record for the declaration of f.

This behavior can be implemented in different ways. One elegant method that can be easily realized in our metalanguage Elm is the use of a so-called *closure*, which is a piece of code paired with an environment (given by the current stack) that provides definitions for unbound (that is, non-local) variables. The idea of a closure is, as the name suggests, to "close" the definition of a function by closing the holes that non-local variables leave open. By storing the current definitions for non-local variables, a closure prevents dynamic changes of these variable values through other declarations, which becomes possible when the code of the function is executed in different contexts.

To illustrate how static scoping can be implemented, we extend the definition of eval from Figure 6.4. The result is shown in Figure 6.7.

First, we need to add two constructors to the Expr data type to represent anonymous functions (Fun) and function application (App). Then we have to use a Val data type as a result type for eval, since we need to distinguish between integers (I) and closures (C), which represent function values. We also integrate errors into the Val type directly (using a constructor Error) to simplify pattern matching a bit compared to the use of Maybe Val.

A closure stores the parameter and body of the function (through the Name and Expr arguments) plus the stack that exists at the time the function is defined.

```
type Expr = Num Int | Plus Expr Expr | Let Name Expr Expr | Var Name
          | Fun Name Expr | App Expr Expr

type Val = I Int | C Name Expr Stack | Error
type alias Stack = List (Name,Val)

eval : Stack -> Expr -> Val
eval s e = case e of
    Num i        -> I i
    Plus e1 e2  -> case (eval s e1,eval s e2) of
                        (I i,I j) -> I (i+j)
                        _         -> Error
    Var v        -> getVar v s
    Let v e1 e2 -> eval ((v,eval s e1)::s) e2
    Fun v e1     -> C v e1 s
    App e1 e2   -> case eval s e1 of
                        C v e3 s1 -> eval ((v,eval s e2)::s1) e3
                        _         -> Error
```

Figure 6.7   An evaluator for the Expr language that implements static scoping.

These two constructors of the Val type are scrutinized in eval in the second and last case to ensure that the arguments for + are integers and an applied expression evaluates to a function value (that is, a closure).

Note that the definition of getVar has to be adapted to account for the changed Val type.

```
getVar : Name -> Stack -> Val
getVar n s = case s of
    []        -> Error
    (m,v)::s1 -> if n==m then v else getVar n s1
```

To understand the use of closures, remember that the definition of a function happens in a let expression. For example, the part of the definition

```
let f y = x+y in ...
```

is represented in the abstract syntax as

```
Let "f" (Fun "y" (Plus x y)) ...
```

The case for Let shows that this definition leads to the following evaluation (where s is the current stack [("x",I 1)]).

```
eval (("f",eval s (Fun "y" (Plus x y)))::s) ...
```

The case for Fun shows how functions are evaluated to closure values. Specifically, eval s (Fun "y" (Plus x y)) leads to the following closure. Here we use the name savedStack for the current stack [("x",I 1)] to distinguish it from later occurrences of the name s.

```
C "y" (Plus x y) savedStack
```

The closure "freezes" the current values of all non-local variables and attaches the frozen package to the code. Later when the code is activated, the variable definitions will be "thawed" to come back to life.

This closure is used as a binding for f, which is pushed onto s, and the evaluation continues with this extended stack.

When the evaluation later encounters the expression f 0 (represented in abstract syntax as App (Var "f") (Num 0)), the stack s at that point contains the binding for f and also the second binding for x.

```
[("x",I 2), ("f",C "y" (Plus x y) savedStack), ("x",I 1)]
```

The definition for eval requires the evaluation eval s (Var "f"), which will retrieve the closure value with the help of getVar (see Figure 6.4). The closure contains the saved stack with the frozen variable values. Evaluation continues with the following computation (where I 0 is the result of eval s (Num 0)).

```
  eval (("y",I 0):savedStack) (Plus x y)
= eval [("y",I 0),("x",I 1)] (Plus x y)
```

By using the saved stack, the evaluation basically skips over the later definition for x and uses the statically visible earlier one.

We can also illustrate the static scoping evaluation using the trace notation.

```
    let x=1 in let f y=x+y in let x=2 in f 0  |   []
⇒        let f y=x+y in let x=2 in f 0        |   [x=1]
⇒             let x=2 in f 0                  |   [f=(\y->x+y,[x=1]),x=1]
⇒                   f 0                       |   [x=2,f=(\y->x+y,[x=1]),x=1]
⇒                   x+y                       |   [y=0,x=1]
                     2
```

Most programming languages have adopted static scoping because it is easier to reason about: under static scoping non-local variables have a fixed reference that can be understood by looking at the program text, whereas under dynamic scoping the value referred to by a variable can change dynamically and is unpredictable. Some older versions of Lisp adopted dynamic scoping, and Perl lets the programmer choose between static and dynamic scoping.

Exercise 6.4

Consider the following program.

```
 1 { int x;
 2   x := 2;
 3   { int f(int y) {
 4       x := x*y;
 5       return (x+1);
 6     };
 7     { int x;
 8       x := 4;
 9       x := f(x-1);
10     };
11   };
12 }
```

Show the runtime stacks that result immediately after the statements on lines 8, 4, and 9 have been executed.

(a) Show the stacks using dynamic scoping.

(b) Show the stacks using static scoping.

Exercise 6.5

Show the development of the runtime stack for following two programs.

```
{ int y;
  int z;
  y := 1;
  z := 0;
  { int f(int x){return y+x};
    { int g(int y){return f(2)};
      z := g(3);
    };
  };
}
```

```
{ int z;
  z := 0;
  { int f(int x){return x+1};
    { int g(int y){return f(y)};
      { int f(int x){return x-1};
        z := g(3);
      };
    };
  };
}
```

(a) Show the stacks using dynamic scoping.

(b) Show the stacks using static scoping.

(c) What is the final value of z?

7 Parameter Passing

Chapter Summary

How arguments are passed to functions. A generic parameter-passing schema for comparing and explaining all the major parameter-passing schemas. Tracing function calls and parameter passing with the runtime stack. A detailed comparison of parameter passing schemes and their features.

Parameter passing is a core component of computing. A function definition (or any similar programming language abstraction for representing algorithms) provides the static description of (many different but similar) computations. But computation doesn't happen yet. Only when a function is applied to arguments does the dynamic semantics turn the function loose and create a computation. During the computation the arguments are referred to by the parameters in the function's body. While it may seem obvious at first what happens when functions are called, there are several questions that a language definition has to answer to define a precise semantics.

For example, what kind of programming elements can be passed as arguments to parameters? Only values, or also expressions? What about variables? If we pass a variable, do we copy its value, or do we use the parameter as an alias? If we pass an expression, do we evaluate the expression once and pass the resulting value, or do we keep the expression and evaluate it every time the parameter is referenced (which makes a difference when the expression contains variables whose value could change)? And what is the effect of assignments to

Programming Language Fundamentals: A Metalanguage Approach in Elm, First edition. Martin Erwig.
© 2024 Martin Erwig. Published 2024 by John Wiley & Sons Inc.
Companion website: www.wiley.com/go/ProgrammingLanguageFun

Name	Abbrev.	What is passed	What is stored
Call-by-value	VAL	Expression	Value
Call-by-reference	REF	Variable	Pointer
Call-by-value-result	INOUT	Variable	Value
Call-by-name	NAME	Expression	Expression
Call-by-need	NEED	Expression	Expression/value

Table 7.1 Parameter passing schemas.

parameters? Can they change parameters temporarily? Do they change the arguments? The purpose of this chapter is to explore answers to these questions.

To better understand and compare the different forms of parameter passing, it is helpful to describe, on a generic level, what happens when a function call is executed. In general, a function application has the following form.

```
f e
```

Here f is the name of a function that is defined by a single equation as follows.[1]

```
f x = d
```

The name x is f's *parameter*,[2] and d is f's *definition* or *body*. We can distinguish three different kinds of bindings that can appear on the runtime stack.

Value bindings	x=v
Variable bindings (or references)	x=y
Expressions bindings	x=e

The five major parameter passing schemas shown in Table 7.1 can be distinguished by what is passed as an argument and what is stored and potentially manipulated on the runtime stack.

The evaluation steps that occur for a function call depend on the parameter passing schema. Figure 7.1 shows in a generic form how f e is evaluated. Everything that happens can be explained by the effect it has on the runtime stack,

---

[1]A function with multiple parameters can always be defined in curried form with one parameter and a function of the remaining parameters as a result (see Section 2.3.2). This pattern also covers functions in imperative programming languages where definitions have the form f(x){ ...; return e} (or something similar).

[2]The parameter x is also sometimes called the *formal parameter*, and the argument e is also sometimes called the *actual parameter*. Since these two names can be easily confused, and since "parameter" and "argument" are two perfectly good names, we'll stick to the latter.

Evaluation of f e

1	{VAL: Evaluate e}
2	Create binding {VAL: x=v} {REF+INOUT: x=y} {NAME+NEED: x=e}
3	Evaluate d, where:
4	{NEED: After first reference to x, replace x=e by x=v}
5	{INOUT: Use x=w to update y=w}
6	Remove binding for x

Figure 7.1   A generic parameter passing schema for the evaluation of f e where f is defined as f x = d. The argument e is a variable y or evaluates to a value v (that is, eval e = v). All references to bindings refer to bindings on the runtime stack. Steps 1 and 2 happen before control is transferred to the execution of the function code, which is described by steps 3 and 4. Steps 5 and 6 occur at the end of the function call. The notation {PAR: s} means that step s happens only for the parameter passing schema PAR.

and we can group the activities into three phases, depending on *when* they happen, that is, *before* (steps 1 and 2), *during* (steps 3 and 4), and *at the end* (steps 5 and 6) of the evaluation of d.

In the following sections we discuss each parameter passing schema in more detail. Note that throughout this chapter we assume *static scoping*.

7.1   Call-by-Value

Call-by-value is the simplest, and probably most intuitive, parameter passing schema. Many, if not most, programming languages employ call-by-value. Under call-by-value, first the argument expression e is evaluated, and then the resulting value v is passed to the function, that is, a binding x=v is created on the runtime stack, which makes the argument value accessible to the function through the parameter name x. As an example, consider the following function definition.

```
f x = x+x
```

Here is a trace for the evaluation of the function call f (3+4) that illustrates call-by-value parameter passing.

Call-by-value

1	Evaluate e to v
2	Create binding x=v
3	Evaluate d
6	Remove binding x=u

Figure 7.2 Call-by-value parameter passing schema. Steps 4 and 5 of the generic schema are not relevant. The parameter may have been a assigned a different value (u), but it is forgotten at the end.

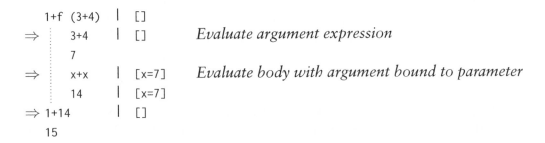

In a functional language the evaluation of a function application f e with f x = d is equivalent to the evaluation of the expression let x=e in d. Under call-by-value the let expression simplifies to let x=v in d where v = eval e. One can also understand call-by-value via textual substitution, that is, substitute the value v of the argument expression for all references to the parameter x in the body of the function definition (but not for other locally defined variables x), and then execute the function body.

In addition to references, an imperative language may or may not allow assignments to a call-by-value parameter. Even if this is allowed, the final value of the parameter is lost once the activation record for the function call is popped off the runtime stack. A function call can have no effect on the call site through a call-by-value parameter. The call-by-value parameter passing schema is summarized in Figure 7.2 as an instance of the generic schema from Figure 7.1.

An example of an imperative program with a call-by-value function call can be found in Figure 7.3. We are using a few additional notational conventions in the trace presentation.

- We don't show the code of functions on the stack. In most implementations the code is not stored on the stack anyway. Instead we show an entry f=· to indicate the existence of the binding and its nesting position with respect to other bindings. An implementation would also store a pointer (called an *access link*) to the place on the stack where the statically scoped

```
 1  { int z;                          1   [ z=? ]
 2      int y;                        2   [ y=? ,z=?]
 3      y := 5;                       3   [y= 5 ,z=?]
 4      { int f(int x){               4   [ f=· ,y=5,z=?]
 5          x := x+1;                10   >> f(y)
 6          y := x-4;                        [ x=5 ,f=·,y=5,z=?]
 7          x := x+1;                 5    [x= 6 ,f=·,y=5,z=?]
 8          return x;                 6    [x=6,f=·,y= 2 ,z=?]
 9      };                            7    [x= 7 ,f=·,y=2,z=?]
10      z := f(y)+y;                  8    [ <<7 ,x=7,f=·,y=2,z=?]
11    };                             <<
12  }                               10   [f=·,y=2,z= 9 ]
                                     11   [y=2,z=9]
                                     12   []
```

Figure 7.3 Example trace of an imperative program showing a *call-by-value* function call. The code is shown on the left, and the trace of the runtime stack on the right shows the stack after each line of code is executed. The changes in each stack version from the previous one are marked with a gray background.

bindings for the non-local variables in f can be found. In most cases these are simply the entries on the stack to the right of f.

- The notation >> f(y) indicates the jump to the code of the function f, which is called with the argument y.
- Evaluations of functions are indented, which is particularly helpful when tracing multiple nested function calls.
- The notation <<v on the stack indicates the value v that is returned from the function. This value will effectively be substituted for the function call at the call site.
- The notation << indicates the jump back from the function call.

Most of the steps should be clear from the explanations and previous examples. Step 1 of the general schema is trivial in this example, since the argument is simply a variable. The reason for choosing the example in this way is to be able to use one program with different parameter passing schemas to get a better sense of their differences. Since call-by-reference as well as call-by-value-result both require the argument to be a variable, a variable had to be used.

Note that the jump from line 4 to line 10 (in the fifth line of the trace) is due to the fact that the function definition extends from line 4 to line 9. In line 10, the assignment requires the computation of the result of f(y)+y, triggering the function call f(y), which causes the binding x=5 to be created on the stack.

Call-by-reference

2	Create binding x↦y
3	Evaluate d
6	Remove binding x↦y

Figure 7.4 Call-by-reference parameter passing schema. Steps 1, 4, and 5 of the generic schema are not relevant. The notation x↦y for variable bindings indicates that all references and assignments to x are effectively redirected to the passed variable y.

After that the code of the function body starting in line 5 is executed, and the corresponding changes to the runtime stack are shown indented. The return statement in line 8 has the effect of pushing the value of x onto the stack, where it is available (for a brief moment) after the return from the function call in line 10 to complete the computation of f(y)+y, which therefore results in 7+2 = 9. After the return value has been consumed, it will be removed together with f's activation record (x=7) from the runtime stack.

We will use the same program again in Sections 7.2 and 7.3 to illustrate how call-by-value, call-by-reference, and call-by-value-result compare.

7.2   Call-by-Reference

Call-by-reference parameter passing is used in imperative languages to allow assignments in a function to affect (potentially many different) external variables. It is useful for performing systematic modifications (captured in a function) of large data structures without having to copy the data structure. Instead, the function is effectively handed a pointer to the data structure, and the update operations on a call-by-reference parameter directly modify the referenced data.

Only variables can be arguments for a call-by-reference parameter, and the parameter effectively acts as an alias for the argument variable, that is, any operation on x that is performed during the execution of the called function is de facto performed on y. Where call-by-value can be understood by *substituting a value* for all references of the parameter in the function body, one can understand call-by-reference as *renaming the parameter* to its argument variable name (assuming the function doesn't define a local variable of the same name as the passed parameter), which effectively turns the function body into code that refers to the argument variable as a non-local variable. The call-by-reference parameter passing schema is summarized in Figure 7.4 as an instance of the generic schema from Figure 7.1.

```
1   { int z;                              1    [ z=? ]
2       int y;                            2    [ y=? ,z=?]
3       y := 5;                           3    [y= 5 ,z=?]
4       { int f(int x){                   4    [ f=· ,y=5,z=?]
5           x := x+1;                     10   >> f(y)
6           y := x-4;                              [ x↦y ,f=· ,y=5,z=?]
7           x := x+1;                      5    [x↦y,f=· ,y= 6 ,z=?]
8           return x;                      6    [x↦y,f=· ,y= 2 ,z=?]
9       };                                 7    [x↦y,f=· ,y= 3 ,z=?]
10      z := f(y)+y;                       8    [ <<3 ,x=7,f=· ,y=3,z=?]
11      };                                      <<
12  }                                     10   [f=· ,y=3,z= 6 ]
                                          11   [y=3,z=6]
                                          12   []
```

Figure 7.5   Example trace of the imperative program from Figure 7.3 showing a *call-by-reference* function call. The variable binding x↦y amounts to storing in x a pointer to y with the effect that any assignments and references to x are redirected to the passed parameter y.

As an example we consider again the program from Figure 7.3 and show in Figure 7.5 how it leads to a different trace under call-by-reference. The notation x↦y for variable bindings on the runtime stack suggests that x itself cannot be changed and that it acts solely as an indirection to the variable y. Similarly, x does not store a value that could be retrieved, which means all references to x effectively retrieve the value of y. The corresponding behavior can be observed in the trace, where changes only affect y and x remains unchanged throughout the execution of the function call.

Exercise 7.1

Show the development of the runtime stack for following program using (a) call-by-value and (b) call-by-reference. What is the final value of z in each case?

```
 1   { int x;
 2     int z;
 3     int f(int y){
 4       x := y-4;
 5       y := y+1;
 6       return y;
 7     };
 8     x := 5;
 9     z := x+f(x);
10   }
```

7.3 Call-by-Value-Result

Call-by-value-result parameter passing was introduced by the programming language Ada and combines aspects of call-by-value and call-by-reference: Like call-by-reference, only variables can be passed as arguments to a call-by-value-result parameter, but unlike call-by-reference and like call-by-value, the value of the argument variable is copied to create a local binding for the functions call. Also like call-by-value, all assignments made to the parameter affect the parameter directly and *not* the variable passed as argument as in call-by-reference. Step 5 at the end of the function call, in which the final value of x is copied back to y, is unique to call-by-value-result.

The call-by-value-result parameter passing schema is summarized in Figure 7.6 as an instance of the generic schema from Figure 7.1. The two steps at the beginning and end of the function call of copying the value of y into the function and then back out give this parameter passing schema its alternative name, *copy-in-copy-out*.

As can be seen in Figure 7.7, the copy-in-copy-out behavior leads to different computations than with call-by-value or call-by-reference. Under call-by-value the value of z after the function call is 9, whereas under call-by-reference it is 6. Under call-by-value-result we instead obtain the value 14.

There is a further semantic subtlety to be considered here. Figure 7.7 shows an additional version of the runtime stack after line 9, which illustrates that the value of y is 7 when we compute the sum of f(y) and y. This is because f(y) is evaluated *before* y, which means the effect of f on y takes place before

Call-by-value-result

2	Create binding x=u by copying u from the existing binding y=u
3	Evaluate d
5	Use x=w to update binding for y to y=w
6	Remove binding x=w

Figure 7.6 Call-by-value-result parameter passing schema (also called copy-in-copy-out). Steps 1 and 4 of the generic schema are not relevant. A local copy of the passed variable is created, and all assignments apply to this copy. During step 3, the variable y remains unaffected. After executing the function code, the final value of x is copied back to y.

```
1    { int z;
2        int y;
3        y := 5;
4        { int f(int x){
5            x := x+1;
6            y := x-4;
7            x := x+1;
8            return x;
9        };
10        z := f(y)+y;
11       };
12   }
```

```
1    [ z=? ]
2    [ y=? ,z=?]
3    [y= 5 ,z=?]
4    [ f=· ,y=5,z=?]
10   >> f(y)
         [ x=5 ,f=·,y=5,z=?]
5    [x= 6 ,f=·,y=5,z=?]
6    [x=6,f=·,y= 2 ,z=?]
7    [x= 7 ,f=·,y=2,z=?]
8    [ <<7 ,x=7,f=·,y=2,z=?]
9    [<<7,x=7,f=·,y= 7 ,z=?]
     <<
10   [f=·,y=7,z= 14 ]
11   [y=7,z=14]
12   []
```

Figure 7.7 Example trace of the imperative program from Figure 7.3 showing a *call-by-value-result* function call.

y is evaluated. If the order of the summands in the assignment in line 10 were reversed and we had to compute z := y+f(y) instead, the value of y used would be 5, and the result for z would be 12.

Exercise 7.2

Show the development of the runtime stack for following program using call-by-value-result. What is the final value of z?

```
 1   { int x;
 2     int z;
 3     int f(int y){
 4       x := y-4;
 5       y := y+1;
 6       return y;
 7     };
 8     x := 5;
 9     z := x+f(x);
10   }
```

Call-by-value and call-by-reference are two common parameter passing schemas that are used in most imperative programming languages. Call-by-value-result is a combination of the two that was introduced in Ada specifically to better control the behavior of variables when used in multi-processor environments or with remote procedure calls.

7.4 Call-by-Name

In contrast to the parameter passing schemas considered so far, which have their origins in imperative programming languages, call-by-name and call-by-need have their origins in the foundations of functional programming, in particular in the operational semantics of lambda calculus. Call-by-name was also available in the programming language Algol 68.

The main idea behind call-by-name is *not* to immediately evaluate the expression e that is passed as an argument, but to evaluate it whenever the parameter x is accessed in the body of the function. Call-by-name is similar to call-by-value in that the value of the argument expression is used whenever the parameter is accessed. However, there are two important differences.

- Assignments to call-by-name parameters are *not allowed*.

Call-by-name

2	Create binding x=e
3	Evaluate d
6	Remove binding x=e

Figure 7.8 Call-by-name parameter passing schema. Steps 1, 4, and 5 of the generic schema are not relevant. Instead of a value or a reference, an expression is stored on the runtime stack. This expression will be evaluated whenever the parameter x is accessed during step 3. Since e may contain variables whose value can change between different accesses to x, the value of x may change as well. This fact can be exploited to simulate function parameters through expressions with variables.

- The number of times the argument expression e is evaluated is, in general, not known in advance (for example, when the parameter x is accessed within a conditional or loop).

The latter fact has two significant implications. First, since e may be evaluated never, once, or more than once, call-by-name can be more efficient, as efficient, or less efficient than call-by-value.

Second, in situations when e is evaluated more than once, it might result in different values when variables that occur in e change their values in between. This can, of course, only happen in an imperative language with assignment operations and side effects. This behavior can be exploited to simulate the effect of higher-order functions. For example, passing an expression e that contains the variable y amounts to passing an anonymous function \y->e.

The call-by-name parameter passing schema is summarized in Figure 7.8 as an instance of the generic schema from Figure 7.1.

Figure 7.9 shows an example trace of a function call with call-by-name parameter passing. Since the argument expression y+3 contains a variable whose value changes during the evaluation of the function, the two references to the function parameter x produce different values.

In a functional language (or any language without assignments and side effects), call-by-name behaves mostly like call-by-value if we disregard the efficiency aspect mentioned above. One exception is that call-by-name can terminate with a value in some situations when call-by-value either doesn't terminate or yields a runtime error. Consider the following two function definitions.

```
forever x = forever x
ignore x = 42
```

The function forever won't terminate for any argument. Under call-by-value, ignore (div 1 0) will cause a runtime error, and ignore (forever "young") will not

```
1   { int y;                          1   [ y=? ]
2       y := 4;                       2   [y= 4 ]
3       { int f(int x){               3   [ f=· ,y=4]
4           y := 2*x;                 7   >> f(y+3)
5           return (y+x);                     [ x=y+3 ,f=·,y=4]
6       };                            4       [x=y+3,f=·,y= 14 ]
7       y := f(y+3);                  5       [ <<31 ,x=y+3,f=·,y=14]
8       };                               <<
9   }                                 7   [f=·,y= 31 ]
                                      8   [y=31]
                                      9   []
```

Figure 7.9 Example trace of an imperative program illustrating a function call with *call-by-name* parameter passing. The argument expression y+3 remains on the stack unevaluated the whole time the function is active. The two accesses to the parameter x yield two different results (4 and 14, respectively), since the variable y is changed in between.

terminate. Under call-by-name both expressions evaluate without problem because the argument expression is never evaluated.

```
> ignore (forever "young")
42
> ignore (div 1 0)
42
```

7.5 Call-by-Need

Call-by-need is almost identical to call-by-name with one important difference: after the first access to the parameter x, its binding to e is replaced with the value of e (as it is determined at that time). Figure 7.10 shows call-by-need as an instance of the generic schema from Figure 7.1.

Call-by-need can be thought of as an optimized version of call-by-name (since the argument expression is not evaluated repeatedly) or a "delayed" version of call-by-value (since the argument expression is only evaluated if needed). The functional programming language Haskell uses call-by-need parameter passing. More generally, in Haskell the evaluation of any expression, not just arguments passed to parameters, is systematically delayed until its value is needed. This evaluation strategy is also called *lazy evaluation* and can be employed in many interesting ways. In contrast, Elm uses so-called *eager evaluation*, which corresponds to call-by-value parameter passing.

Call-by-need

2	Create binding x=e
3	Evaluate d, where:
4	After first reference to x, replace x=e by x=v
6	Remove binding x=*

Figure 7.10 Call-by-need parameter passing schema. Steps 1 and 5 of the generic schema are not relevant. Instead of a value or a reference, an expression is stored on the runtime stack. This expression will be evaluated when the parameter x is accessed during step 3 for the first time, after which e is replaced by its value.

```
1   { int y;
2       y := 4;
3       { int f(int x){
4           y := 2*x;
5           return (y+x);
6       };
7       y := f(y+3);
8       };
9   }
```

```
1   [ y=? ]
2   [y= 4 ]
3   [ f=· ,y=4]
7   >> f(y+3)
            [ x=y+3 ,f=·,y=4]
    4   [x= 7 ,f=·,y= 14 ]
    5   [ <<21 ,x=7,f=·,y=14]
    <<
7   [f=·,y= 21 ]
8   [y=21]
9   []
```

Figure 7.11 Example trace of an imperative program illustrating a function call with *call-by-need* parameter passing. The argument expression y+3 remains on the stack unevaluated until the parameter x is accessed. At that point the expression is replaced by its value.

The difference[3] between call-by-need and call-by-name is visible only in imperative languages where the values of variables referenced by the argument expression can change between successive accesses. The different behavior is illustrated in Figure 7.11, which shows the trace for the example from Figure 7.9 with call-by-need parameter passing. The change to variable y has no effect, since the result of y+3 is remembered after the first evaluation.

---

[3]The difference in computed values, that is. The difference in runtime can be observed in any case.

	Call-by-value	Call-by-reference	Call-by-value-result	Call-by-name	Call-by-need
Restriction on arguments		Only variables	Only variables		
Restriction on parameter use				No assignments	
Direction of value flow	In	In & out	In & out	In	In
Stored on the runtime stack	Value	Pointer	Value	Expression	Expression, then value
Parameter access	Lookup	Dereference	Lookup	Evaluation	Evaluation, then lookup
At the end of function call			Copy parameter to argument		

Table 7.2   Comparison of parameter passing schemas.

Exercise 7.3

Show the development of the runtime stack for following program using (a) call-by-name and (b) call-by-need. What is the final value of a in each case?

```
1   { int a;
2     a := 3;
3     int f(int b){
4       a := 2*b;
5       return (a+b);
6     };
7     a := f(a-1);
8   }
```

7.6 Summary

A high-level comparison of the different parameter passing schemas is presented in Table 7.2. The table uses six aspects of parameter passing to highlight the commonalities and differences between the different approaches.

Logic Programming with Prolog

8

Chapter Summary

An introduction to the basics of logic programming with Prolog. Answering queries with the Prolog interpreter. Basic Prolog terminology. Formulation and evaluation of goals. Expressing relationships through rules. Recursion and a tree model of tracing. A detailed look at Prolog's search procedure. How to represent data structures with terms and, in particular, how to program with lists. The special role of arithmetic. Modifying Prolog's search method using the cut. Negation and its idiosyncrasies.

In Chapter 2 we have already seen that computation doesn't have to be understood as a sequence of state transformations. Specifically, functional programming regards computation as a sequence of *expression simplifications*. The transformation of an expression is similar to imperative programming in that it happens linearly, step-by-step (although it is also possible to simplify independent subexpressions in parallel). However, a crucial difference is that a functional program transforms an *expression*, whereas an imperative programs transforms a *state*.

Logic programming in general, and Prolog in particular, provides yet another view on computation. First, in addition to representing data as (trees of) values, which is similar to functional programming, Prolog also supports the explicit representation of relationships among values. Second, running a Prolog program means to construct an answer to a query about the relationships by searching for facts and linking them together using rules.

Programming Language Fundamentals: A Metalanguage Approach in Elm, First edition. Martin Erwig.
© 2024 Martin Erwig. Published 2024 by John Wiley & Sons Inc.
Companion website: www.wiley.com/go/ProgrammingLanguageFun

Concept	Prolog	Elm	C, Java, etc.
Algorithm	Set of rules	Function	Program
Instruction	Term	Expression	Statement
Input	Value argument	Function argument	read statement
Output	Variable binding	Function result	print statement
Iteration	Recursion	Recursion	Loop
Step	Term unification	Expression simplification	State update
Computation	Tree search	Sequence of steps	Sequence of steps

Table 8.1 How algorithmic concepts are realized in Prolog compared to functional and imperative programming languages (an extension of Table 2.1).

But note that Prolog is untyped and that it is a first-order language, that is, we can only formulate queries about specific relationships and not express queries that determine, for example, what relationships hold between objects.

Table 8.1 extends Table 2.1 from Section 2 and gives a high-level overview of the differences between logic, functional, and imperative languages with regard to how they realize algorithmic concepts (see also Section 1.5).

In essence, *writing* a Prolog program is declaring facts and defining rules about objects and their relationships, and *running* a Prolog program is asking questions about the relationships defined in the program.

8.1 Getting Started

As with Elm, Prolog programming consists of two separate activities that happen in two different environments: First, *writing* Prolog programs is done with an editor and involves editing fact and rule definitions in a file (which must have the extension .pl). Second, *executing* a Prolog program happens in a Prolog interpreter where definitions are loaded from Prolog files to set the context for formulating and answering so-called *queries* or *goals*.

The left part of Figure 8.1 shows a small example Prolog program that defines *facts* about the hobbies of two people as well as a *rule* that classifies people based on their hobbies. A fact defines a single *relationship* between a tuple of objects. For example, the fact in the first line states that a relationship called hobby exists between the objects alice and reading. A *relation* is a set of relationships, which can be defined by a collection of individual facts or by rules. The three hobby facts together constitute a so-called *predicate* definition. Sometimes the terms "relation" and "predicate" are used synonymously, but they are dif-

```
hobby(alice,reading).
hobby(alice,running).
hobby(bob,running).

runner(P) :- hobby(P,running).
```

hobby	
alice	reading
alice	running
bob	running

runner
alice
bob

Figure 8.1   On the left: the file hobby.pl, which contains facts that define a binary predicate hobby and a rule that defines a unary predicate runner. In the middle: the relation denoted by the hobby predicate. On the right: the relation denoted by the runner predicate.

ferent things: a predicate is a syntactic Prolog object whose semantic value is a relation. Moreover, a predicate is used like a function,[1] that is, it is applied to a tuple of arguments and is evaluated to a Boolean value that says whether or not the tuple is an element of the relationship denoted by the predicate.

The rule definition in the last line defines another predicate, runner, that denotes the unary relation of all people who have running as a hobby. (We will look at the details of rule definitions a little later.) In addition to the predicate definitions, Figure 8.1 also shows the relations denoted by the predicates.

In the following I will use the SWI-Prolog implementation, which can be downloaded from www.swi-prolog.org/download/stable. After starting the interpreter,[2] we are presented with a message (shortened here), followed by an input prompt.

```
Welcome to SWI-Prolog (threaded, 64 bits, version 9.0.4)
...

?-
```

To answer queries, we first have to load the definitions from the Prolog file, which is done by entering the file name[3] (without the .pl extension) in square brackets, followed by a period.

```
?- [hobby].
true.
```

Loading a file is considered to be a goal or query like any other in Prolog,[4] and thus the response true means that the goal of loading the file could be achieved.

---

[1]For each set S, the corresponding predicate $P_S(x) :\Longleftrightarrow x \in S$ is called the *characteristic function* of S. In Prolog, a predicate is the characteristic function of a relation.

[2]On Linux and Unix systems, including Mac OS, this is done by entering the command swipl in a terminal window.

[3]If your file name starts with an uppercase letter, you have to enclose the name in double quotes so that Prolog doesn't confuse it with a variable name.

[4]You may think of it as a polite request, *Is it possible to load the definitions from the file?*

Similar to Elm (and other interpreter-based language systems), a Prolog program loaded into `swipl` can be used to perform a number of different computations, which in Prolog means to repeatedly formulate queries (or goals). A query extracts information from the relations defined by the program. For example, we can check for specific elements by stating relationships as hypotheses that are then either confirmed or rejected by the interpreter.

```
?- hobby(alice,running).    ?- runner(alice).    ?- hobby(bob,reading).
true.                       true.                 false.
```

As expected, the first two hypotheses are confirmed, while that third one is rejected because no fact mentions that Bob has reading as a hobby, and there is no rule for deriving that relationship either.

In addition to letting Prolog confirm specific relationships (which quickly gets kind of boring), we can also use variables to pose more interesting queries. For example, we can ask who has running as a hobby by using a variable[5] for the first component of the relationship.

```
?- hobby(P,running).
P = alice ▮
```

The Prolog interpreter responds by generating variable bindings that satisfy the given goal. In this example we are presented with the binding `P=alice`, after which the interpreter waits for the user to respond, which is indicated by a (blinking) cursor at the end of the line. If we are satisfied with the answer, we can hit the Return key, in which case the interpreter stops looking for more answers.

```
?- hobby(P,running).
P = alice.
```

Alternatively, we can type a semicolon if we would like to see more solutions for `P`, in which case another solution is produced.[6]

```
?- hobby(P,running).
P = alice ;
P = bob.
```

Since Prolog can tell that in this example there can be no more solutions, it stops automatically.

Looking at the program `hobby.pl` we can notice that the goal `hobby(P,running)` is actually the same as the definition of the predicate `runner`. Thus, we could have used the goal `runner(P)` instead to compute the same results.

---

[5]Note that variables must start with an uppercase letter.

[6]The semicolon acts as a logical or. In this situation one can think of it as an "Or? Anything else?" question posed in response to a Prolog answer.

```
?- runner(P).
P = alice ;
P = bob.
```

Rules are the main programming abstraction in Prolog and are often used to abbreviate more complex goals that are needed repeatedly. To leave the Prolog interpreter, enter:

```
?- halt.
```

The take-away message of this very brief introduction is this: Prolog programs consist of predicate definitions (denoting relations) that can be loaded into the Prolog interpreter. The definitions set the context for answering queries from within the interpreter. Queries can be distinguished from definitions by the preceding ?- prompt, and the interpreter responds either with true or false (followed by a period) or with a variable binding as a solution. A sequence of responses is indicated by a ; after each individual solution.

Exercise 8.1

Alice eats pizza and salad, Bob only likes burgers, and Carol's meals consist of salad.

(a) Capture these facts by defining a binary predicate diet.

(b) Write a goal to determine whether Bob eats salad.

(c) Write a goal that finds all people who eat salad.

(d) Write a goal that finds everything Alice eats.

8.2 Predicates and Goals

A Prolog program consists of predicate definitions, which are used to represent data as well as algorithms. This conceptual simplicity can sometimes lead to confusion, which is compounded by the fact that the Prolog syntax relies on a single concept of so-called *compound terms* (or *structures*) to represent predicates as well as complex objects (that is, data structures). A simplified version of the core Prolog syntax is shown in Figure 8.2.

The terminology can be quite confusing because the same concept often has different names, depending on whether we are referring to its specific Prolog syntax, its semantics, or its use. For example, runner(P) is, syntactically, a *compound term*. In the file hobby.pl it appears as the *head* of a rule. When entered in the Prolog interpreter, it is a *goal* or *query*, and its semantics is a *relation*.

$$program ::= rule^*$$
$$rule ::= structure\ [\text{:-}\ structure^+].$$
$$structure ::= atom(term, \ldots, term)$$
$$term ::= structure\ |\ atom\ |\ var\ |\ int$$

Figure 8.2 Simplified Prolog syntax. The building blocks of a Prolog program are so-called *structures* or *compound terms*, which are atoms (that is, names that start with a lowercase letter) applied to tuples of (general) terms where a term can be an atom, a variable (a name that starts with an uppercase letter), an integer, or itself a structure. A non-empty list of structures constitutes a *rule*, and a Prolog program consists of a set of rules. Rules have a *head* (left of :-) and an optional *body*. A rule without a body is called a *fact*.

Similarly, hobby(bob,running) is again a compound term. In the file hobby.pl it appears as a *fact*, and its semantics is a single relationship. When used in the Prolog interpreter, it is also a *goal* or *query*.

Therefore, it is important to be precise in the use of terminology when talking about the different concepts. While most of the definitions are straightforward, note that we *don't* use the words "relation" and "relationship" synonymously. As already indicated in Section 8.1, the term *relation* refers to a set, while the term *relationship* refers to a tuple that is an element of a relation. As summary of some important terms is given in the box *Prolog Terminology*.

8.2.1 Predicates

In Prolog, a predicate can be defined by *facts* and *rules* (to be discussed in Section 8.3). A fact typically defines a single relationship by applying (or attaching) a name of a relationship to a tuple of arguments for which the relationship is said to hold. If one or more of the arguments are variables, then the fact defines multiple relationships, as for example in hobby(P,reading), which states that everyone has reading as a hobby.

Notably, all the names in the definition of hobby start with a lowercase letter. These names are called *atoms*, and they can represent objects (such as alice or reading) and *functors* when they are used as a name for a predicate (such as hobby or runner). On the other hand, names that start with an uppercase letter are *variables*. An example is the variable P used in the definition of the predicate runner. Like in other programming languages, variables in Prolog are placeholders for values, and the use of a variable in a term allows this term to be instantiated to different terms by substituting objects (or terms) for the variable.

> **PROLOG TERMINOLOGY**
>
> When talking about Prolog programming, it is important to understand the difference between the closely related terms *relation*, *relationship*, and *predicate*.
>
> *Relation*: a set of tuples that all have the same number of components, which defines the *arity* of the relation. A set of pairs is called a *binary relation*, and a set of triples is called a *ternary relation*. A special case is a set of single values, which is called a *unary relation*. A relation is represented in Prolog by a *predicate*.
>
> *Relationship*: a tuple that belongs to a relation. A tuple may belong to different relations. For example, (bob,car) is a tuple that can be an element of the relation owns, indicating that Bob owns a car, as well as an element of the relation sell, indicating that he wants to sell his car. The two relationships are distinguished by their names as given in the corresponding predicate definitions, such as owns(bob,car) and sell(bob,car). The tuple components are also called the *arguments* of the predicate.
>
> *Predicate*: a collection of Prolog facts or rules that share a common name. The Prolog name of a predicate is called a *functor*.
>
> *Goal*: a (compound) term used as a query in the Prolog interpreter. If the goal can be satisfied, Prolog will respond with one or more answers.
>
> *Clause*: a fact or a rule.

For example, by substituting alice for P in hobby(P,running), we obtain the term hobby(alice,running), which happens to be a fact in the program hobby.pl.

8.2.2 Goals

Any term can be used as a query, or goal, but goals with variables typically represent more interesting queries. When Prolog answers a query such as hobby(P,running), it tries to find substitutions, or bindings, for the variables in the goal that lead to relationships that are defined in the program through facts or rules. In this case, hobby(alice,running) is a fact in the program, and thus the binding P=alice is a solution for the goal.

Of course, variables can be used for any argument of a predicate. So we can ask what the hobbies of Bob are by formulating the following goal.

```
?- hobby(bob,H).
H = running.
```

Prolog is able to figure out that there is only one solution and presents the corresponding binding. Can we also use variables for both arguments? Absolutely!

```
?- hobby(P,H).
P = alice,
```

```
H = reading ;
P = alice,
H = running ;
P = bob,
H = running.
```

First, we can observe that Prolog delivers three answers and that each answer consists of two bindings. Not surprisingly, by calling the predicate with variables for all of its arguments we have produced – interactively – the relation denoted by the predicate.

The interactive scanning of predicates might work well for small examples, but it can become annoying pretty quickly. Prolog provides several predicates that allow the collection of multiple answers in a list. For example, the findall predicate takes three arguments: (i) the variable, say X, whose solutions we want to collect, (ii) the goal to be satisfied (which should contain X), and (iii) a variable to collect all the solutions computed for X. With findall we can gather all names and hobbies from the hobby predicate as follows.

```
?- findall(P,hobby(P,H),L).
L = [alice, alice, bob].

?- findall(H,hobby(P,H),L).
L = [reading, running, running].
```

By supplying a term with multiple variables as a first argument, we can also produce a list of relationships.

```
findall(hasHobby(P,H),hobby(P,H),L).
L = [hasHobby(alice,reading), hasHobby(alice,running), hasHobby(bob,running)].
```

We can also collect the relationships simply as tuples, without assigning them a name.

```
?- findall((P,H),hobby(P,H),L).
L = [(alice, reading),  (alice, running),  (bob, running)].
```

Note that Prolog is a so-called *first-order* language, which means that variables can only be used for arguments of predicates and not for predicates themselves. Thus, we cannot express queries about what relationships hold between objects. For example, the following query is *not allowed* in Prolog.

```
R(alice,running).    % Invalid goal.
```

The simple hobby predicate can also help illustrate an important difference between logic and functional programming. Consider how we could represent the facts about hobbies in Elm. Since different persons can have different numbers of hobbies, we can't define a function of type `Person -> Hobby`. Instead, to capture the variability in the number of relationships, we need to employ a list (or some other data structure). For example, we could define the following function.

```
hobbies : Person -> List Hobby
hobbies p = case p of
    Alice -> [Reading,Running]
    Bob   -> [Running]
    _     -> []
```

A significant difference between logic and functional (and imperative) programming becomes apparent when we consider how we can use function and predicate definitions for computations. In both functional and imperative languages, we apply functions to arguments to produce results. For example, we can use the function `hobbies` to determine the hobbies of Alice as follows.

```
> hobbies Alice
[Reading,Running] : List Hobby
```

However, functions can only be used in one direction, that is, we *cannot* use the inverse of the function and compute the persons who have a specific hobby. In contrast, since relations are not directed, Prolog can use predicates in either direction, and we can easily find out who has running as a hobby.

```
?- hobby(P,running).
P = alice ;
P = bob.
```

We will see later (for example, in Section 8.7) that the relational nature of logic programming is quite powerful and expressive.

8.2.3 Repeated Variables (aka Non-linear Patterns)

As in any programming language, the actual choice of names as variables does not matter, and instead of `P` and `H` we could just as well choose `X` and `Y`, `Person` and `Hobby`, etc. However, what happens if we chose the *same* variable for two arguments in a rule or goal? In most programming languages, this would not be allowed. In contrast, Prolog *does* allow it. In the hobby example, such a query won't produce any result.

```
?- hobby(X,X).
false.
```

This query asks for the reflexive subset of the `hobby` relation, which is empty. Or when viewed as a graph with objects as nodes and relationships as edges, the query asks for all loops in the graph. Only homogeneous binary relations – that is, binary relations over one set – can be reflexive, but since hobby relates people and activities, it can't contain any reflexive relationships (unless we use names of people as hobbies or vice versa).

As an example of a relation that admits reflexivity, consider the definition of the predicate trust with facts about who trusts in the judgment of whom.

```
trust(bob,alice).
trust(alice,alice).
```

The query trust(P,P) asks for people who have trust in themselves. In other words, the query finds people with self confidence.

```
?- trust(P,P).
P = alice.
```

Reflexivity can also apply to projection on two columns of a relation with more than two columns. As a simple example consider a predicate river that describes a ternary relation with facts about the states of their source and mouth.

```
river(mississippi,mn,la).
river(riogrande,co,tx).
river(willamette,or,or).
```

Here we could be interested in rivers that start and end in the same state, which we can list with the following query.

```
?- river(R,S,S).
R = willamette,
S = or.
```

The interesting point about both of these examples is that the use of the same variable at different places in a goal is not only perfectly fine but also provides an expressive query mechanism.

8.2.4   Conjunction

One way of creating more complex goals is to compose queries with logical connectives such as *and* and *or*. For example, to find out whether both Alice and Bob could go out together for a run, we would like to know whether they both have running as a hobby. We can create a corresponding query by joining two individual hobby queries using a comma, which works as a logical *and*.

```
?- hobby(alice,running), hobby(bob,running).
true ▮
```

The result itself is not surprising. What may come as a surprise, however, is that the `swipl` interpreter waits for user input. If we enter ; to request further solutions, we are told that there are none.

```
?- hobby(alice,running), hobby(bob,running).
true;
false.
```

Now, one might wonder what other solutions could possibly exist. The answer is that there might be other facts to satisfy the goal, and maybe the user is interested in those. In this case, this is unlikely, since the goal doesn't contain any variables and therefore the answer doesn't contain any bindings for which alternatives could be of interest. However, even in this simple scenario it is in principle possible to have alternative evidence for the goal. For example, assume that we duplicate the fact `hobby(bob,running)`. In this case the query evaluation looks slightly different.

```
?- hobby(alice,running), hobby(bob,running).
true ;
true ;
false.
```

Here the two (identical) facts act as two pieces of evidence for the goal. Again, since no bindings are generated, this is not really useful in this case.

8.2.5 Expressing Joins

We can obtain more interesting queries using conjunction to connect information from different relations. To illustrate this and some related aspects, let's add the following facts to the `hobby.pl` program.

```
sport(running).
sport(swimming).
```

Suppose now we would like to know who has a sport as a hobby. We can envision two strategies for generating answers. First, we could find out which hobbies are sports by consulting the `sport` predicate, and then find for each sport facts in the `hobby` relation. Concretely, we can formulate the following Prolog goal.[7]

```
?- sport(H), hobby(P,H).
```

---

[7]From now on, I will omit ";-followed-by-`false`." responses (indicated by ending the last response *without* a period) for brevity.

```
H = running,          H = running,
P = alice ;           P = bob
```

We could also go through the facts of the hobby relation and keep only those for which the hobby is a sport. While the query results in the same bindings, the order of variables is reversed.

```
?- hobby(P,H), sport(H).
P = alice,            P = bob,
H = running ;         H = running
```

This kind of query, which combines tuples from two (or more) relations based on the equality of values in the columns of the relations, is called an *equi-join*. The equality of values is expressed using the same variable in the two different predicates. The name "equi" indicates that the values of the relations to be joined are required to be equal. More general forms of joins result from using other relationships between the values. An example follows after the next exercise.

Exercise 8.2

Continuing Exercise 8.1:

(a) Define a unary predicate healthy through facts about healthy food.

(b) Write a query that finds people who eat (at least some) healthy food.

(c) What is missing in the query from (b) to find people that *only* eat healthy food?

We can also join a relation with itself. Consider, for example, the task of formulating a query to find out who has more than one hobby. To this end, we can join the hobby relation with itself based on the name column. We also have to use two different variables for the activity column. But this is not enough, because without further constraint, different variables can be bound to the same value. Therefore, we have to explicitly force the two hobby values to be different using the \= operator.

```
?- hobby(P,H1), hobby(P,H2), H1 \= H2.
P = alice,            P = alice,
H1 = reading,         H1 = running,
H2 = running ;        H2 = reading
```

As expected, we get only Alice as a result, since she is the only one with two hobbies. However, this result is presented twice, and it's instructive to understand why. To construct responses to queries, Prolog systematically traverses the facts (and rules) of the current program to identify candidates for results that are then subjected to potential constraints in the query. We explore how this works next.

Exercise 8.3

Continuing Exercises 8.1 and 8.2:

(a) Write a goal that finds pairs of people who share the same hobby.

(b) Write a goal that finds people who eat more than one thing.

(c) Write a goal that finds people with a healthy life style, that is, people who eat something healthy and have a sport as a hobby.

8.2.6   A Simple Operational Evaluation Model for Prolog

As an operational model for how Prolog answers queries, one can imagine that a series of nested loops is created, one for each predicate that appears in the goal. Each loop ranges over possible relationships for the predicate and creates bindings for the variables used.

In the two-hobbies query, the first (outer) loop starts by creating the bindings P=alice and H1=reading for the first fact. Since the second (inner) loop reuses the variable P, it is constrained by the value and can only range over facts that match the current value for P. Therefore, the loop only creates bindings for the single variable H2. Starting at the top, this yields H2=reading. With the binding for the three variables we can now test the condition H1 \= H2, which is not true in this case. Therefore, the current binding is rejected.

In the next step, the inner loop advances one fact and creates the binding H2=running. Since now H1 \= H2 is true, the three bindings are reported as a result. Then the inner loop advances to the third fact, which is immediately rejected because the name bob doesn't match the current value of P.

Since the inner loop is completed, it is reset, and the outer loop advances to the second fact, where it creates the bindings P=alice and H1=running. The inner loop restarts with the first fact, again creating the binding H2=reading. Since H1 \= H2 is true, the three bindings are reported as the second result. The only difference is that the values of H1 and H2 are swapped. After that, it's easy to see that none of the remaining cases yield any more results.

Sometimes the results produced by Prolog can be surprising, in particular, when expectations are guided by structural assumptions rooted in the application domain that are not exactly reflected in the formulation of predicate definitions or queries. In this example, we were, strictly speaking, looking for people who have a *set*, or *unordered pair*, of two (or more) hobbies, but the query was searching for an *ordered pair*.

Exercise 8.4

Suppose we omit the inequality constraint from the two-hobbies query, which leads to the following goal.

```
?- hobby(P,H1), hobby(P,H2).
```

How many results does Prolog produce and what bindings?

The example has shown that using the same variable in different predicates implicitly expresses an equality predicate, whereas using different variables doesn't express any constraint on the generated bindings. Note that we can always express equality constraints explicitly, that is, we can express the two-hobby query also as follows.

```
?- hobby(P1,H1), hobby(P2,H2), P1 = P2, H1 \= H2.
```

However, queries and programs are generally more readable when using repeated variable names to express equality.

8.3 Rules

We can define predicates by explicitly listing facts for all individual relationships. With rules we can define predicates that are derived from other predicates. We have already seen how to derive relations with queries. Rules allow us to define an interface for queries, that is, we can provide them with names and potential parameters.

As summarized in Figure 8.2, a rule consists of two parts that are syntactically separated by the :- symbol (called the *neck* operator in the SWI-Prolog glossary):

- A *head* that defines the name and parameters of the predicate.
- A *body* given by a query that defines the resulting relation.

Our first example rule was for the predicate runner, shown in Figure 8.1. The head of that rule is runner(P); runner is the *name* of the predicate, and P is its *parameter*. The body of the rule is given by the term hobby(P,running), which defines a query on the hobby relation that depends on the value of the parameter P.

In Section 8.2.5 we have discussed the query for determining people who have a sport as a hobby. We can define the following predicate based on this query.

```
sportHobby(P) :- hobby(P,H), sport(H).
```

The body of this rule consists of a conjunction of terms that express a join. A rule can be understood as an "if-then" rule that is read from right to left with subgoals connected by an "and," that is, the above rule can be read as:

if P has a hobby H **and**
   H is a sport
then
   P has a sport hobby

We have seen these rules before in Section 5.2.2 where we used the visual notation of inference rules from Section 5.1 to present them. Prolog rules can be viewed as inference rules in the same way, that is, we can write the rule also in the following way.

$$\frac{\texttt{hobby(P,H)} \qquad \texttt{sport(H)}}{\texttt{sportHobby(P)}}$$

This view is helpful, in particular, for understanding how Prolog tries to satisfy goals by constructing a proof tree, a topic to be discussed in Section 8.4.1.

We can use the newly defined predicate sportHobby in two ways. First, we can supply an atom as an argument and check whether the expressed fact is true.

```
?- sportHobby(alice).
true.
```

Second, we can use the predicate to find all people with a sport as a hobby by using a variable as an argument. Note that the name of this variable can be arbitrary. In particular, it doesn't have to be the name of the parameter.

```
?- sportHobby(Anyone).
Anyone = alice ;
Anyone = bob.
```

It is instructive to compare the result with the results from Section 8.2.5. The sportHobby predicate only produces bindings for the names of people, whereas the plain query also produced bindings for the hobbies. Thus, rules are not just convenient abbreviations for complex or repeatedly used goals, the head of a

```
hobby(alice,reading).      diet(alice,pizza).      sport(running).
hobby(alice,running).      diet(alice,salad).      sport(swimming).
hobby(bob,running).        diet(bob,burger).
hobby(carol,reading).      diet(carol,salad).      veggie(salad).
hobby(carol,chess).
```

Figure 8.3 Extended Prolog program `hobby.pl`.

rule also provides control over the amount of information that is revealed from the query in the body.

A related, intriguing aspect of the sportHobby rule is that the variable H in the body is *unbound* (or *free*). Usually, unbound variables are considered a programming mistake and are reported as type errors. Not so in Prolog (which is untyped): here unbound variables are programming features that can be understood as an instruction for Prolog to find a suitable binding that can satisfy the goal(s) that use the free variable.[8] And, as indicated in Section 8.2.6, Prolog's underlying search mechanism can generate such bindings.

If we want to show the hobby in addition to the person, we could easily do this by adding H as a parameter to the head.

```
sportHobby(P,H) :- hobby(P,H), sport(H).
```

With this definition the goal sportHobby(P,H) produces the same results as the query in Section 8.2.5.

To support some more interesting queries, we add a few facts to the hobby relation and add a new predicate about people's diets, see Figure 8.3.

Suppose we want to find out who has a healthy life style, which we assume is having a sport as a hobby or vegetables in one's diet. We can define a corresponding predicate healthy by giving *two* rules, one for each condition.

```
healthy(P) :- diet(P,F), veggie(F).
healthy(P) :- sportHobby(P).
```

The second rule makes use of the sportHobby predicate defined earlier. As with auxiliary functions in Elm, it is often a good idea to build an application gradually by identifying several relevant logical properties and capturing those in predicates. Similar to sportHobby, we could also have defined and used a predicate veggieDiet for the goal of the first rule. In any case, with this definition we find that everyone is healthy.

```
?- healthy(P).
P = alice ;
P = carol ;
P = alice ;
P = bob
```

---

[8]In terms of first-order logic, unbound variables are existentially quantified.

Notice that Alice occurs twice in the result, since she satisfies both rules for being healthy: she eats veggies and has a sport hobby. However, the reasons for being healthy are not reported in the results, because the head of healthy only includes one parameter for persons. We can, of course, change this by adding another parameter, one for hobby in the first rule, and one for food in the second rule, but we then have to replace the reference to sportHobby by its definition.

```
healthy(P,F) :- diet(P,F), veggie(F).
healthy(P,H) :- hobby(P,H), sport(H).
```

If we run the query again with this extended definition, the bindings include the reason for being healthy.

```
?- healthy(Who,Why).
Who = alice,      |   Who = carol,      |   Who = alice,      |   Who = bob,
Why = salad ;     |   Why = salad ;     |   Why = running ;   |   Why = running
```

Multiple rules, like multiple facts, define alternative ways to satisfy a predicate, that is, multiple rules effectively realize an *or* operation (or disjunction) on the conditions expressed by each body, whereas the terms in each body of a rule are connected by an *and*.

Exercise 8.5

(a) Define a unary predicate brainy, similar to sport, that classifies hobbies that are intellectual.

(b) Define a binary predicate buddies, that identifies pairs of people who have the same hobby. *Note*: Don't forget to add a constraint (as the last term) that prevents people being reported as their own buddies.

(c) How many results do you expect do get for the goal buddies(P1,P2) when using only the initial small set of hobby facts?

```
hobby(alice,reading).
hobby(alice,running).
hobby(bob,running).
```

Execute the queries in swipl. Did you predict correctly? Explain the results.

(d) How many results do you get when you remove the inequality constraint from your rule definition? Test your prediction, and explain the result.

The fact that Alice is reported twice suggests the definition of another predicate veryHealthy, which is true if your diet includes vegetables and you have a sport hobby.

```
veryHealthy(P) :- diet(P,F), veggie(F), sportHobby(P).
```

As expected, according to this definition only Alice is very healthy.

```
?- veryHealthy(P).
P = alice
```

Spoiler alert! If you haven't worked on Exercise 8.5 on page 169, do it before continuing to read. A typical definition for the predicate buddies looks as follows.

```
buddies(P1,P2) :- hobby(P1,H), hobby(P2,H), P1 \= P2.
```

With this definition we might expect to get only one result. However, as discussed at the end of Section 8.2.5, we get *two* results, since Prolog doesn't know that the buddies relation is symmetric and can't exploit this fact.

```
?- buddies(P1,P2).
P1 = alice,          P1 = bob,
P2 = bob ;           P2 = alice
```

We can avoid such duplicate results for symmetric relations by strenghtening the constraint on result pairs. Specifically, we can exploit the built-in ordering of atoms (implemented in the @< operator) and only return ordered pairs.

```
buddies(P1,P2) :- hobby(P1,H), hobby(P2,H), P1 @< P2.
```

With this definition we get only one result.

```
?- buddies(P1,P2).
P1 = alice,
P2 = bob
```

Exercise 8.6

For this exercise, we use the extended fact base from Figure 8.3.

(a) Define a predicate foodmates that finds people who like to eat the same food. Since foodmates describes a symmetric relation, use the @< operator to exclude unnecessary duplicates.

(b) Define the predicate friends that holds for two people if they are buddies or foodmates.

(c) The use of the @< operator in both buddies and foodmates avoids returning duplicate pairs. Explain why the goal friends(P1,P2) still returns one pair of people as a result twice.

Since facts are rules without a body, we can use rules and facts together to define predicates. For example, to add the information that Bob and Carol are friends, even though they have no hobby or food interest in common, we can simply add a corresponding fact to the predicate definition.

```
friends(P1,P2) :- ...
friends(carol,bob).
```

Finally, we should mention that predicates can be overloaded, that is, we can use the same name for predicates with different numbers of parameters. For example, in addition to the unary sport predicate, we can also have a binary predicate of the same name that says how many people one needs to play the sport.

```
sport(running,1).
sport(tennis,2).
sport(soccer,22).
```

Therefore, predicates have to be distinguished by name and arity. In Prolog we refer to a specific overloaded predicate by adding the arity to the predicate name. For example, sport/1 refers to the unary sport predicate, whereas sport/2 refers to the binary one.

One can debate whether it is a good idea to overload predicate names. In any case, the possibility of overloading presents a potential source of programming errors. For example, if you supply the wrong number of arguments for a predicate, this will generally not produce an error message, but Prolog may assume that you are referring to a different predicate, which, if not defined, will simply lead to failure in satisfying goals.

8.4   Recursion

The examples in Section 5.1 illustrate that inference rules can be recursive. Similarly, we can use recursion in Prolog rules to define predicates. We will come back to the factorial example later in Section 8.8 when we discuss the special requirements for arithmetic in Prolog. For now, consider as an example the facts about spatial containment shown in Figure 8.4, defined through the predicates inside and in. While inside/2 is solely defined through facts, in/2 is defined by two rules, one of which is recursive, and computes the transitive closure of inside.

With these definitions, we can try to find out whether we have milk in the house by formulating the following goal.

```
inside(bathroom,house).
inside(kitchen,house).
inside(fridge,kitchen).        in(X,Y) :- inside(X,Y).
inside(milk,fridge).           in(X,Z) :- inside(X,Y), in(Y,Z).
```

Figure 8.4   Prolog program house.pl. The second rule of the predicate definition for in makes use of recursion.

```
?- in(milk,house).
true
```

We may ask ourselves now *why* this it true and how Prolog can figure it out. For this goal, which doesn't involve variables, we can construct an answer by repeatedly replacing goals with new goals, as required by rules, until we are left with a set of (true) inside facts. We can describe this process through a trace that shows the step-by-step expansion of subgoals. For each step we show on the right which rule was applied.

```
    in(milk,house)
⇒ inside(milk,fridge), in(fridge,house)                                    | in₂
⇒ inside(milk,fridge), inside(fridge,kitchen), in(kitchen,house)           | in₂
⇒ inside(milk,fridge), inside(fridge,kitchen), inside(kitchen,house)       | in₁
```

The final entry in the trace, which consists only of facts from the program, provides a justification for the truth of the goal: milk is in the house because milk is inside the fridge, the fridge is inside the kitchen, and the kitchen is inside the house.

8.4.1   Trees as Computation Traces

We can give a more visual representation of the justification in the form of a tree that has the goal as a root and in which all leaves are facts. The internal nodes are subgoals that are defined by rules and require the truth of their subgoals.

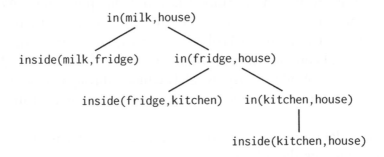

The structure of the tree reflects the rules of the program that were used to answer the goal. Specifically, if the rule H :- B1, ..., Bk was used in the computation to justify the term T in the tree (using a binding σ as a substitution with $\sigma(\text{H}) = T$), then T has children $T_1, \ldots, T_k$ in the tree, where T_i is an instance of the term Bi of the rule's body, that is, $\sigma(\text{Bi}) = T_i$, (for $1 \leq i \leq k$).

For example, the subgoal in(fridge,house) is an instance of the rule head in(X,Z) with $\sigma = \langle \text{X=fridge, Y=kitchen, Z=house} \rangle$. Using the second rule for the predicate in to satisfy this subgoal[9] leads to the two children $\sigma(\text{inside(X,Y)}) = $ inside(fridge,kitchen) and $\sigma(\text{in(Y,Z)}) = $ in(kitchen,house) in the tree. While it is clear that the bindings for X and Z are created by the arguments that are passed to the subgoal in(fridge,house), it is not so clear where the binding for Y comes from. Since Y is a free variable in the second rule for in, its binding is determined by Prolog's built-in search mechanism, which we'll discuss soon.

Using the inference rule notation, the same tree can also be written as a so-called *proof tree*, which can show the rules that were used at each branch.

$$
\cfrac{\text{inside(milk,fridge)} \qquad \cfrac{\text{inside(fridge,kitchen)} \qquad \cfrac{\text{inside(kitchen,house)}}{\text{in(kitchen,house)}}\ \text{in}_1}{\text{in(fridge,house)}}\ \text{in}_2}{\text{in(milk,house)}}\ \text{in}_2
$$

Both representations show the dynamic nature of rules in generating new goals during query evaluation. We will look into the Prolog evaluation mechanism in more detail in the next section.

8.4.2 Left Recursion

The possibility for recursively defined queries distinguishes Prolog from most database query languages (such as SQL) and turns it into a fully fledged, powerful programming language – with all the dangers that come with the territory. An important caveat about recursion in Prolog is this.

Rules should not be left recursive.

The term *left recursion* describes the situation when the recursive use of a predicate appears as the first term in the body of a rule, in a form that matches the head of the rule. For example, suppose we change the order of subgoals in the second rule for in as follows. (And we also exchange the order of the two rules.)

```
in(X,Z) :- in(Y,Z), inside(X,Y).   % Left recursion! Avoid!
in(X,Y) :- inside(X,Y).
```

---

[9] We can't use the first rule, since we don't have a fact inside(fridge,house) in our program.

Now the evaluation of the goal in(milk,house) goes into an infinite loop, and after some time the interpreter runs out of memory and stops with a runtime error. This is because in order to satisfy in with the first rule (which is tried first), another subgoal for in is generated that Prolog then tries to satisfy by using the first rule for in, etc.

If we change the order of rules back to the original but keep the left recursion, the effect is a bit more subtle: Prolog produces the result true, but if we then ask for more results, we'll end up in an infinite loop anyway. For queries involving variables the situation is very similar.

The bottom line is that you should be aware of left recursion and avoid using it. In fact, it is always a good strategy to put fact subgoals first in the body of rules.

Exercise 8.7

Consider the following directed, unlabeled graph in which nodes are represented by lowercase letters.

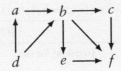

(a) Define the graph as a binary predicate edge.

(b) Define a binary predicate path so that path(X,Y) is true when there is a path from X to Y in the graph.

(c) How many results does the goal path(a,f) produce? Explain why.

(d) Write a goal that finds all nodes that are reachable from node *b*.

(e) Define a unary predicate cycleAt that yields true if the graph contains contains a cycle that starts and ends with at node X.

(f) A *join* is a constellation of three distinct nodes such that two are predecessors of the third. Define a corresponding predicate join/3. How many joins does the graph contain?

8.5   Prolog's Search Mechanism

In the previous section we have seen how the result for a Prolog query can be represented in a tree that captures a trace of the rules that were involved in generating the result. But how does Prolog actually find the results? To describe the method in general, note that a goal can be satisfied by a fact or a rule. In the first case, the goal is satisfied and the search and computation has come to a successful end. If instead Prolog finds a rule whose head matches the goal, the terms of the body of this rule are added as additional subgoals (instantiated by applying the potential bindings that result from matching the head of the rule).

In terms of our tree model, the new subgoals are added as children of the currently processed goal. Then Prolog continues trying to satisfy a new subgoal (which has to be a leaf in the tree because goals in internal nodes are already being processed).

This process is repeated until either all leaf nodes could be matched to facts and thus are satisfied (in which case all internal nodes and the goal in the root of the tree are also satisfied) or we encounter a leaf that cannot be satisfied. In the latter case, we remove that goal and continue the search for an alternative fact or rule that can be used. If none can be found, we remove the parent goal and continue to look for an alternative for that one, etc. This process of removing intermediate goals is called *backtracking*. If backtracking proceeds all the way to the original goal in the root, and we run out of alternatives for that goal, the process fails, and the goal cannot be satisfied.

The search process can be described more precisely as a step-by-step transformation of a search state. This state consists of:

- A search tree with n nodes, each representing a goal.
- A pointer to a current goal in the tree.
- n pointers to facts and rules in the program, one for each goal.
- Sets of bindings (or substitutions), one set for each node.

In the following we will illustrate Prolog's search process by showing how the result for the example query in(milk,house) is built. But before we do that, we have to explain how bindings are constructed when a rule is matched against a goal.

8.5.1 Unification

When a goal is entered, Prolog scans the current program for rules whose heads match the goal. More precisely, Prolog actually finds rules whose head can be *unified* with the goal. What does that mean?

We have seen examples of pattern matching in Elm, where a term built by data constructors is matched against a pattern when a function is applied to it. When a pattern matches a term, bindings for the variables in the pattern are generated. For example, the list [2,3,4] successfully matches the pattern x::xs and creates the binding ⟨x=2, xs=[3,4]⟩. In Prolog we can compare terms and patterns directly in the interpreter. Lists are written similarly to Elm lists, but patterns have a slightly different syntax, in particular, the pattern x::xs would be written in Prolog as [X|XS] (we will discuss this in more detail in Section 8.7). Therefore, we can express the pattern matching example as follows.

```
?- [2,3,4] = [X|XS].
X = 2,
XS = [3, 4].
```

The list [2,3,4] doesn't match the patterns [] or 1::xs (since the first element in the list, 2, doesn't match the constant 1 in the pattern) and thus doesn't generate any binding. We can directly verify this in Prolog.

```
?- [2,3,4] = [].
false.
```

```
?- [2,3,4] = [1|XS].
false.
```

Pattern matching always matches a term that contains only values against a pattern, which is a term that in addition to values may also contain variables.

Unification is a generalization of pattern matching that takes two patterns and tries to find a substitution for variables that, when applied to both patterns, makes them equal. For example, we can ask whether the two lists [X,3,4] and [1|XS] can be made equal.

```
?- [X,3,4] = [1|XS].
X = 1,
XS = [3, 4].
```

We observe that, unlike in Elm, in Prolog we can have variables in both terms, and Prolog finds a substitution if it exists. This process is called *unification*, and the resulting substitution that makes the two terms equal is called a *unifier*.

Now how about the two lists [X,Y,4] and [1|XS]? Can we also make them also equal?

```
?- [X,Y,4] = [1|XS].
X = 1,
XS = [Y, 4].
```

Yes, and we can see that (i) no substitution for Y is generated and (ii) the substitution term for XS contains itself a variable. This is because any other solution (such as substituting 3 for Y) is less general and could be obtained as a special case from the more general one.

In fact, the unification algorithm employed by Prolog is always able to compute what is called the *most general unifier*, which is a substitution from which all other valid substitutions can be obtained by adding further substitutions.

8.5.2 Scan, Expand, and Backtrack

With unification as the basic tool for finding rules that can satisfy a goal, we can now illustrate the Prolog search process in more detail. We represent the state of the search as a tree where each node is annotated in one of two ways:

(a) A circled number ⓝ that indicates the position of the pointer in the program. The number says that currently the nth rule/fact of the marked predicate is being examined.

(b) A bullet • that indicates that all rules/facts for the marked predicate have been tested and that the goal cannot be satisfied, which means the goal has to be retracted in the next step.

We also sometimes include the names of bound variables in goals for easier tracking. The current goal is always the leftmost leaf that contains an unsatisfied goal.

When we try to satisfy in(milk,house), we first try the first rule for in, which leads to the subgoal inside(milk,house), which cannot be satisfied by any of the inside facts. Thus, we are stuck at this point and have to retract this goal, which also means to advance the pointer for the in predicate to the next, that is, second rule, which causes the creation of two new subgoals as children.

Next we need to satisfy the inside(milk,Y) goal. Scanning the inside facts we find a match for the fourth fact.

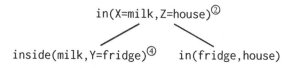

This match creates the binding Y=fridge and instantiates inside(fridge,house) as the next subgoal to be satisfied. Starting with the first rule for in creates inside(fridge,house) as a new subgoal, which, however, cannot be satisifed.

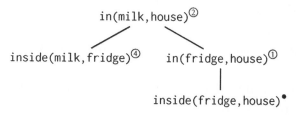

Therefore, we have to backtrack and retract the last inside goal as well as advancing the in goal to the second rule, which leads to the two new subgoals inside(fridge,kitchen) and in(kitchen,house). We find the third inside fact as a match for the first subgoal, which creates the binding Y=kitchen. To satisfy the newly generated in subgoal we start with the first rule for in, which creates inside(kitchen,house) as a new subgoal, which can finally be satisfied by the second inside fact.

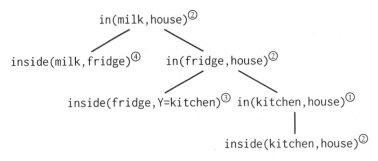

At this point, all goals are satisfied, and the result can be reported. In this example, it is only the token true. For goals that contain variables, the generated bindings will be reported as well. For example, if we are wondering where the milk is, we could ask:

```
in(milk,Where).
```

A difference to the previous goal is that we have passed the variable Where as an argument, which generates a binding of one variable to another one. This binding effectively establishes the two variables as synonyms for whatever value will be bound to either one. We can observe this behavior directly in the Prolog interpreter.

```
?- Y=Where, Y=fridge.
Y = Where, Where = fridge.
```

Therefore, we can consider Y and Where as aliases. Otherwise, the query is processed in much the same way as the previous one: the goal matches the head of the first in rule and generates the subgoal inside(milk,Where), which can then be satisfied by the fourth inside fact.

At this point, the binding that was generated for the variable provided in the goal will be reported as a result.

```
?- in(milk,Where).
Where = fridge ▮
```

Rejecting the result by entering ; and asking for a different solution forces Prolog to backtrack. The effect is the removal of the inside goal as well as the binding for Where. Advancing the in goal to the second rule creates the two new subgoals inside(milk,Y) and in(Y,Where). The first subgoal can again be satisfied by the fourth inside fact, which instantiates the second subgoal through the produced binding for Y and generates another inside subgoal by following the first in rule.

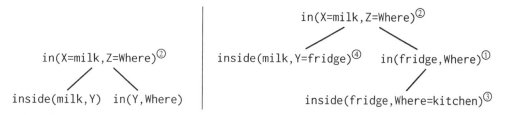

The third inside fact satisfies the last goal and produces the new binding for Where that is reported as a result.

```
?- in(milk,Where).
Where = fridge ;
Where = kitchen ▮
```

The final result house can be produced in a similar way.

Exercise 8.8

Draw a sequence of trees that explain the computation of the results for the following queries.

(a) in(What,kitchen)

(b) path(b,f) (see Exercise 8.7)

8.6   Structures

A structure, or compound term, can represent a fact or be part of a rule, in which case it is interpreted as part of the definition of a relation. But structures can also serve as data structures and represent complex data, such as person records, geometric objects, trees, or arithmetic expressions.

```
person(name(jon,doe),dob(1,1,2000))

line((1,1),(3,4))

node(3,leaf(1),node(5,leaf(4),leaf(7)))

+(2,*(3,4))
```

Note that none of these terms is a fact, and they do *not* represent relationships but simply structured objects.[10] The functors (person, name, etc.) play a role that is similar to that of Elm's data constructors. An important difference (apart from starting with a lowercase letter) is that functors are *untyped* and can be applied to arbitrary arguments. Therefore, they don't need to be introduced through a type definition either.

To participate in a computation, compound terms will have to occur as part of predicates. The main use of compound terms is to provide a structured representation that can be exploited by queries. Assume, for example, that we have a program that represents facts about objects on a map.

```
map(road, line((1,1),(3,4))).
map(blvd, line((2,3),(2,4))).
map(river,line((1,2),(1,4))).
map(city, point(3,4)).
```

If we want to search the map, say for vertical objects, we can express the verticality constraint by using a the same variable X for the *x* coordinate of both line end points and use the following query.

```
?- map(Object,line((X,Y1),(X,Y2))).
Object = blvd,        |    Object = river,
X = 2,                |    X = 1,
Y1 = 3,               |    Y1 = 2,
Y2 = 4 ;              |    Y2 = 4.
```

The use of the functor line acts as a filter that picks out only facts with line objects as second arguments, which is similar to pattern matching against constructors in Elm. Another example is a query to find line objects that end in a position where a point object can be found.

---

[10]They could be turned into facts, though. For example, placing the fact person(name(jon,doe), dob(1,1,2000)). into a Prolog program defines a binary predicate person. Carefully note the period at the end! The functor person then becomes the name of a predicate (while the functors name and dob still only denote terms).

```
?- map(Line,line(_,(X,Y))), map(Point,point(X,Y)).
Line = road,
X = 3,
Y = 4,
Point = city
```

Note the use of the underscore, which is an anonymous variable, much like in Elm, that matches anything but for which no bindings are generated. Here we have used it to simply ignore the coordinates of the line's first point.

A more interesting application is to use terms as an abstract syntax representation, like we used data types in Elm. Concretely, suppose we want to represent the same language as we did in Section 5.3 (see the data type definition on page 110) and implement a type checker for it. Consider, for example, the following program.

```
let x=3 in x+1
```

In Elm we use constructors to represent it as follows.

```
Let "x" (Num 3) (Plus (Var "x") (Num 1))
```

In Prolog, we can represent it as a compound term in much the same way. The only differences are that we are using functors (that start with lowercase letters) instead of constructors and parentheses and commas to separate arguments.

```
let("x",num(3),plus(var("x"),num(1)))
```

While this representation works, it is not very readable. Fortunately, the simple and general structure of Prolog terms allows us to represent the syntax in a much more direct and less convoluted way. First, we can use atoms instead of strings to represent variables names. Second, since we can distinguish atoms from integers, we don't need to tag the latter with num. Third, since arithmetic expressions (see Section 8.8) are represented in Prolog as terms with symbolic operators as functors (that is, x+1 is just syntactic sugar for +(x,1)), we can use them directly in the abstract syntax. Thus, we can represent the expression much more concisely by the following Prolog term.

```
let(x,3,x+1)
```

The types for our language can be represented by the two atoms int and bool.

As explained in Section 5.2.2, the definition of the typing rules relies on the typing judgment $\Gamma \vdash e : T$, which says that in the context of type environment Γ, the type of expression e is T. This typing judgment defines a ternary relation that contains a triple (Γ, e, T) for each valid judgment.

In Prolog we can represent a type assumption as a list of variable/type pairs. For the typing rules we need only two operations on such lists: (i) extending a list (temporarily) by a new assumption, and (ii) looking up the type of a variable. The latter can be achieved by the predicate `lookup/3`, where `lookup(X,G,T)` holds if G contains the pair `(X,T)`. (We will define `lookup` in Section 8.7.) We have already encountered the Prolog notation for extending a list with new elements in Section 8.5.1: to extend G with a pair `(X,T)`, we write `[(X,T)|G]`.

To implement the type system, all we need to do now is translate the visual inference rules into Prolog syntax. To that end we can represent the typing judgment $\Gamma \vdash e : T$ by a predicate `type/3` so that `type(G,E,T)` holds if E has type T given the assumptions G.

Recall the general form of inference rules from Section 5.1.

$$\frac{\mathcal{P}_1 \quad \cdots \quad \mathcal{P}_n}{\mathcal{C}}$$

Such an inference rule can be directly translated into a Prolog rule where the conclusion is represented by the head and the premises are combined using conjunction to define the body.

$$\mathcal{C} \;:\text{-}\; \mathcal{P}_1, \; \ldots, \; \mathcal{P}_n$$

Consider again the typing rule for let expressions, which has two premises.

$$\text{Let } \frac{\Gamma \vdash e_1 : U \qquad \Gamma, x : U \vdash e_2 : T}{\Gamma \vdash \text{let } x{=}e_1 \text{ in } e_2 : T}$$

Using the `type/3` predicate, this inference rule therefore translates into the following Prolog rule.

```
type(G,let(X,E1,E2),T) :- type(G,E1,U), type([(X,U)|G],E2,T).
```

It is an instructive exercise at this point to disentangle the different notations/languages with their symbols and their meanings. For example, we have the following three different representations of the example let expression.

```
let x=3 in x+1                           Concrete syntax
Let "x" (Num 3) (Plus (Var "x") (Num 1))  Abstract syntax in Elm
let(x,3,x+1)                             Abstract syntax in Prolog
```

In addition, we also have two different representations of the typing rule, namely, as an inference rule and as a Prolog rule.

Let's consider the different versions of "x" that are being used here. First, the lowercase, typewriter x is a variable of the object language, but it's also a Prolog atom that is used in the Prolog abstract syntax representation of the example. In the Elm abstract syntax the variable is represented in two different ways: as a string "x" where it is defined and as Var "x" where it is used. The inference rule representation of the typing rule uses the italic x as a metavariable that can match any variable of the object language, whatever the concrete name. This metavariable is given in the Prolog representation of the typing rule as an uppercase, typewriter X. Thus, the differences in notation for x, "x", Var "x", x, and X matter; they are quite important, since each representation has a specific role to play.

These kinds of considerations are helpful in avoiding confusion of object language and metalanguage.

Exercise 8.9

Explain the differences between let, Let, and LET and their different roles.

The complete type system is shown in Figure 8.5. Note that the last rule is for explicitly assigning a type error to type-incorrect expressions. We don't necessarily need such a rule, because if we omit it, type-incorrect expressions will simply fail the type checker. For example, with the last rule we get the following.

```
?- type([],not(2),T).
T = error.
```

In contrast, without the last rule the typing predicate simply fails for the goal.

```
?- type([],not(2),T).
false.
```

It is generally good programming practice to distinguish error values of the application (in this case type errors) from runtime errors that result from failure to apply rules.

Compared with the Elm implementation (see Figure 5.1), the Prolog implementation is shorter and provides a more direct realization of the typing rules. The Elm implementation is more verbose for two main reasons. First, Elm uses a typed representation of the abstract syntax, whereas in Prolog we can reuse much of Prolog's own syntax (that is, the syntax of the metalanguage) as the syntax for the object language. Second, in the Elm implementation type errors are distinguished from proper types (Just vs. Nothing), which causes some overhead in managing the typing of subexpressions. This could be avoided to some

```
type(G,E1 + E2,int)     :- type(G,E1,int), type(G,E2,int).
type(G,E1 = E2,bool)    :- type(G,E1,T),    type(G,E2,T).
type(G,not(E),bool)     :- type(G,E,bool).
type(G,let(X,E1,E2),T)  :- type(G,E1,U), type([(X,U)|G],E2,T).
type(G,X,T)             :- lookup(X,G,T).
type(_,I,int)           :- integer(I).
type(_,_,error).
```

Figure 8.5 The type system from Figure 5.1 expressed in Prolog. The typing rules for the judgment $\Gamma \vdash e : T$ are implemented by Prolog rules defining the predicate type(G,E,T). The built-in predicate integer/1 is true for integer objects only.

degree by representing a type error by a constructor Error that is part of the type Type, but the resulting code would be more intricate and arguably harder to follow.

On the other hand, while the Prolog implementation is very succinct and quite close to the formal definition by inference rules, it can behave in unexpected ways and is also prone to errors. Consider the following example.

```
?- type([],let(x,1,let(x,2=3,x)),T).
T = bool ▮
```

As expected, the result type is bool, the type derived for the x defined in the inner let expression. But curiously, Prolog offers us to enter ; with the prospect of another result, and if we take up that offer, we find, surprisingly, the following answer.

```
?- type([],let(x,1,let(x,2=3,x)),T).
T = bool ;
T = int.
```

That seems to suggest that x can have both types bool *and* int, but that should not be the case according to the typing rules, since the binding for the inner let expression hides the outer one. The reason for this behavior is that backtracking allows Prolog to find alternative answers (in this case through the hidden binding in the type assumption). But we can get conflicting answers in even the most basic cases, as the following example illustrates.

```
?- type([],2,T).
T = int ;
T = error.
```

This seems to say that the type of 2 is int, which is correct, but also that it is a type error, which is definitely not the case. In this example, it is easy to see what's going on: first, Prolog identifies the second-to-last rule for type to show that the type of 2 is int. But when forced by ; to backtrack, the search advances to the next rule, which succeeds and yields error as another solution. Backtracking allows the catch-all case to be reached, even when another case was executed already.

This behavior can be prevented by using !, the so-called *cut*, which is a predicate that succeeds, but prevents backtracking when reached. Concretely, if we change the second-to-last rule as follows, the last rule cannot be reached after the int rule has been successfully matched.

```
type(_,I,int) :- integer(I), !.
```

The result is as expected.

```
?- type([],2,T).
T = int.
```

We will discuss the cut in Section 8.9.

And to illustrate how the lack of typing in Prolog facilitates semantic errors, consider the following example.

```
?- type([],x+2,T).
T = error.
```

Just as we expect, x+2 is type incorrect, since x is undefined. But suppose we mistyped int in the body of the first rule and used Int instead, like so.

```
type(G,E1 + E2,int) :- type(G,E1,Int), type(G,E2,Int).   /* INCORRECT! */
```

Now we can observe the following strange behavior.

```
?- type([],x+2,T).
T = int
```

Why is x+2 all of a sudden considered to be of type int? Since Int is a Prolog variable, the first subgoal of the changed rule, type([],x,Int), will succeed, creating the binding Int=error, since it can be satisfied with the last rule. The second subgoal then instantiates to type([],2,error), which also succeeds due to the last rule, which means the query type([],x+2,T) succeeds binding int to T.

Exercise 8.10

Why doesn't adding a cut to the second-to-last rule change this behavior? Shouldn't the second subgoal be typed to be int in that case and the last rule not be reached? Apparently, this reasoning is wrong; the last rule is reached despite a cut. Why is that?

Note that the typo in the program does *not* lead to a compiler or even a runtime error but to a semantic error that might be very difficult to find. These kinds of programming mistakes are caught by type systems and could not happen in Elm, which illustrates the trade-off between succinctness and programming convenience on the one hand versus more correctness guarantees on the other.

Exercise 8.11

This exercise is a continuation of Exercise 5.5. Extend the Prolog program in Figure 8.5 by rules for typing (potentially nested) pairs of expressions. Add rules for the construction of pairs (such as (2,2=3)) and the operations swap and fst. Here are several test cases.

```
type([],(2,2=3),(int,bool)).
type([],let(x,1,let(y,2=3,(x,y))),(int,bool)).
type([],swap(swap((2,2=3))),(int,bool)).
type([],fst(swap((2,2=3))),bool).
type([],swap(fst(((2,2=3),3))),(bool,int)).
```

8.7 Lists

Like in Elm, lists are probably the most important and widely used data structures in Prolog. Moreover, just as in Elm lists are just ordinary data types with special syntax, Prolog lists are ordinary terms with special syntax.

As in Elm, the empty list in Prolog is represented by the atom []. The role of the cons constructor :: is played in Prolog generally by the dot functor .; however, SWI-Prolog uses the functor '[|]',[11] so that the inductive representation of the list [3,5] is written in Elm, Prolog, and SWI-Prolog, respectively as follows.

```
> 3::5::[]        | ?- L = .(3,.(5,[])).   | ?- L = '[|]'(3,'[|]'(5,[])).
[3,5]             | L = [3, 5].            | L = [3, 5].
```

Luckily, we almost never construct or deconstruct lists using the dot functor (or SWI-Prolog's version), since Prolog provides a generalized form of cons pattern that is expressive and convenient to use. The syntax has a list of elements separated by the bar symbol | from the list tail.

list ::= [*term* , ... , *term* | *term*]

---

[11] For an explanation of this design, see https://www.swi-prolog.org/pldoc/man?section=ext-lists.

To illustrate this notation, here are several alternative ways to denote the list [3,4,5].

```
[3,4,5]
[3|[4,5]]
[3,4|[5]]
[3,4,5|[]]
```

Note that [3,4|5] is a valid Prolog term, but it is different from [3,4,5]. In fact, it is not a proper list, since it doesn't end with an empty list.

Since Prolog is untyped, lists don't have to be homogeneous, and we can form lists of atoms and numbers as well as nested lists.

```
[4,privet_drive]    |    [1,(2,2),[1,(2,2)]]    |    [[],1,[[]],2,[[[]]],3]
```

Exercise 8.12

Consider the following fact.

```
book([george,orwell],[nineteen,eighty,four]).
```

Create goals that produce exactly the following results. Note that you can use the wildcard symbol _ to match terms without producing a binding.

(a) Author = orwell,
    Book = [nineteen, eighty, four].

(b) Century = nineteen.

(c) Year = [eighty, four].

(d) X = nineteen,
    Y = eighty,
    Z = four.

Note: Try to express each query *twice*: using a list pattern with and without a bar. For one query this does *not* work. Which one?

One of the most basic predicates on lists is member/2, which takes an element and a list and returns true if the element is contained in the list. The predicate is defined as follows.

```
member(X,[X|_]).
member(X,[_|XS]) :- member(X,XS).
```

The first rule expresses the fact that the first element in a list is a member of that list, and the second rule says that an element can be also a member of a list if it is a member of the list's tail. Note that we don't need a base case for empty lists, because member should always fail for empty lists, which is the behavior when no rule is found.

We can use the member predicate in *three* different ways. First of all, we can of course test membership of specific list elements.

```
?- member(3,[2,3,4,3]).
true ;
true.
```

The response shows that the goal can be satisfied *twice*, which is not surprising, because 3 occurs twice in the list, that is, when forcing Prolog to retract the first answer and continue to search for another piece of evidence, it will find it in the last list element. When we formulate a member goal with an element that occurs only once in the list, only one result is produced.

```
?- member(4,[2,3,4,3]).
true ;
false.
```

Exercise 8.13

Change the definition of the predicate member so that it produces at most one answer.

Hint: Think about a condition that constrains the second rule: when should it *not* be used?

So far we have used Prolog almost exclusively to derive information from relations represented by predicates. The member predicate is different in that it computes information for input data. It is therefore the right time to highlight an important relationship between predicates and their corresponding functions in imperative or functional languages:

A function of n arguments with a result type that is *not* Bool is represented in Prolog by a predicate of $n + 1$ arguments.

A function of n arguments with result type Bool is represented in Prolog by a predicate of n arguments.

The reason for the second special case is that a Bool result type of a function is not needed for a corresponding Prolog predicate, because it is captured by the success or failure of the predicate. This is why the function succ : Int -> Int would be represented by a binary predicate succ/2, whereas a function even : Int -> Bool would be represented by a unary predicate even/1. And it explains why

member is a binary predicate, whereas the corresponding Elm function List.member
: a -> List a -> Bool has two arguments and a Bool result.

The shown usage scenario for member, providing two arguments and getting a
Boolean as a result, is the only one that Elm offers through the function member.
In contrast, Prolog offers two more uses. For example, we can employ a variable
as the first argument to enumerate elements from the list. To make the example
a bit more interesting, let's add a condition as a filter for the elements.

```
?- member(X,[2,3,4,3]), X>2.
X = 3 ;
X = 4 ;
X = 3.
```

As illustrated in Section 8.2.2, instead of interactively enumerating the results,
we can use findall to collect all results in a list.

```
?- findall(X, (member(X,[2,3,4,3]),X>2), L).
L = [3,4,3].
```

As a third application scenario for member, we can also employ a variable for the
list argument (and provide an example element that should be in the list). This
will lead to the following results.[12]

```
?- member(3,L).
L = [3|A] ;
L = [A,3|B] ;
L = [A,B,3|C]
```

To understand the results, we first have to understand the query, which asks,
What list is 3 *a member of*? Prolog's first answer is a pattern that matches any
non-empty list with 3 as its first element and an arbitrary tail. Prolog's second
answer matches any list of two or more elements with 3 as its second element
and an arbitrary first element and tail, and the third answer describes lists of at
least three elements that have 3 as their third element.

How does Prolog produce these answers? The search starts by matching the
goal member(3,L) against the first rule for member, which produces the bindings
⟨X=3, L=[3|A]⟩, where the binding for X is reused in the one created for L. Also,
Prolog always generates fresh variable names as a representation for the underscore (in this instance, A). With the substitutions for X and L, the goal can be
satisfied using the first rule, which produces the first answer. This state of the
search is captured by the search tree consisting of just one node shown in Figure
8.6 on the left.

---

[12]Instead of A, B, and C, swipl will generate numbered variable names that start with an underscore.

member(X=3,[3|A]=L)①   member(X=3,[A|XS]=L)②   member(X₁=3,[A|XS₁]=L)②
                                      | |
                            member(X=3,[3|B]=XS)①   member(X₂=3,[B|XS₂]=XS₁)②
                                                                   |
                                                         member(X₃=3,[3|C]=XS₂)①

Figure 8.6   Search trees for the first three solutions for the goal member(3,L).

When we force it to retract the result, Prolog tries the second rule, which creates the bindings $\langle$X=3, L=[A|XS]$\rangle$ in the head of the rule and then uses it to create the subgoal member(3,XS) as required by the body of the rule. This subgoal can be satisfied by the first rule for member, which is solved as before and produces the additional bindings $\langle$X=3, XS=[3|B]$\rangle$. If we substitute the binding thus generated for XS in the binding for L, we obtain the second answer. This state of the search is represented by the search tree in the middle of Figure 8.6.

Note that each recursive instance of a predicate that is created as a subgoal has its own set of variable bindings. In this second step we actually have two bindings for X, which we don't have to distinguish, since they don't differ. To see that it generally *does* matter to distinguish the variable bindings in different rule instances, consider how the solution for the third answer is generated. In this case backtracking revokes the latest instance of the first rule and tries to solve the subgoal member(3,XS) using the second rule, which, in particular, passes XS as the second argument to be unified with the term [_,XS]. But this latter variable XS refers to a different tail than the previous one. Therefore, to distinguish the different variable instances, we index them with the level of the search tree from which they originate, as shown in the search tree in Figure 8.6 on the right. The next result is computed in the same way as before, except with a new set of bindings. In particular, we now match XS₁ against [B|XS₂] in the head of the second rule and then match XS₂ against [3|C] in the body. Altogether this produces three bindings for X plus the bindings $\langle$L=[A|XS₁], XS₁=[B|XS₂], XS₂=[3|C]$\rangle$. Substituting the binding for XS₂ in the binding for XS₁ produces XS₁=[B,3|C] (note that in this notation the bar has to "shift over" the single element 3 to properly separate the single elements from the list), and then substituting this binding in the binding for L yields L=[A,B,3|C] as the third result.

In Section 8.6 we have used the predicate lookup/3 in the definition of the typing rules. The definition of lookup is very similar to that of member. The main difference is that the list to be searched must contain pairs, and the condition for a successful lookup is that the searched element matches the first component of the pair, in which case the second component is "returned" as the result value.

> ### Exercise 8.14
>
> Consider the following goal.
>
> ```
> member(3,L), member(4,L).
> ```
>
> Predict the first three answers. Then test your prediction, and explain the output produced by Prolog.

```
lookup(X,[(X,T)|_],T).
lookup(X,[_|G],T) :- lookup(X,G,T).
```

I have put "returned" in quotes because, as we have just seen with member, Prolog predicates do not generally have dedicated input and output parameters, that is, we can very well use lookup with a result value as input. For example, we can use lookup not only to find values using keys but also ask, *What key do I have to use to find* 3 *in the list* [(a,2),(b,3)]?

```
?- lookup(X,[(a,2),(b,3)],3).
X = b
```

And we can even leave the list unspecified.

```
?- lookup(X,L,3).
L = [(X,3)|A] ;
L = [A,(X,3)|B] ;
L = [A,B,(X,3)|C].
```

While this use case is somewhat contrived, it shows that Prolog predicates generally can produce many answers if parameters are underspecified, which can be a feature, but can also sometimes produce unwanted or even incorrect results (as discussed in Section 8.6).

> ### Exercise 8.15
>
> Define a predicate del/3, such that del(X,L1,L2) holds when L2 is equal to the list L1 with the first occurrence of X removed.
>
> Consider *all* results produced for the goal del(a,[a,b],L). If your predicate definition leads to more than one result, explain why, and then add a suitable condition so that only one result is produced.

Another frequently used list predicate that can be elegantly used in a relational way is append/3, defined as follows.

```
append([],L,L).
append([X|L1],L2,[X|L3]) :- append(L1,L2,L3).
```

The first rule says that an empty list appended to any list L is the same as L. The second rule says that when we append a non-empty list with first element X to another list L2, the resulting list starts with X, and its tail L3 is obtained by appending the tail of the first list L1 to the second list L2.

Again, we can use append in different ways. The simplest case is the functional use for appending two lists.

```
?- append([2,3],[a,[c],d],L).
L = [2,3,a,[c],d].
```

More interestingly, we can use the predicate to solve list concatenation equations. For example, we can ask, *What list do I have to append to* [2,3] *to get the list* [2,3,a,[c],d]?

```
?- append([2,3],L,[2,3,a,[c],d]).
L = [a,[c],d].
```

This works similarly for the first parameter. Providing a value for the third ("result") parameter and using a variable for an "argument" parameter effectively allows us to compute inverse functions. And we get those for free!

But there is more. For example, by leaving both argument parameters as variables, we can ask for all decompositions of a list.[13]

```
?- findall(X+Y,append(X,Y,[3,4,5]),L).
L = [[]+[3,4,5], [3]+[4,5], [3,4]+[5], [3,4,5]+[]].
```

We can observe here a fundamental strength of logic programming: whereas programs in imperative and functional programming languages are primarily about deriving output from input, logic programming can additionally use the same programs to generate data in a systematic way as input for further computation. This aspect shows up especially in applications of Prolog to solve puzzles. It can also be exploited in simpler scenarios, as illustrated by the next exercise.

Exercise 8.16

Define a predicate sublist/2, such that sublist(S,L) holds if the list S is a sublist of L, which is the case when L could be obtained by adding a prefix and suffix to S.

Hint: S is a sublist of L if L can be split into Prefix and Rest, where Rest can be split into S and Suffix. Use append to express the decomposition conditions.

---

[13]Note that I am using + here simply as a functor to build terms of two lists that are a bit easier to read than pairs. Other symbols that Prolog recognoizes as operators such as - or ^ work as well.

8.8 Numbers and Arithmetic

Numbers and numerical expressions enjoy special treatment in Prolog. We have already seen in Section 8.6 that an expression such as 2+3*4 is simply a term (whose functors are operators). This is easy to verify.

```
?- 2+3*4 = +(2,*(3,4)).
true.
```

While we can directly evaluate such an expression in the Elm interpreter, trying to evaluate it in swipl leads to an error complaining that + is not a defined predicate.

```
?- 2+3*4.
ERROR: Undefined procedure: (+)/2
```

To evaluate numerical expressions, Prolog provides a built-in predicate is/2, which is typically used in infix notation and whose first argument is a variable that will be bound to the result of evaluating the second argument.

```
?- X is 2+3*4.
X = 14.
```

In order to succeed, the second argument must be instantiated, that is, if it contains variables, they must be bound to numerical terms.

```
?- Y=3*4, X is 2+Y.     ?- Y is 3*4, X is 2+Y.     ?- Y=Z*4, Z=3, X is 2+Y.
Y = 3*4,                Y = 12,                     Y = 3*4,
X = 14.                 X = 14.                      Z = 3,
                                                     X = 14.
```

Note that without the binding for Y (and Z), the goal would fail. Moreover, the bindings for Y and Z must exist *before* they are used (directly or indirectly) in the second argument of is. In the third example, while Z must be bound before is can be evaluated, its definition could come after the one for Y. The variations of the example also show the crucial difference between = and is, namely = unifies terms (recall Section 8.5.1), while is evaluates expressions.

   With is we can now implement predicates that perform arithmetic computations, for example, for computing squares.

```
sqr(X,Y) :- Y is X*X.
```

The use of is in the definition of sqr restricts its use – we can supply only instantiated terms as the first argument. It is possible to supply a number for Y, in which case `is` checks whether its second argument evaluates to that number, but a term passed as an argument for Y will not be evaluated.

```
?- sqr(3,Y).        ?- sqr(3+1,Y).       ?- sqr(3,9).        ?- sqr(3,8+1).
Y = 9.              Y = 16.              true.               false.
```

In particular, since `is` works only in one direction and cannot be used to invert computations, we *cannot* use it to solve equations.

```
?- sqr(X,9).
ERROR: Arguments are not sufficiently instantiated
```

We are now ready to define a predicate for computing factorial numbers. Recall the inference rules from Section 5.1.

$$\frac{}{fac(1,1)} \qquad \frac{fac(n-1,m)}{fac(n,n\cdot m)}$$

While Prolog rules are very similar to inference rules, we have to be careful when dealing with arithmetic and ensure that arguments to `is` are sufficiently instantiated.

```
fac(1,1).
fac(N,F) :- K is N-1, fac(K,M), F is N*M.
```

Note that the order of the subgoals in the second rule is determined by the dependency of the evaluations involved. The definition works as expected, but, again, the predicate can only be used in one direction in goals.

```
?- fac(4,F).          ?- fac(X,24).
F = 24 .              ERROR: Arguments are not sufficiently instantiated
```

Exercise 8.17

Explain what is wrong with each of the following definitions. First, try to predict what will happen when you try to evaluate the goal `fac(3,F)`. Then explain how exactly they go wrong.

(a) `fac(N,F) :- fac(N-1,M), F is N*M.`

(b) `fac(N,N*M) :- K is N-1, fac(K,M).`

(c) `fac(N,N*M) :- fac(N-1,M).`

Exercise 8.18

Define a predicate `length/2`, such that N in `length(L,N)` is equal to the length of the list L.

8.9 The Cut

We have already briefly encountered the *cut* ! in Section 8.6 where we have used it to fine-tune a predicate definition to produce *fewer* results. In general, Prolog's ability to satisfy a goal repeatedly, by using different rules, is a powerful feature that nicely supports the programming of search problems. This behavior is implemented using a general backtracking mechanism that allows Prolog to systematically iterate over all alternatives of a predicate definition.

The cut provides a mechanism to modify this standard search algorithm. Concretely, the cut prevents backtracking and thus the re-satisfying of a subgoal. As an example, consider the following definition of a predicate p that is true for the first three natural numbers. The evaluation, especially, the re-satisfying of goals, should not be surprising: after rejecting the first solution, X=1, Prolog presents the second one, X=2, and then the third one, X=3 . If we add the cut as a subgoal to the first rule, Prolog cannot retract the goal that came before, which means only one answer is computed for the goal p(X). If we add the cut to the second rule, Prolog can retract a goal satisfied by the first but not second rule.

```
p(X) :- X=1.          p(X) :- X=1, !.        p(X) :- X=1.
p(X) :- X=2.          p(X) :- X=2.           p(X) :- X=2, !.
p(X) :- X=3.          p(X) :- X=3.           p(X) :- X=3.

?- findall(X,p(X),L).  ?- findall(X,p(X),L).  ?- findall(X,p(X),L).
L = [1,2,3].           L = [1].               L = [1,2].
```

The example is somewhat contrived, but it illustrates how the cut works. However, the effect of using a cut is not always so obvious. For example, with the definition of member shown earlier in Section 8.7, the goal member(3,[3,3,3,3]) can be satisfied four times. If we add a cut to the first rule, we again only get one solution. This version is more efficient than the more general definition for simply determining list membership, since it terminates computation as soon as a solution is found.[14] This version, however, also generates only one solution for the goal member(3,L).

When we add the cut to the second rule, goals containing member can be satisfied twice, similar to what happened with p earlier.

```
?- member(3,[3,3,3,3]).        ?- member(3,L).
true ;                         L = [3|A] ;
true.                          L = [A,3|B].
```

But what happens with a goal such as member(3,L), member(4,L).?

---

[14]This predicate is predefined in SWI-Prolog and is called memberchk.

```
?- member(3,L), member(4,L).
L = [3,4|A] ;
L = [4,3|A] ;
L = [A,3,4|B].
```

This behavior is not all that obvious and shows that reasoning about goals that employ predicates whose definitions use cuts requires careful thinking about Prolog's execution mechanism.

The cut can also easily lead to inconsistent predicate definitions. Consider, for example, the following attempt to define xor on the numbers 0 and 1.

```
xor(X,X) :- !, false.
xor(0,1).
xor(1,0).
```

Clearly, the goal xor(0,0) should fail, and xor(0,1) should succeed. And they do, but the queries xor(0,X) or xor(X,0) both fail, which is inconsistent with the two facts.

```
?- xor(0,0).     |   ?- xor(0,1).     |   ?- xor(0,X).     |   ?- xor(X,0).
false.           |   true.            |   false.           |   false.
```

Exercise 8.19

Find *two* different ways to fix the definition of predicate xor (without eliminating the cut).

The cut is used for efficiency and for making computations of Prolog programs (more) deterministic. While powerful and in certain situations indispensable, the cut is ultimately a non-logical, imperative feature that is not easy to use. The cut leaves a somewhat bitter aftertaste, since it abandons the otherwise elegant logic computation model. The bottom line is that the cut should be used very carefully and deliberately.

8.10   Negation

Negation is a critical operation in logic, and it can be employed to make Prolog predicate definitions more precise and eliminate unnecessary duplicates.

Consider again the predicate friends from Exercise 8.6, which says that two people are friends if they are buddies or foodmates. A straightforward definition of the predicate provides the two alternatives as separate rules.

```
friends(P1,P2) :- buddies(P1,P2).
friends(P1,P2) :- foodmates(P1,P2).
```

Exercise 8.20

Consider the following predicate definition.

```
q(a).
q(b) :- !.
q(c).
```

What answers does Prolog produce for the following queries?

(a) q(X).

(b) q(X), q(Y).

(c) q(X), !, q(Y).

There is nothing wrong with this definition per se, but it might not be ideal, because it can provide the same solution several times. In fact, with the facts from Figure 8.3, Alice and Carol are mentioned twice as a result.[15]

```
?- findall(P1+P2,friends(P1,P2),L).
L = [alice+carol, alice+bob, alice+carol].
```

Maybe we can avoid the duplication by using the cut? We could add a cut at the end of the first rule with the goal of preventing a pair that has been produced using the buddies predicate to again be produced by foodmates. However, if we try this, we may be surprised by the result.

```
friends(P1,P2) :- buddies(P1,P2), !.
friends(P1,P2) :- foodmates(P1,P2).

?- findall(P1+P2,friends(P1,P2),L).
L = [alice+carol].
```

While the duplicate was eliminated, we have also lost, incorrectly, the pair Alice and Bob (proving again that the cut is a tricky programming construct).

A correct way of defining the friends predicate is to spell out the three different, non-overlapping cases, which requires the use of not to express the requirement that a specific relationship does *not* hold.

```
friends(P1,P2) :- buddies(P1,P2), not(foodmates(P1,P2)).
friends(P1,P2) :- foodmates(P1,P2), not(buddies(P1,P2)).
friends(P1,P2) :- foodmates(P1,P2), buddies(P1,P2).
```

---

[15]Remember that + is a functor that can be used to build terms. Sometimes the use of infix operators such as + leads to goals and results that are easier to read.

With this definition each pair of friends is produced by a separate case, and we obtain the desired result.

```
?- findall(P1+P2,friendsB(P1,P2),L).
L = [alice+bob, alice+carol].
```

The negation predicate not is actually defined in terms of the cut. The trick is to say that if a predicate P succeeds, then not(P) should definitely fail. Otherwise, that is, if P fails and with it the first rule of not(P), then not(P) should succeed. The cut in the first rule prevents not(P) from succeeding through the second rule when P is true, and it causes not(P) to fail using the predefined predicate fail.

```
not(P) :- P, !, fail.
not(P).
```

This implementation of negation through failure implies what is called the *closed-world assumption*, which means that Prolog considers as true only relationships that can be derived from the predicates defined in the currently active program and correspondingly considers everything else to be false. Consider, for example, the evaluation of the following query.

```
?- sport(football).
false.
```

The negative answer should always be qualified and implicitly prefixed by "according to the facts known from the currently loaded Prolog program."

While not is a convenient programming tool, it also has to be deployed carefully. We'll consider two examples to illustrate this point. For example, we could be tempted to try to solve the barber's paradox with Prolog. The paradox is given by the following riddle.

> *In a town, the barber (who is male) shaves all males who do not shave themselves.*
> *Does the barber shave himself?*

Here is a straightforward representation of the information through two predicates shaves and male.

```
shaves(barber,X) :- male(X), not(shaves(X,X)).

male(barber).
```

A solution would be given by an answer to the following goal.

```
?- shaves(barber,barber).
```

But as you can imagine, Prolog is unable to come up with an answer. It will enter an infinite recursion that will cause the interpreter to eventually run out of stack space. We can employ our tree model to understand how the goal satisfaction unfolds. First, the goal shaves(barber,barber) leads to the subgoal not(shaves(barber,barber)).

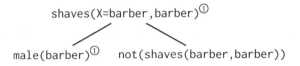

Second, the first rule for not applies, which creates three new subgoals, the first of which is the original goal – a case of left recursion!

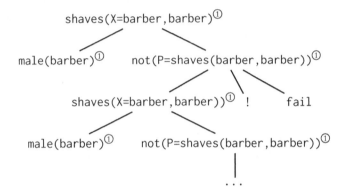

Since Prolog satisfies subgoals from left to right, the recursion continues, and Prolog tries to solve shaves(barber,barber) again. Thus, we will never reach the cut or fail, and the goal cannot be satisfied. This example is an instance of recursion without a base case, which has no well-defined semantics. The implication for philosophical puzzles in general is that we can't compute our way out of paradoxes.

A final problem with the treatment of negation in Prolog is the interaction with the quantification of variables. To illustrate the issue, suppose we want to find out what hobbies people have that are not considered sports. We can express this query with the following goal (recall the definitions from Figure 8.3 on page 168).

```
?- hobby(_,H), not(sport(H)).
H = reading ;
H = reading ;
H = chess.
```

The result is as expected. But consider what happens if we reorder the goals to ask basically the same question, namely, *Which of the non-sports are hobbies that people have?*

```
?- not(sport(H)), hobby(_,H).
false.
```

This result is surprising. Why do we not get any result? The comma represents the logical *and* operation, which is commutative. Therefore, we might expect the same result as before.

The different behavior is a consequence of the fact that free variables are existentially quantified in Prolog. For example, the query hobby(_,H) is interpreted as $\exists H.hobby(\_,H)$. The bindings for H are generated by Prolog's search mechanism with values taken from the predicate hobby. The additional condition not(sport(H)) then acts as a filter on the generated bindings, and the logical formula becomes the following.

$$\exists H.hobby(\_,H)) \wedge not(sport(H))$$

The crucial aspect is that at the time not is evaluated, the referenced free variable H is already bound.

When we change the order of the goals, Prolog first tries to satisfy not(sport(H)), which, following the first rule for not, leads to the three subgoals sport(H), the cut, and fail. The first subgoal succeeds (with the binding H=running), which means that the cut succeeds. This leads to fail, which causes the failure of not(sport(H)) and the whole goal.

The problem is that since H is unbound when not is evaluated, it causes H to be bound to a value for which sport succeeds, which then leads not to fail. It is similar to the following query.

```
?- not(sport(running)), hobby(_,running).
false.
```

By choosing running as an argument for sport, not and the whole query is bound to fail. If we could magically guess a value for which sport is false but that is part of hobby, the goals could succeed, as in the following example.

```
?- not(sport(chess)), hobby(_,chess).
true.
```

But that is not how Prolog works. By filling the unbound variable H with values from sport, the call of the not predicate will always fail. The bottom line is that, like the cut, negation has to be employed carefully, and it is a good strategy to reorder subgoals so that not is only applied to goals whose variables are already bound.

Index

Symbols _____

∃, *see* variable, quantification,
    existential

∀, *see* variable, quantification, forall

⟨·⟩, *see* activation record

⟦·⟧, *see* semantics, hollow square
    brackets

⇓, *see* inference rule examples,
    evaluates to

⇒*, *see* derivation, multi-step

::=, *see* grammar, production

!, *see* inference rule examples, *fac*

|, *see* grammar, production,
    alternatives

:, *see* judgment, *has-type*

<, *see* inference rule examples, *less than*

⊥, 76–78, 82

+, *see* grammar, plus notation

*, *see* grammar, star notation

∶, 77, 101

⊢, 106

𝔹, 74

𝕊, 75

ℤ, 74, 102

Γ, *see* type environment

ε, *see* grammar, production, ε

Σ, *see* grammar, terminal symbol

σ, 173

,, *see* Prolog, logical and

->, *see* function type

;, *see* Prolog, logical or

[], *see* list, empty

_, *see* pattern, wildcard

\, *see* lambda abstraction

:-, 166

A _____

abstract syntax, 58, 62
    vs. concrete syntax, 58, 62
    data type representation, 58
    factoring, 63–65
    idioms, 62
    recursion elimination, 65–68
    set of syntax trees, 58, 62
    term representation, 181

abstract syntax examples
    Conditio, 60
    Cond, 59, 63–65
    Expr, 58, 76, 87, 110, 130
    Prog, 93
    SNum, 70
    Stmt, 59, 68, 89, 94

abstract syntax tree, 57, 71
    vs. parse tree, 57, 58
    linear representation, 58, 59

abstraction, 3
    hierarchy, 3
    users and creators, 5

abstraction examples
    abstract syntax, 57
    algorithms, 3
    automata, 3
    big O notation, 3
    functions, 14
    parse trees, 52
    programming languages, 3

Programming Language Fundamentals: A Metalanguage Approach in Elm, First edition. Martin Erwig.
© 2024 Martin Erwig. Published 2024 by John Wiley & Sons Inc.
Companion website: www.wiley.com/go/ProgrammingLanguageFun

rules, 157
   star notation, 65
   syntax trees, 52
   types, 3, 121
access link, 142
activation record, 124, 132, 133
actual parameter, 140
Ada, 146, 148
Algol 68, 148
algorithm, 1
alias, 144
ambiguity, *see* syntax, ambiguity
anonymous function, 27
assignment, 13, 124
AST, 57, 78, 124
atom, *see* Prolog, atom
axiom, *see* inference rule, axiom, 105
axiomatic semantics, 75

B _____

backtracking, 11, 175, 190, 195
barber paradox, 198–199
binary tree, 42
binding, 11, 19, 22, 124, 159, 173
   expression, 140
   value, 140
   variable, 140, 156
block, 124
   body, 124
   declaration, 124
   entering, 133
   inclusion, 125
   leaving, 133
   nested, 125, 128, 130
block path, 126
bottom element, 76–78, 82
   see also CPO

C _____

C program, 30
case expression, 22, 36, 43
   see also pattern matching

characteristic function, 155
closed-world assumption, 198
closure, 135, 136
complete partial order, *see* CPO
compound term, *see* Prolog, term,
     compound
computation, 1, 9
computer science, 2, 4
   vs. programming, 4
   vs. software engineering, 4
concrete syntax, 58, 61
   vs. abstract syntax, 58, 61, 71
   key words, 61
   set of sentences, 62
   white space, 61
conditional
   expressions vs. statements, 18
conjunction, *see* Prolog, logical and
cons, 34
constructor, *see* data constructor
context-free, *see* grammar, context-free
CPO, 76, 79
   bottom element, 76
currying, *see* function, definition,
     curried
cut, *see* Prolog, cut

D _____

data constructor, 34, 40, 180
   immutability of, 41
data structure, 25, 34, 40, 179
   containing functions, 28
   Elm
     changes, 41, 42
   functional, 42
   in Elm, 40
   in Prolog, 157, 179
   list, 34
   tree, 42
data type, 34
   polymorphic, 35
denotational semantics, 8, 75, 76

derivation, 51
   choice of productions, 52
   multi-step, 51
   one-step, 51
disjunction, *see* Prolog, logical or
divide-and-conquer, 17
   see also recursion
dynamic scoping, 135
dynamic type checking, 88

E

eager evaluation, 150
Elm, 13
   (data) type definition, 40, 103
   basic types, 18
   evaluating expressions, 16
   installation, 14
   interpreter, 15
   loading definitions, 16
   module, 16
   predefined constructors
     ::, 21, 34
     False, 41
     Just, 37, 83
     Nothing, 37, 79, 83
     True, 41
     [], 21, 34
   predefined functions
     ++, 21, 24, 36
     <<, 46–47, 93
     Dict.empty, 90
     Dict.get, 90, 92, 111
     Dict.insert, 90, 93
     List.all, 69
     List.member, 189
     List.tail, 38
     Maybe.map2, 84
     Maybe.map, 84
     Tuple.first, 25
     Tuple.second, 25
     &&, 30
     foldr, 45–46
     map, 44–45
     min, 27
     range, 35, 40
     sqrt, 26
   predefined types
     Bool, 18, 40, 74
     Char, 18
     Dict.Dict, 90
     Either, 81
     Float, 16, 18, 25
     Int, 16, 18, 25, 74
     List, 21, 34
     Maybe, 37, 47, 70, 81, 83
   program, 15
   REPL, 15
   shadowing, 19
   type alias, 15, 103
Elm examples
   Grade, 16
   ListProperty, 104
   Pair, 104
   Points, 16
   Pos, 104
   Property, 104
   Tree, 42, 43
   TyEnv, 111
   Type, 111
   Val, 87
   alice, 16
   both, 86, 113
   check, 113
   dbl, 28
   evalSafe, 116
   eval, 116, 131, 135
   fac, 32–34, 46, 95, 110, 127
   getVar, 131, 136
   grade, 16
   head, 37–38
   hobbies, 161
   inorder, 43
   isEmpty, 36
   isEven, 46

isOdd, 46
keepUntil, 69
mapIII, 88
min3, 29
onJust, 47
pow2, 28
recip, 28
removeUntil, 69
replFst, 42
rev, 21, 33
semCount, 86
semE, 92
semVC, 86
sem, 76, 77, 85, 88, 89, 92
snd, 39
suc, 28
sum, 38, 46
tc2, 113
tc, 111–114, 116, 120
see also abstract syntax examples
equi-join, 164
expression binding, 140
expression simplification, 12, 154

F

fact, *see* Prolog, fact
factorial, 30, 95, 99, 127
filler symbol, *see* grammar, terminal
symbol, filler
first-order logic, 11
formal parameter, 140
function, 26
vs. Prolog predicate, 188
anonymous, 27, 149
see also lambda abstraction
application, 16
partial, 27
precedence of, 22, 26
typing rule, 105
argument type, 26
body, 14
composition, 46–47, 93

see also Elm, predefined
functions, <<
definition, 29, 140
curried, 27, 32
higher-order, 10, 44, 91, 149
inverse, 161
parameter, 13, 28, 139
partial, 37, 79
result type, 26, 33
type, 26
see also lambda abstraction
function type, 26
functional programming, 10, 13, 148,
153, 154
functor, 193

G

goal, 157
goto, 31
grammar, 50
ambiguous, 56, 61
context-free, 8, 50, 79
formal definition, 51
non-terminal symbol, 50, 77
optional elements, 70
plus notation, 67
production, 50
ϵ, 53
alternatives, 52
LHS, 50
name, 50
RHS, 50
recursion, 65
refactoring, 56
repetition, 65–68
square bracket notation, 70
star notation, 65–68
start symbol, 51
terminal symbol, 50, 78
filler, 61, 62, 67
translation into data type, 71
grammar examples

move, 72, 81, 82
switch, 63
zoo, 50
arithmetic expressions, 55, 58, 77
assembly language, 72
binary digit sequences, 52–54, 57
Boolean expressions, 57, 80
conditions, 59
let expressions, 68
Prolog, 158
signed numbers, 70
statements, 59, 68, 102
while loop, 59

H
Haskell, 150
higher-order function, *see* function,
    higher-order
homonym, 124

I
imperative program
    nested block, 128, 134
    trace, 133, 134
imperative programming, 10, 14, 148,
    154
    semantics, 74, 89, 90
    state transformation, 10, 153
incremental programming, 17
inference rule, 98, 105, 167, 182
    as Prolog rule, 167, 182
    axiom, 99
    example uses of, 98–102
    recursive, 99, 171
inference rule examples
    evaluates to, 101
    even, 99
    expr, 101
    fac, 99, 100, 110, 194
    less than, 100
    see also typing rule examples
infix notation, 26

interpreter
    see also Elm, interpreter

J
join, 164
judgment, 98
    conclusion, 98
    premise, 98
judgment examples
    evaluates to, 101
    even, 99
    fac, 99
    has-type, 105, 106

K
key words, *see* concrete syntax, key
    words

L
lambda abstraction, 27, 92
lambda calculus, 3, 10, 148
language
    defined by grammar, 51
    first-order, 154, 160
    set of sentences, 49, 58
lazy evaluation, 150
left recursion, *see* Prolog, rule, left
    recursive
let expression, 7, 124, 142, 182
    body, 19
    evaluation, 20
    multiple definitions, 20
    nested, 20, 125
    recursive, 127
    shadowing, 19
    syntax, 68
let expressions, 19
LHS, *see* grammar, production, LHS
list
    (data) constructors, 34
    data type, 34
    empty, 22, 34, 35, 38, 186

functor, 186
   homogeneous, 35, 187
   pattern, 22, 186
   terms (in Prolog), 186
logic programming, 11, 154

M _____

metalanguage, 8, 112
   Elm data types, 58
   Elm, 9, 79
   grammar, 8, 50
   inference rules, 101
   Math, 79
metavariable, 77, 105, 183
modus ponens, 99
most general unifier, 176

N _____

name, 7, 19, 123
   see also variable
non-termination, 76
nonterminal (symbol), *see* grammar,
      nonterminal symbol
nontermination, 33, 150, 174, 199
notation, *see* syntax

O _____

object language, 8, 112, 183
operational semantics, 75
overloading, 18

P _____

parameter, 140
   renaming, 144
   substitution, 3, 14, 144
parameter passing, 7, 140
parameter passing schema, 141
   call-by-name, 14, 140, 148–150
   call-by-need, 14, 140, 148, 150,
      151
   call-by-reference, 140, 144, 145

call-by-value, 14, 140–143, 148,
      150
   call-by-value-result, 140, 146, 147
   copy-in-copy-out, 147
parametric polymorphism, 104
parentheses, 61
   of metalanguage, 61
parse tree, 54
   vs. abstract syntax tree, 57, 58
   obtained from derivation, 54
parser, 54
partial function application, 27
   for binary operations, 28
pattern, 22
   functions in, 39
   invalid, 39
   list, 22, 175
      Elm vs. Prolog, 176
   nested, 39
   repeated variables, 40, 161, 162,
      164, 166, 180
   wildcard, 39, 181
pattern matching, 22, 36, 175, 180
   programming tool, 39
   see also case expression
pointer, 144
predicate, *see* Prolog, predicate
predicate calculus, 3, 11
predicate logic, 11
prefix notation, 26
problem, 1
product domain, 86
product type, 40
production, *see* grammar, production
program
   correctness, 74
program generator, 95
program state, 31
programming language, 2
programming paradigm, 9
   functional, 10
   imperative, 10

logic, 11
Prolog, 153
  arithmetic, 193
  atom, 158
  compound term, 157
  cut, 185, 195–198
  fact, 154, 158
  functor, 158, 159, 180, 197
  goal, 159
  interpreter, 155, 157
  logical and, 162
  logical or, 156, 162
  negation, 196–201
  predefined predicates
    @<, 170
    \=, 164
    fail, 198, 199
    findall, 160, 189
    integer, 184
    is, 193
    memberchk, 195
    not, 198
  predicate, 154, 158, 159
    arity, 171
    name, 166
    parameter, 166
  predicate definition, 157
  program, 157, 158
  rule, 158, 166
    body, 158, 166
    head, 158, 166
    if-then, 167
    left recursive, 173
  search mechanism, 165, 173–175,
      177–179, 189–190, 195
  structures, 157
  syntax, 158
  term, 154, 158
    compound, 154, 158, 179
    numerical, 193
    unification, 154, 158
  terminology, 157, 158

  variable, 158
Prolog examples
  append, 191
  diet, 168
  fac, 194
  healthy, 168, 169
  hobby, 154, 155, 168
  inside, 171
  in, 171
  lookup, 182, 190
  map, 180
  member, 187, 189, 195, 196
  not, 198
  river, 162
  runner, 155
  sportHobby, 167, 168
  sport, 163, 168
  trust, 162
  type, 182, 184
  veggie, 168
proof tree, 108, 173
proposition, 99
propositional formula, 99

Q
quantification, 199
query, 156, 157

R
recursion, 10, 154, 199
  base case, 33
  describing a loop, 32
  in function definitions, 33
  in grammars, 65
  in inference rules, 99, 171
  inductive case, 33
reference, see binding, variable
reflexivity, see relation, reflexive
relation, 99, 154, 155, 157–159
  arity, 159
  binary, 159, 162
  reflexive, 161

symmetric, 170
ternary, 159, 181
unary, 99, 159
relationship, 154, 158, 159
REPL, 15
representation, 1, 2
RHS, *see* grammar, production, RHS
rule, *see* grammar, production;
    inference rule; Prolog, rule;
    typing rule
runtime error, 74, 82, 116, 118, 121,
    149, 174, 183
runtime stack, 124, 130, 140
    growing and shrinking of, 130

S

scope, 126
scoping
    static vs. dynamic, 7, 135, 137
semantic domain, 75, 76, 79, 90
semantic function, 75–77, 79, 90
semantics, 6, 8, 73
    vs. syntax, 73
    benefits of, 73
    denotational vs. operational vs.
        axiomatic, 75
    hollow square brackets, 78, 101
sentence, 51
    ambiguous, 49
    structure, 49
sentential form, 51
shadowing, 19, 126
side effect, 21, 42, 91
smart constructor, 64
software engineering, 4
SQL, 173
stack frame, 132
start symbol, *see* grammar, start
    symbol
static scoping, 135
    implementation, 136
static typing, 36

termination, 119
structure, *see* Prolog, term, compound
substitution, 142, 159, 173
sum type, 40
SWI-Prolog, 155
synonym, 124
syntactic sugar, 22, 27
syntax, 8, 49
    vs. semantics, 73
    ambiguity, 6, 49, 58
    parentheses, 61
    see also concrete syntax; abstract
        syntax
syntax tree, *see* abstract syntax tree
systematic transformation, *see*
    algorithm

T

term, *see* Prolog, term
terminal (symbol), *see* grammar,
    terminal symbol
termination, 76, 119, 150
trace, 12, 22–24, 131, 132, 137, 142,
    172
    tree, 172
tuple, 25
    component, 25
    element of relation, 154, 158, 159
    nesting, 25
Turing machine, 3, 10
type, 16, 29, 102
    language, 102
    polymorphic, 104
    programmer intention, 29
type alias, *see* Elm, type alias
type assumption, 106
type checker, 102, 109, 115
type checking, 6, 102
    static vs. dynamic, 6, 117–120
    see also static typing
type checking algorithm, 109
type constructor, 80, 103

binary, 103
unary, 103
type correctness, 118
type environment, 106, 111
type error, 36, 74, 87, 102, 108, 111, 118
type expression, 103, 104
type inference algorithm, 109
type safety, 115, 118
type soundness, 74
type synonym, 103
type system, 102, 112, 118
benefits of, 97
in Prolog, 184
type variable, 16, 25, 35, 36, 104
typing context, 106
typing judgment, 106, 110, 181
typing rule, 102, 105
typing rule examples
App, 105
Cond, 119
Equal, 113
Let, 107, 182
Not, 112
Plus, 113
Var, 107

U
undefined, *see* ⊥; CPO, bottom element
unification, 176
vs. pattern matching, 176
unifier, 176
union domain, 87

V
value binding, 140
variable, 13, 19, 124
call-by-reference parameter, 144
call-by-value-result parameter, 146
definition, 127, 128
free, 168, 173, 200
quantification, 199
existential, 168, 200
reference, 127
unbound, 168
use, 127, 128
local vs. non-local, 128
see also name; Prolog, variable
variable binding, 140
variant type, 40

W
while loop, 30
white space, *see* concrete syntax

Printed and bound by CPI Group (UK) Ltd, Croydon, CR0 4YY

27/10/2024

14580677-0003